T0319825

Asia beyond the Global Economic Crisis

Asia beyond the Global Economic Crisis

The Transmission Mechanism of Financial Shocks

Edited by

Satoshi Inomata

Project Director, International Input–Output Project and Director, Microeconomic Analysis Group, Development Studies Center, IDE-JETRO, Japan

Edward Elgar

Cheltenham, UK • Northampton, MA, USA

Published by
Edward Elgar Publishing Limited
The Lypiatts
15 Lansdown Road
Cheltenham
Glos GL50 2JA
UK

Edward Elgar Publishing, Inc.
William Pratt House
9 Dewey Court
Northampton
Massachusetts 01060
USA

A catalogue record for this book
is available from the British Library

Library of Congress Control Number: 2010934048

ISBN 978 1 84980 764 7

Typeset by Servis Filmsetting Ltd, Stockport, Cheshire
Printed and bound by MPG Books Group, UK

Contents

List of contributors vii
Foreword by Pascal Lamy ix
Preface xi

Introduction 1
Satoshi Inomata

1 The triangular trade: the shock transmission mechanism in the Asia-Pacific region 11
Ikuo Kuroiwa, Hiroshi Kuwamori and Hajime Sato

2 Impact of the global economic crisis on employment in the Asia-Pacific region 51
Bo Meng and Satoshi Inomata

3 International trade and real transmission channels of financial shocks in global production networks: an Asian–USA perspective 73
Hubert Escaith and Fabien Gonguet

4 Vertical specialization at the time of economic crisis 106
Yoko Uchida and Satoshi Inomata

5 The impact of the financial crisis on Factory Asia 125
Kazunobu Hayakawa

6 To what extent will the shock be alleviated? The evaluation of China's counter-crisis fiscal expansion 144
Nobuhiro Okamoto and Satoshi Inomata

7 An input–output analysis of post-crisis rebalancing in the Asia-Pacific economy 169
Peter A. Petri

8 Explanatory notes 191
Satoshi Inomata

Index 209

Contributors

Hubert Escaith is the World Trade Organization's Chief Statistician and a Research Fellow at the DEFI, Faculty of Economics and Management, Université de la Méditerranée in France. He holds a doctorate in Mathematics Applied to Economics (1982) from the University of Toulouse (France) and a Master's in Management Information and Decision Support Systems (1988) from the Ecole Supérieure de Sciences Economiques et Commerciales in Paris. After a research position in economics and statistics at Toulouse University, he joined the United Nations in 1982. In October 2006, he left his post as Director of the ECLAC Statistics and Economic Projections Division to join the WTO.

Fabien Gonguet holds an advanced graduate degree from the Ecole Polytechnique (France) and a Master's in Forecasting and Economic Policy from the Ecole Nationale de la Statistique et de l'Administration Economique (France). He also holds a Master's in International Affairs from Sciences Po Paris (France).

Kazunobu Hayakawa is a Research Fellow at the Inter-disciplinary Studies Center, IDE-JETRO. He received his doctorate from Keio University in 2008 with a dissertation on intermediate goods trade. His main research areas are international economics and economic geography. He has published in journals such as the *Journal of the Japanese and International Economies* and the *North American Journal of Economics and Finance*.

Satoshi Inomata is the Project Director of the International Input–Output Project and Director of the Microeconomic Analysis Group, Development Studies Center, IDE-JETRO. He received his MSc in Development Economics from the University of Oxford. His major research interests include input–output analyses and BRICs economies. He has been involved in the construction of the Asian International Input–Output Tables for 1990, 1995 and 2000.

Ikuo Kuroiwa is the Director-General, Development Studies Center, IDE-JETRO. He received his PhD from the University of Pennsylvania. His current research interests include the industrial development of East Asia, regional economic cooperation and integration. He has previous experience in the construction and analysis of international input–output tables and has served as an economic adviser for the Japan Bank for International Cooperation.

Hiroshi Kuwamori is the Deputy Director of the Microeconomic Analysis Group, Development Studies Center, IDE-JETRO. He received his MA degree in Economics from the University of Pittsburgh. His major research interests include input–output analyses and international trade. He has been involved in the construction of the Asian International Input–Output Tables for 1990, 1995 and 2000.

Bo Meng is a Visiting Research Fellow at the Organisation for Economic Co-operation and Development on secondment from IDE-JETRO. He received his PhD in Information Science from Tohoku University. He works on international (inter-regional) input–output analyses and spatial CGE models. He is co-author of 'The transport sector and regional price differentials: a spatial CGE model for Chinese provinces' (*Economic Systems Research*, **21** (2), pp. 89–113, 2009).

Nobuhiro Okamoto is an Associate Professor at the Faculty of International Relations in Daito Bunka University. He received his PhD (Economics) from the People's University of China in 2000. He has recently been studying regional development in China by using an inter-regional input–output model. His recent work (co-edited with Satoshi Inomata and Hiroshi Kuwamori) includes *The Emergence of the Chinese Economy and Re-organization of the Asian Industrial Structure* (IDE-JETRO, 2007).

Peter A. Petri is the Carl J. Shapiro Professor of International Finance at the Brandeis International Business School (IBS) and Senior Fellow of the East–West Center in Honolulu, Hawaii. He received AB and PhD degrees in Economics from Harvard University. His research focuses on international trade, finance and investment, primarily in the Asia-Pacific region and his recent publications include *Asian Regionalism and the World Economy: Engine for Dynamism and Stability* (co-editor, Edward Elgar, 2010) and *Inclusive, Balanced, Sustained Growth in the Asia-Pacific* (editor, ISEAS, 2010).

Hajime Sato is an Associate Senior Research Fellow at IDE-JETRO. He received his PhD from the University of London. He carries out research on the industrial development of Asia.

Yoko Uchida is an Associate Senior Research Fellow at the Development Studies Center, IDE-JETRO. Her research interest lies on international trade issues in the Asia-Pacific region. She received her MA from the Osaka School of International Public Policy at Osaka University.

Foreword

The book *Asia beyond the Global Economic Crisis*, produced by the Institute of Developing Economies, offers an important contribution to the empirics of the new trade economy. The analysis focuses on the importance of economic interactions in explaining the modern global economy, and the role of international production networks.

In today's world, the complexity of productive and commercial relationships has dissociated the localization of final production units from the location of the value added included in the final product. Global manufacturing, characterized by the vertical integration of productive processes and the off-shoring of industrial tasks, has led to an increase of trade flows in intermediate goods, especially in the manufacturing sector. The traditional notion of country of origin, so dear to traditional trade statisticians, is gradually becoming obsolete as various operations from the design of a product to the manufacture of its components, their assembly and related marketing have spread across the world. Nowadays more products are '*Made in World*' rather than '*Made in*' a specific country. This trade in parts, components and accessories relates to the exchange of goods sent abroad for further processing, or 'trade in tasks' that add value along the production chain.

As the recent crisis indicates and the book illustrates compellingly, this closer interdependency was also behind the fast and synchronized transmission of shocks the world economy experienced after the financial crisis of September 2008. It is also behind the strong recovery that international trade has been experiencing in 2010, after the coordinated efforts from the largest developed and developing economies to sustain demand when the crisis was at its deepest.

Many analysts have been caught off guard by the speed and the synchronization of the process. This is partly due to the lack of proper statistical indicators to properly analyse trade and the creation of value along the global supply chains. This volume offers an important contribution towards this aim, and represents one facet of the fruitful partnership between IDE-JETRO and the WTO to measure vertical specialization and trade in value added. Measuring accordingly the international chain of value will provide relevant information on the new business model behind global manufacturing, where trade in goods is progressively substituted by 'trade in tasks'.

Among all the interesting results presented by the various authors using the very technical point of view of input–output analysis, I wish to highlight one, which is of particular importance for policy makers: in the face of such a complex global production system, the appropriate counter-crisis policy should not isolate the national economies within some out-dated protectionist measures, but should look at devising systemic and cross-national programmes.

Pascal Lamy
Director-General
World Trade Organization
2011

Preface

The financial crisis from the United States, as triggered by the collapse of Lehman Brothers, has rapidly spread to the real side of the economies. Many advanced nations were trapped in persistent downward spirals and felt the painful cost of seeking an exit strategy. The story, of course, was not irrelevant to the emerging economies in Asia, despite the unprecedented growth they had enjoyed over the last decade or so. In particular, China, the 'Factory of the World', lost its foreign customers and currently faces the urgent need to redirect its products towards the domestic market.

For many, the term 'globalization' still remains a key concept in describing the world economy. The rapid development of cross-national production networks has significantly deepened economic interdependency in various parts of the globe. The production process has become fragmented and exchanged between countries according to the rule of comparative advantage, to facilitate the efficient division of labour and enhance resource allocation. There is no doubt that the expansion of international production chains, assisted by sophisticated management skills and advanced logistic technology, has played an important role in boosting the contemporary world economy. But then, what do we see today?

When we consider the nature of the recent crisis, we may refer to the close analogy of the conjuncture to the day-to-day problems that we face in the age of the Internet. The development of information technology and the worldwide web have undoubtedly improved the mode of communications, and the benefit of increased efficiency for global knowledge exchange is undeniable. Simultaneously, however, over-exposure to anonymous users has invited the immediate danger of cyber attacks and contagion, revealing the structural vulnerability of the system to which we belong. What has happened to the world economy over the past few years, from the Lehman shock to the Greek debt crisis, or even to the Tohoku Earthquake Disaster in Japan, presents a strong resemblance to such an intertwined cyberspace; an economic shock that occurs in one country is quickly and widely transmitted to the rest of the world through extensive cross-border supply chains. The rapid contraction of world trade and output is nothing but the negative outcome of such a complex global production system.

There *is* an important difference, however. While the antidote to a computer virus infection is simply to disconnect the terminal from the Internet and individually give anti-virus treatment, the counter-crisis measure here, in contrast, is *not* to isolate the economy. History is supposed to have taught us this point, yet the recent protectionist movement is a frustrating, albeit somewhat predictable reaction of misguided countries.

What is required is internationally concerted action on the basis of a firm understanding of how the system works (or not, as the case may be) in times of crisis. The 'Economics of the crisis', therefore, entails a detailed examination of the mechanics of shock transmission, by probing the labyrinth of complex supply networks among the countries. This book investigates the nature of the global economic crisis from the perspective of cross-national production systems based on international input–output analyses, and aims to envisage the prospect of the post-crisis Asian economy.

On this occasion, I would like to express my sincere gratitude to the researchers of international organizations/academic institutions who have kindly offered us the opportunity to present the preliminary research results, in response to which we were able to receive invaluable feedback from specialists in various fields for the further elaboration of the study, including particularly, but by no means limited to the following: Ludovico Alcorta and Nobuya Haraguchi of the UN Industrial Development Organization (UNIDO), Carlo Filippini of Bocconi University, Jose M. Rueda-Cantuche of the IPTS European Commission, Masataka Fujita of the UN Conference on Trade and Development (UNCTAD), Tuomas Peltonen and Gabor Pula of the European Central Bank, Kiichiro Fukasaku of the Organisation for Economic Co-operation and Development (OECD), Michel Fouquin of Centre d'Etudes Prospectives et d'Informations Internationales (CEPII), Machiko Nissanke of the School of Oriental and African Studies, University of London (SOAS), and Gabriele Suder of SKEMA Business School, while the ardent logistic support of Yutaka Hashimoto and Tomoharu Mochizuki is highly appreciated, without which the mission could not have been completed successfully.

We are also indebted to Yosuke Noda, who kindly assisted us in the laborious computation of numerous trade statistics.

Satoshi Inomata
Director of the International Input–Output Project
IDE-JETRO
2011

Introduction

Satoshi Inomata

The characteristic feature of the recent global economic crisis is the speed and extent of the shock transmission. The rapid development of cross-national production networks over the past several decades has significantly deepened the economic interdependency between countries, and a shock that occurs in one region, whether positive or negative in nature, will be swiftly and widely transmitted to the rest of the globe. The sudden contraction of world trade and output was, indeed, a negative outcome of this intertwined global economic system.

The major focus of this book is directed at the analysis of 'triangular trade through China', which is considered to have formed the principal mechanism of shock transmission in the Asia-Pacific region under the crisis.

The USA, one of the main players of the 'triangular trade', has always been the largest customer for the products of the region. Its consumption demand, backed by enormous purchasing power, was a leading catalyst for regional output growth.

In the first decade of the twenty-first century, China became a major trade partner for the United States, and rapidly increased its exports of final consumption goods to US markets to meet their unlimited consumption demand. Here, China specialized in the final assembling stage of the production process, since its technical requirement is quite labour-intensive and hence advantageous for a country with a massive labour force.

The growth of China's manufacturing export is supported by the supply of intermediate inputs from other Asian countries. In contrast to China, other emerging economies in the region specialized in the production of parts and accessories, which usually require higher levels of technology and sophisticated management skills.

Therefore, the 'triangular trade through China' assumes a structure of product flows whereby: (1) Asian countries (including Japan) produce parts and accessories and export them to China; and (2) China assembles them into final goods; (3) which are further exported to the US markets for consumption (see Figure I.1).

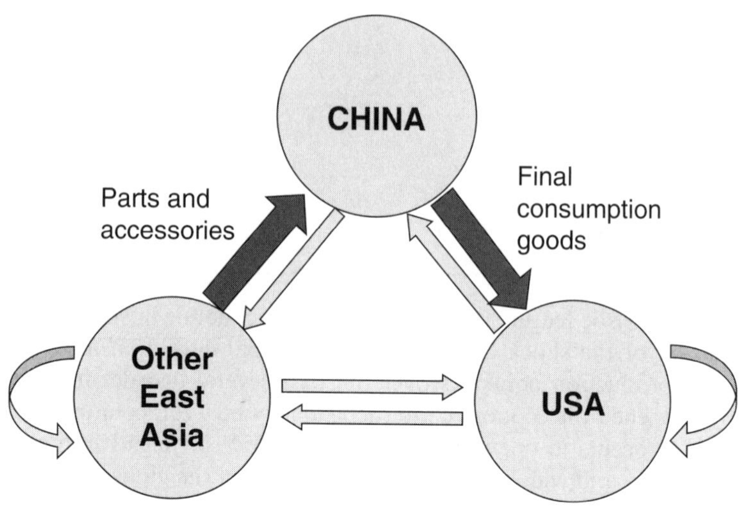

Source: Drawn by the author.

Figure I.1 Triangular trade through China

There is no doubt that the 'triangular trade through China' prevailed as a primary growth engine for the Asia-Pacific region. The opposite picture, however, is equally possible and valid. The collapse of US consumption demand under the crisis caused a significant decline of Chinese exports to the United States, which further reduced China's import demand for intermediate inputs from neighbouring Asian countries. The negative shock of the economic crisis propagated quickly and extensively throughout the region via complex production networks among countries, yet, on top of this, the 'triangular trade through China' is considered to have functioned as the US–Asia 'turnpike' for the shock transmission within the region.

The direct impact of the contraction of the US import demand can be measured by a simple reference to the change in trade statistics, but the entire effect of the impact on industries, both through direct and indirect channels, can be examined only by probing the intertwined production networks among the countries (see Figure I.2). The Asian International Input–Output Tables (AIO tables), constructed by the Institute of Developing Economies, JETRO, are used for this particular purpose, and they enable us to capture all recursive impacts of negative demand shock, both direct and indirect, on every industry of every country in the Asia-Pacific region.[1]

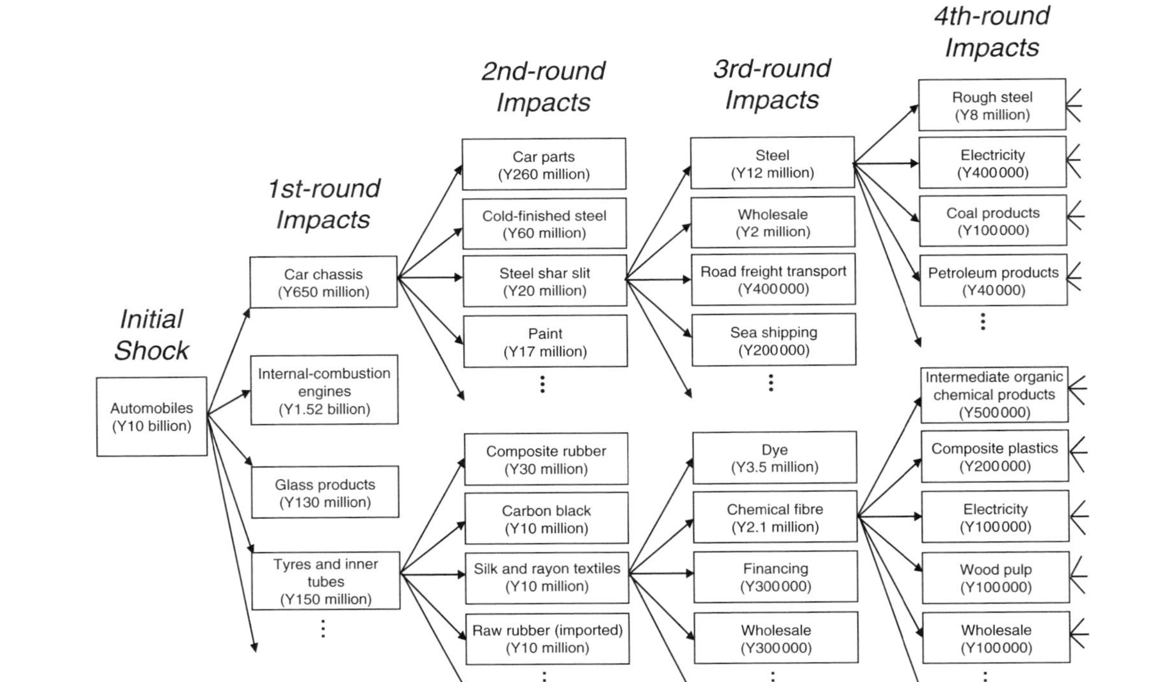

Source: Drawn by the author.

Figure I.2 Image of shock propagation

CHAPTER 1: THE TRIANGULAR TRADE: THE SHOCK TRANSMISSION MECHANISM IN THE ASIA-PACIFIC REGION

Chapter 1 attempts to measure the impact of the crisis by a simple multiplier analysis using an orthodox international input–output model. A change or 'shock' that occurs in one industry in one country will be transmitted and amplified through complex cross-national production networks, and inflict a larger and wider impact on the rest of the region. This is called a multiplier effect. By decomposing the multiplier effect into three types according to the shock transmission channels (the domestic linkage channel, the 'triangular trade' channel, and other inter-country linkage channel), the chapter reveals that the shock delivered by the 'triangular trade through China' caused significant damage to the entire Asia-Pacific region.

For the analysis at the industrial level, it emerges that the output of manufacturing products with complex architecture, such as computer equipment and electrical appliances, was seriously affected by external shocks. The production of these goods is more prone to offshoring since its manufacturing process is separable into several stages and the parts and accessories are relatively compact and lightweight (and can hence be easily delivered across countries). Consequently, the production activities of these goods, extensively connected to regional production networks, became highly vulnerable to shocks coming from outside.

CHAPTER 2: IMPACT OF THE GLOBAL ECONOMIC CRISIS ON EMPLOYMENT IN THE ASIA-PACIFIC REGION

Chapter 2 continues the analytical focus of Chapter 1, yet shifts its attention to employment issues. It devises the indices of 'employment gain potential' and 'employment give-out potential', which present a balance sheet of employment opportunities for each country brought about by the engagement in international trade. The combination of both indices shows that, in the Asia-Pacific region, China is the biggest receiver of job opportunities, while the USA is the most benevolent provider. From 2000 to 2008, however, there was a marked structural change in the gain/give-out relationship of the region. China continues to benefit from the USA's strong demand for its exports, yet started to give out job opportunities to other neighbouring countries through the increase in its import demand for intermediate goods from the same. Here, the emergence of 'triangular trade through China' is observed again. What happened in the commodity markets was echoed in the labour markets in the Asia-Pacific region.

Chapter 2 also contributes to the analysis by calculating the impact of the crisis on regional employment. By using the same analytical framework as in Chapter 1 but extending the model of 'employment multipliers', the chapter simulates the potential number of job losses in each country for the years 2008 and 2009. A particular focus is placed on the 'transfer of unemployment' between countries, in which China is found to be the main transmission hub for Asian countries.

CHAPTER 3: INTERNATIONAL TRADE AND REAL TRANSMISSION CHANNELS OF FINANCIAL SHOCKS IN GLOBAL PRODUCTION NETWORKS: AN ASIAN–USA PERSPECTIVE

The analyses in the first two chapters are based on the demand-driven model, generally known as the 'Leontief model'. The contraction of final demand leads to a decline in the output of final goods, which reduces the demand for and thus the production of parts and accessories, which further induces the output decline of sub-parts and materials, and so on. The negative impact is transmitted 'backward' along production chains from downstream to upstream industries.

The impact can also propagate in the opposite direction. The change that occurs at a certain point in the vertical chain is recurrently transferred to the subsequent stages of the production process, moving 'forward' all the way down to the terminals of supply-demand circuits. The analytical model used to capture such transmission mechanism is of the supply-driven type, known as the 'Ghosh model', which forms a dual counterpart of the Leontief model.

Unlike the other studies conducted in this book, Chapter 3 deals uniquely with the price effect of the financial crisis by employing the supply-driven model. Its analytical focus is devoted to the impact of the credit crunch, the global conjuncture of the current state, which is anticipated to disrupt the smooth functioning of vertical production networks.

After the sub-prime shock, many small-scale manufacturers are finding it increasingly difficult to gain access to credit markets, and at some point may choose to shut down factories lacking operational finance. The sudden stop in the supply of key intermediate products will force downstream clients to seek other sources, yet switching from one supplier to another is a difficult task for the producers of differentiated products, especially of high-tech industries, which use highly knowledge-intensive parts and components and require specific production technologies. Finding an appropriate alternative involves considerable costs (searching costs, transaction costs, training costs and so on). Consequently, the unit cost of production is bound to increase. The increase in production cost is a typical example of supply-side shocks, which will reverberate and propagate to other industries by cumulative price mark-ups along the vertical production chains.

Applying the supply-driven model to the AIO tables, the chapter simulates the mark-up effect of a price shock for the selected Asian countries in the face of the contagious credit crunch. By doing so, it attempts to bridge the real and monetary sides of the economies under the crisis.

The simulation results show that the relative size of the shock on the domestic economy depends on its degree of openness, and also on the relative size of the originating industrial sector in relation to the rest of the economy. As for the cross-national transmission of price shocks, Japan is found to be the largest exporter of potential inflation, while Malaysia and Thailand are the most vulnerable to such shocks, apparently due to the considerable foreign orientation of the manufacturing sector. From 2000 to 2008, China increased its influence as an exporter of the price shock, yet its vulnerability to imported shocks remained relatively stable.

CHAPTER 4: VERTICAL SPECIALIZATION AT THE TIME OF ECONOMIC CRISIS

The last few decades have been marked by the rapid development of vertical production networks within the Asia-Pacific region. Manufacturing goods are no longer produced in a single country. Production processes are fragmented into several stages, and countries specialize in each production stage according to their own comparative advantages.

Chapter 4 is devoted to investigating the impact of the crisis on the vertical production networks of the Asia-Pacific region, by adopting the Vertical Specialization (VS) index. The VS index measures a country's degree of participation in cross-national production networks by calculating the amount of 'imported inputs used for producing a good that is subsequently exported'. The chapter, however, extends the model by employing the AIO tables as principal data, the unique feature of which enables the VS index to be decomposed into two indices: 'VS_i' and 'VS_f'.

VS_i is the VS index of exports for intermediate usage in foreign countries, which shows the level of participation in the production of parts and components. VS_f, on the other hand, is the VS index of exports for overseas final consumption, which is thus considered to indicate the degree of engagement in the final assembly process.

From the viewpoint of vertical production chains, whether a country is mainly exporting intermediate goods or final consumption goods is directly related to the country's technological profile within the international division of labour. It is generally considered that the production of parts and components requires sophisticated technology with qualified logistics management for just-in-time delivery. The assembly of components required to complete the final consumption goods, in contrast, entails relatively simple routines with low working skills. So, by comparing the values of VS_i and VS_f, one can profile the technological development of the countries concerned.

The calculation results show that the upstream production process of intermediate goods (as measured by the VS_i index) was relatively 'resistant' to the impact of the crisis, compared to the assembly process at the end of the production chains (as measured by the VS_f index), which was directly and immediately affected by the contraction of final demand.

The analysis also confirms the prevalence of the 'triangular trade through China', yet with a striking new finding. The 'triangular trade' presumed China's role to be a mere assembler of final products. The comparison of VS_i and VS_f indices of China, however, reveals that the country has already 'stepped up' the technological ladder and recently promoted its position within the regional production networks from a simple assembler of final goods to a producer of parts and components. The 'triangular trade through China' has undergone a significant qualitative change in recent years, and its contents are no longer the same as a decade ago.

CHAPTER 5: THE IMPACT OF THE FINANCIAL CRISIS ON FACTORY ASIA

Now, based on the VS analysis of Chapter 4, the importance of production networks for intermediate goods is very apparent. They determine the length of the vertical production chains and the complexity of supply–demand networks. In order to envisage the post-crisis production system in the Asia-Pacific region, there is a need for detailed analysis of the trade mechanism of intermediate goods.

Chapter 5 contributes to this subject. This chapter employs a conventional regression analysis with the Ordinary Least Squares method, in order to identify the determinants of trade in intermediate products. The design of the equation system is based on the popular gravity model, yet the originality and strength of the study resides in its treatment of datasets.

Usually, it is quite difficult to obtain consistent time series data for intermediate goods trade. The UN trade statistics, for example, are often criticized in that the definition of intermediate products is rather arbitrary and goods are categorized in an ad hoc fashion. The research of this chapter instead focuses on the unique features of the AIO tables. These tables offer a complete and harmonized set of panel data for the trade of intermediate goods in four dimensions: the country of origin, the country of destination, the industrial sector, and the reference year. The regression model of the study is constructed in such a way as to optimally exploit these international I–O table properties.

Another characteristic of the study is that it includes the financial aspect of international trade in the model. It refers to the data provided by *Institutional Investor*, upon which the credibility of the financial markets of each country concerned is constructed as an explanatory variable. This is a very strong and important formulation for our research since the financial meltdown in the United States was the main trigger of the crisis.

Empirical results show that the regional production networks of Asia, or 'Factory Asia', have begun to develop without relying on external forces such as the US consumption demand. Its robust production system, backed by the sound operation of financial markets, is expected to enhance regional self-sufficiency and improve its resistance to external shocks. The finding is along the lines of support for the prediction of the VS analysis in Chapter 4, which suggests the possible re-organization of the 'triangular trade' structure that has dominated the Asia-Pacific region throughout the last decade.

CHAPTER 6: TO WHAT EXTENT WILL THE SHOCK BE ALLEVIATED? THE EVALUATION OF CHINA'S COUNTER-CRISIS FISCAL EXPANSION

So, what will be the key element of the post-crisis 'Factory Asia'? No one can deny the importance of China in bringing Asia back on track. Chapter 6 considers the potential of the Chinese economy for regional economic growth, by evaluating the effect of China's counter-crisis fiscal measures, which were recently implemented on an unprecedented scale.

The chapter adopts an orthodox I–O model of impact multipliers for its study, yet the data used for the analysis is especially unique. It is the *Transnational Interregional Input–Output Table between China and Japan*, the newest product of the Institute of Developing Economies. In this dataset the inter-regional I–O tables of both China and Japan are harmonized and interlinked in a single matrix, so that the cross-national transmission of impact from one sub-region in China, say Huanan, to one sub-region in Japan, say, Hokkaido, can be consistently measured. Feeding the data into the analysis enables us to see the 'intra'-regional multiplier effect and 'inter'-regional multiplier effect individually, and thus we are able to probe the detailed, region-to-region linkage structure from a geographical perspective.

The empirical results indicate that the production of export-driven districts such as Huadong and Huanan significantly declined during the crisis, and induced drops in output, not only in neighbouring Huazhong and Huabei, but also further in other Asian economies such as Japan, South Korea, Taiwan and ASEAN countries.

The recent fiscal measure adopted by the Chinese government, however, is expected to turn the situation around. The study reveals that the policy mainly functions to stimulate the economies of inland regions such as Xinan and Huazhong, although Huabei and Huadong in coastal areas may also benefit through inter-regional economic linkages. Moreover, the impact of fiscal expansion transcends international borders and reaches other Asian countries through extensive trade channels in the Asia-Pacific region.

CHAPTER 7: AN INPUT–OUTPUT ANALYSIS OF POST-CRISIS REBALANCING IN THE ASIA-PACIFIC ECONOMY

The increasing influence of China and other emerging economies in determining the global distribution of wealth, as seen in the preceding chapters of the book, has brought wide attention to the issues of rebalancing the world economy. Chapter 7 completes our research by considering the post-crisis rebalancing of expenditures among and within surplus and deficit countries as a key policy priority.

The chapter examines the implications of rebalancing expenditure categories in ten Asia-Pacific countries for the structure of production. An aggressive rebalancing scenario (based on 2007 current account data) is constructed, and its detailed production implications are analysed using the inter-country I–O framework.

The analysis reveals that changes associated with eliminating excessive international imbalances are modest relative to major expenditure categories in the Asia-Pacific region. Moreover, significant overlaps in the production induced by different types of expenditures dampen the output effects of shifts among them.

This does not mean that rebalancing will be easy – spending reallocations are politically difficult – but the need to 'reinvent' Asia's growth model appears to be overstated. Policy makers should be well comforted by the result of analysis that expenditure adjustments required for rebalancing are attainable without involving serious dislocations in industrial structure or patterns of economic growth.

The book was written to serve both the interests of non-specialists and I–O experts alike, and assumes no preliminary knowledge about international input–output analyses. Readers, however, may like to glance at the 'Explanatory notes' in Chapter 8 before proceeding to the main chapters, which might help deepen understanding of the basic logic behind the arguments.

NOTE

1. Traditionally, the input–output model of impact analysis has been used to measure the effect of positive shock, such as that of the special procurement from the Olympic Games or World Expo. The analysis of positive shock, however, is subject to two practical difficulties. Firstly, shock propagation is bound to stop when the repercussion of extra demand hits the production bottleneck of industries. Secondly, manufacturers may try to meet the extra demand by running down their stocks rather than increasing output, in which case the shock propagation will also come to a halt.

   As for negative shock, in contrast, the transmission of impact does not presume this kind of 'obstacle'. While manufacturers may not be able to produce more due to their production capacity limits, they can always choose to produce less. Also, because retaining stock incurs cost, manufacturers usually opt to reduce production when they face a declining demand for their products, rather than maintaining the same production level and piling up undesired inventory.

   Therefore, the impact analysis seems to be more suitable for analysing negative shock than positive shock.

1. The triangular trade: the shock transmission mechanism in the Asia-Pacific region

Ikuo Kuroiwa, Hiroshi Kuwamori and Hajime Sato

1. INTRODUCTION

The financial meltdown that occurred in the USA in 2008 hit the countries in the Asian region severely. Although the damages sustained by financial institutions in Asia from the sub-prime shock are less serious compared to those in the USA and Europe (IMF, 2009, p. 71), many Asian countries are suffering more badly than the USA, the seismic epicentre of the crisis, on their production side (Figures 1.1a and 1.1b). Although North-east Asian countries had enjoyed sound real GDP growth until 2007, growth rates plummeted in 2008. In particular, Japan's growth rate turned negative, from 2.7 per cent in 2007 to −0.7 per cent in 2008, with a further decline expected in 2009. The growth rates of Japan, Korea and Taiwan are also forecast to become negative and lower than that of the USA. Only China is expected to maintain positive growth, although significantly slowed, from 9 per cent in 2008 to 6 per cent in 2009. Countries in South-east Asia retained positive growth in 2008, yet this is forecast to turn negative in 2009. However, significant variations exist among the countries concerned as regards the impact of the crisis. The growth rate of Indonesia was estimated at −1.3 per cent in 2009, while that of Singapore was −8.8 per cent, much worse than that of the USA.

The purpose of this chapter is to investigate the transmission mechanisms of the US financial crisis to Asian countries. Specifically, two questions will be addressed. First, what is the extent of the impact of the collapse of the US economy on industries in Asian countries? Second, why is this impact so amplified when it reaches Asian shores? In order to explore these questions, this chapter will utilize trade statistics and the Asian International Input–Output Tables (AIO tables) compiled by the Institute of Developing Economies, JETRO.

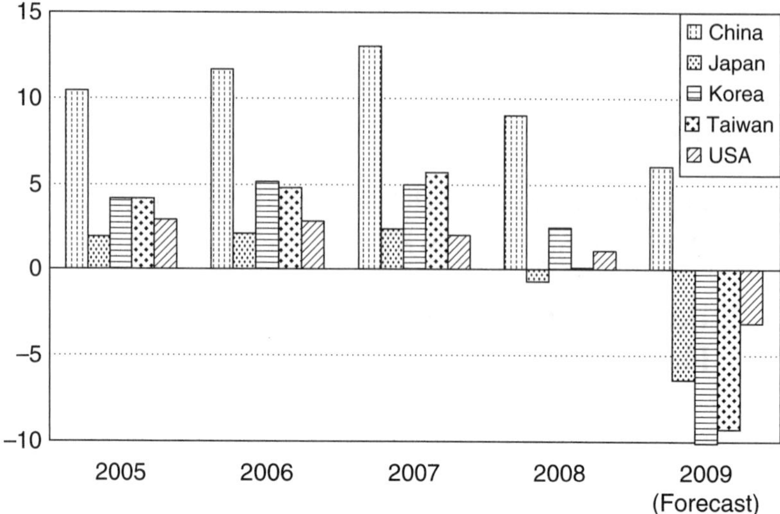

Sources: ADB, Asian Economic Outlook 2009. EIU for 2009 forecast.

Figure 1.1a Real GDP growth (North-east Asia, %)

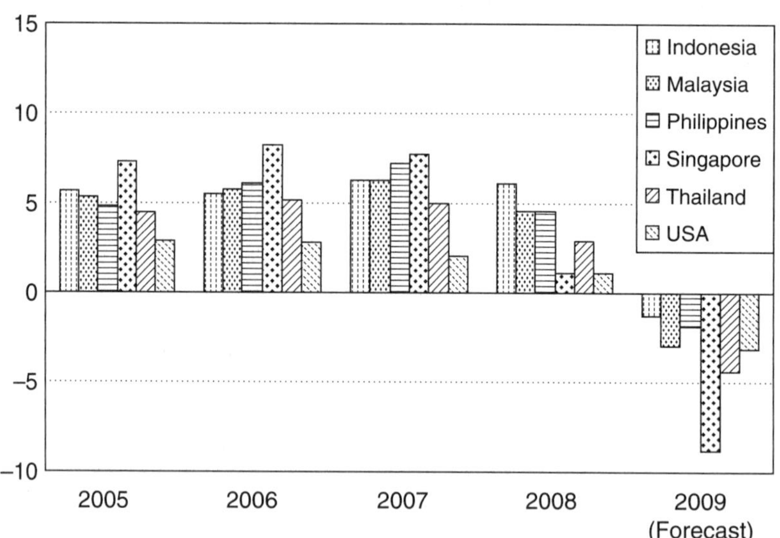

Sources: ADB, Asian Economic Outlook 2009. EIU for 2009 forecast.

Figure 1.1b Real GDP growth (South-east Asia, %)

The analyses in this chapter will measure the quantitative impacts of the decline in US import demand caused by the financial crisis. The analyses will also reveal the international production structure of the Asia-Pacific region, particularly the 'triangular trade', which involves China as an assembly base and the USA as a destination for final products, as the major means by which the impact of the crisis is transmitted. In Asian countries, the impact of the economic crisis has been amplified through this triangular trade, together with the collapse of direct exports to markets in developed countries.

The chapter is organized as follows. Section 2 will reveal the structure of the 'triangular trade' by employing conventional trade statistics. In section 3, the impacts of the drop of US demand on Asian countries will be measured by using the AIO tables, while section 4 investigates the formation of the triangular trade structure in Asian production networks. Finally, the results of the analyses are summarized in section 5.

2. TRANSMISSION MECHANISM OF THE CRISIS: THE TRIANGULAR TRADE

This section analyses the transmission mechanism of the economic crisis of 2008 to the Asian region. As mentioned above, despite the relatively stable conditions of financial institutions, Asian countries were affected by the crisis more severely than the US economy. This indicates that the shock is transmitted not only through the financial markets but also via other channels. International trade is the principal channel linking most Asian countries to the global economy.

Exports became increasingly important in all Asian countries through the 2000s. Table 1.1 presents the exports–GDP ratio of major Asian countries from 1995 to 2007. It shows that all the countries concerned increased their orientation for exports from 1995 to 2007. Except for Japan and the USA, the share of exports reached more than a quarter of GDP in 2007. This indicates that Asian countries are highly exposed to the global economy, and under such circumstances cannot insulate themselves from the shocks that occur in foreign markets. Moreover, although Japan's exports–GDP ratio was relatively lower than those of other countries, it increased most sharply during 2000 and 2007. The sudden collapse in external demand inflicted tremendous damage on the Japanese economy.

One remarkable feature of these Asian countries' exports is their heavy dependence on the exports of manufacturing products. Figures 1.2a and 1.2b depict the composition of exports of Asian countries by major commodity groups.[1] For all countries except Indonesia, 'Electrical machinery'

Table 1.1 Exports–GDP ratio (%)

	1995	2000	2005	2007
China	20.4	20.8	34.0	37.1
Indonesia	22.5	37.6	29.8	26.4
Japan	8.4	10.3	13.1	16.3
Korea	24.2	33.7	35.9	38.3
Malaysia	83.1	108.8	103.3	97.5
Taiwan	48.0	53.8	64.2	73.8
Philippines	23.5	50.2	41.8	35.0
Singapore	140.3	148.6	191.7	185.5
Thailand	33.6	56.1	62.4	62.5
USA	7.9	8.0	7.3	8.4

Sources: Calculated from WDI Online and UN comtrade. ADB Key Indicators (for Taiwan).

and 'Machinery' were the most important exported commodities, in both 2000 and 2007, while for Indonesia, 'Minerals' accounts for the largest share. In Korea and Japan, 'Transport equipment' is also important, and its share increased from 2000 to 2007.

The destination of exports from Asian countries has gradually shifted away from the USA to China through the 2000s. Table 1.2 reports the destinations of major exported commodities of North-east Asian countries in 2000 and 2007. The figures reported in the tables are shares of total exports. It is observed that for China, the USA became a more important destination for all China's major exported commodities. From 2000 to 2007, the share of the USA increased from 3.8 to 4.6 per cent in 'Electrical machinery', from 2.8 to 4.3 per cent in 'Machinery' and 1.8 to 1.9 per cent in 'Textile products' respectively. In contrast, for all other North-east Asian countries, China replaced the USA as the most important destination between 2000 and 2007 for most of the commodities.

Table 1.3 reports the destinations of major export commodities of South-east Asian countries. Although the characteristics of export destinations are not as obvious as the case of North-east Asia, it is observed that China and the ASEAN countries themselves, became more important destinations for South-east Asian countries between 2000 and 2007, while the shares of the USA and Japan dropped during the same period.

In short, from the observations of trade statistics in Tables 1.2 and 1.3, the following trade structure in the Asia-Pacific region can be identified regarding the destinations of major export commodities. From 2000 to 2007, the USA increased its presence as a destination for China's exports,

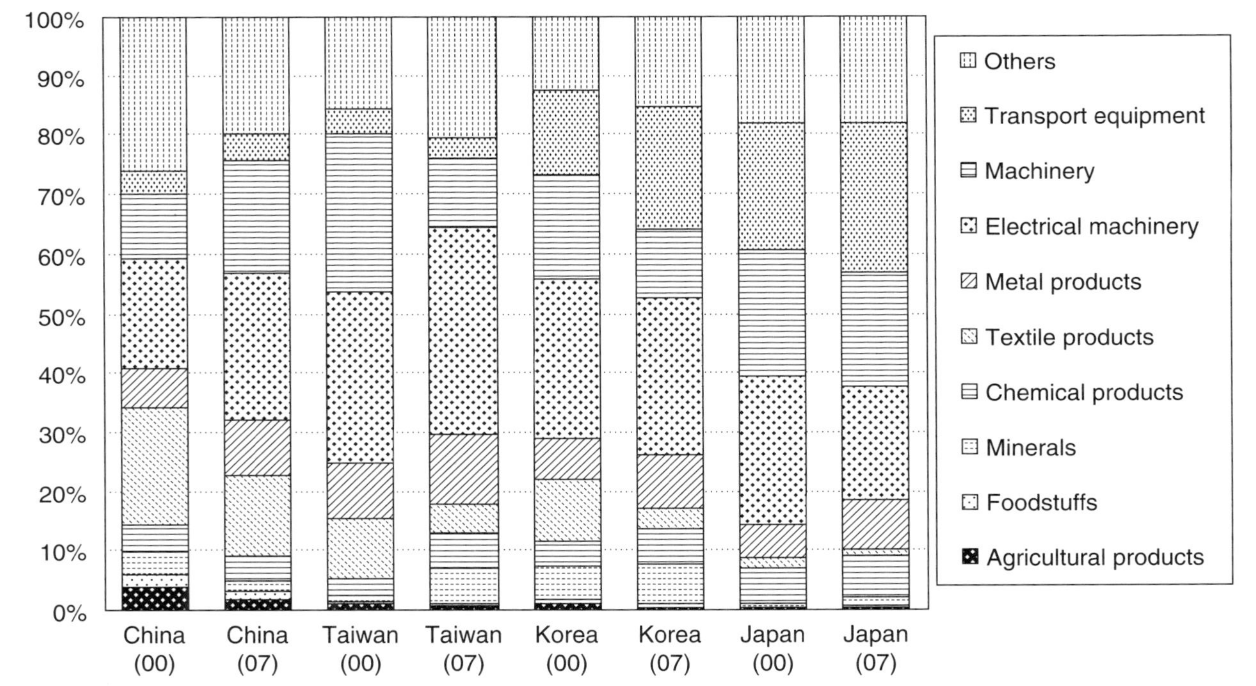

Source: United Nations, UN Comtrade Database.

Figure 1.2a Composition of exports (North-east Asia)

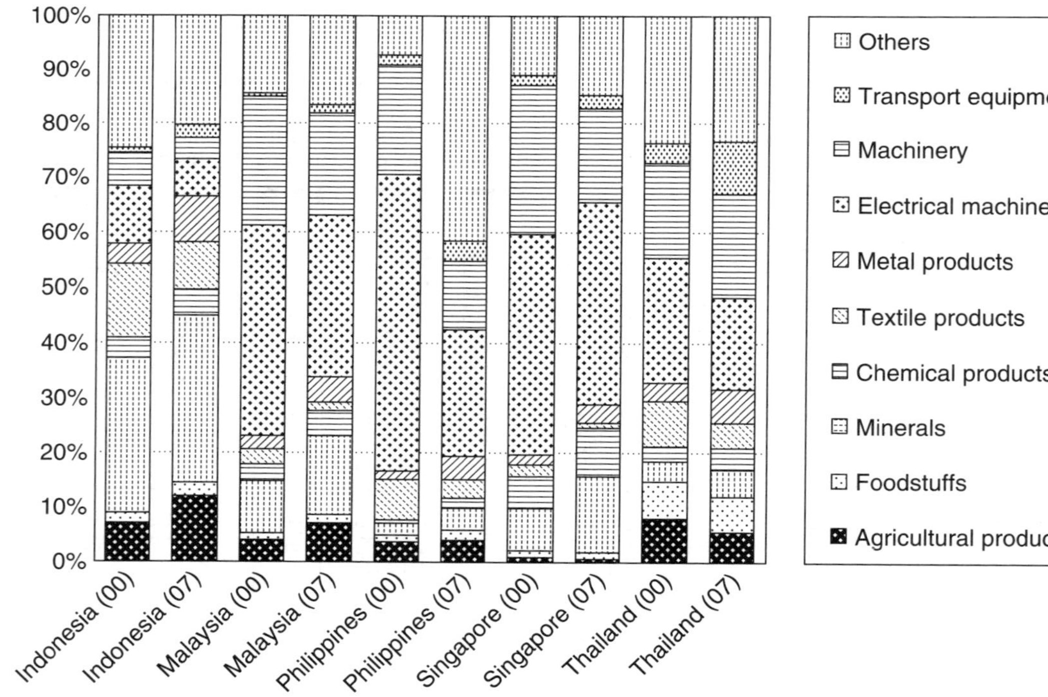

Source: United Nations, UN Comtrade Database.

Figure 1.2b Composition of exports (South-east Asia)

Table 1.2 Destinations of major export commodities (North-east Asia: 2000, 2007)

2000			1st		2nd		3rd	
(Rank)	(Commodity Name)	(Share)	(Country)	(Share)	(Country)	(Share)	(Country)	(Share)
CHINA (Total exports: 249 203 million US$)								
1	Textile products	(19.8%)	Japan	(5.3%)	Hong Kong	(4.5%)	USA	(1.8%)
2	Electrical machinery	(18.5%)	Hong Kong	(4.2%)	USA	(3.8%)	Japan	(2.6%)
3	Machinery	(10.8%)	USA	(2.8%)	Hong Kong	(1.9%)	Japan	(1.0%)
TAIWAN (Total exports: 147 817 million US$)								
1	Electrical machinery	(29.1%)	USA	(6.7%)	Hong Kong	(6.4%)	Japan	(3.1%)
2	Machinery	(26.6%)	USA	(7.7%)	Japan	(3.7%)	Hong Kong	(3.5%)
3	Textile products	(10.2%)	Hong Kong	(3.2%)	USA	(1.7%)	Indonesia	(0.4%)
KOREA (Total exports: 172 267 million US$)								
1	Electrical machinery	(26.9%)	USA	(6.8%)	Japan	(2.7%)	Hong Kong	(2.2%)
2	Machinery	(17.3%)	USA	(5.4%)	Japan	(2.0%)	China	(1.2%)
3	Transport equipment	(14.2%)	USA	(3.8%)	Greece	(0.7%)	Germany	(0.7%)
JAPAN (Total exports: 479 248 million US$)								
1	Electrical machinery	(25.1%)	USA	(6.5%)	Hong Kong	(2.2%)	Korea	(1.9%)
2	Machinery	(21.3%)	USA	(6.4%)	Korea	(1.3%)	China	(1.2%)
3	Transport equipment	(21.2%)	USA	(9.4%)	Panama	(1.3%)	Australia	(0.9%)

Table 1.2 (continued)

2007			1st		2nd		3rd	
(Rank)	(Commodity Name)	(Share)	(Country)	(Share)	(Country)	(Share)	(Country)	(Share)
CHINA (Total exports: 1 217 776 million US$)								
1	Electrical machinery	(24.7%)	Hong Kong	(6.3%)	USA	(4.6%)	Japan	(1.6%)
2	Machinery	(18.8%)	USA	(4.3%)	Hong Kong	(3.0%)	Japan	(1.4%)
3	Textile products	(13.6%)	USA	(1.9%)	Japan	(1.6%)	Hong Kong	(1.5%)
TAIWAN (Total exports: 234 683 million US$)								
1	Electrical machinery	(35.0%)	Hong Kong	(7.7%)	China	(6.2%)	USA	(4.9%)
2	Machinery	(11.5%)	China	(2.3%)	USA	(2.2%)	Hong Kong	(0.9%)
3	Chemical products	(6.1%)	China	(3.2%)	Japan	(0.4%)	Hong Kong	(0.3%)
KOREA (Total exports: 371 477 million US$)								
1	Electrical machinery	(26.2%)	China	(6.7%)	USA	(3.0%)	Hong Kong	(2.5%)
2	Transport equipment	(20.7%)	USA	(3.1%)	Russia	(1.2%)	Germany	(1.2%)
3	Machinery	(11.7%)	China	(2.7%)	USA	(2.0%)	Japan	(0.7%)
JAPAN (Total exports: 714 327 million US$)								
1	Transport equipment	(25.1%)	USA	(8.4%)	Panama	(1.2%)	Russia	(1.2%)
2	Machinery	(19.5%)	USA	(4.1%)	China	(2.8%)	Korea	(1.4%)
3	Electrical machinery	(18.9%)	China	(4.0%)	USA	(2.9%)	Hong Kong	(2.0%)

Note: 'Share' indicates the percentage ratios to total exports.

Sources: United Nations, UN comtrade database. Global Trade Information Services, World Trade Atlas (for Taiwan).

Table 1.3 Destinations of major export commodities (South-east Asia: 2000, 2007)

2000			1st		2nd		3rd	
(Rank)	(Commodity Name)	(Share)	(Country)	(Share)	(Country)	(Share)	(Country)	(Share)
INDONESIA (Total exports: 62 124 million US$)								
1	Minerals	(28.3%)	Japan	(12.9%)	Korea	(5.1%)	China	(1.7%)
2	Textile products	(13.2%)	USA	(3.5%)	U. Kingdom	(0.8%)	Japan	(0.8%)
3	Electrical machinery	(10.4%)	Singapore	(2.9%)	USA	(1.8%)	Japan	(1.7%)
MALAYSIA (Total exports: 98 230 million US$)								
1	Electrical machinery	(38.3%)	USA	(9.2%)	Singapore	(8.9%)	Japan	(4.2%)
2	Machinery	(23.5%)	USA	(6.8%)	Singapore	(4.5%)	Japan	(2.6%)
3	Minerals	(9.7%)	Japan	(3.0%)	Korea	(1.2%)	Singapore	(1.1%)
PHILIPPINES (Total exports: 38 078 million US$)								
1	Electrical machinery	(53.9%)	USA	(15.3%)	Singapore	(6.1%)	Japan	(5.9%)
2	Machinery	(20.2%)	USA	(4.5%)	Japan	(4.5%)	Thailand	(1.6%)
3	Textile products	(7.3%)	USA	(5.3%)	U. Kingdom	(0.3%)	Japan	(0.3%)
SINGAPORE (Total exports: 137 806 million US$)								
1	Electrical machinery	(39.7%)	Malaysia	(9.6%)	USA	(6.3%)	Japan	(3.4%)
2	Machinery	(27.5%)	USA	(8.1%)	Malaysia	(3.0%)	Japan	(2.0%)
3	Minerals	(7.4%)	Malaysia	(1.6%)	Hong Kong	(1.6%)	Viet Nam	(0.7%)
THAILAND (Total exports: 68 819 million US$)								
1	Electrical machinery	(22.5%)	USA	(5.3%)	Japan	(3.8%)	Singapore	(2.6%)
2	Machinery	(17.1%)	USA	(3.3%)	Singapore	(2.9%)	Japan	(2.2%)
3	Agricultural products	(7.9%)	Japan	(1.6%)	USA	(1.4%)	Hong Kong	(0.5%)

Table 1.3 (continued)

2007			1st		2nd		3rd	
(Rank)	(Commodity Name)	(Share)	(Country)	(Share)	(Country)	(Share)	(Country)	(Share)
INDONESIA (Total exports: 114 101 million US$)								
1	Minerals	(30.3%)	Japan	(11.8%)	Korea	(4.8%)	China	(3.6%)
2	Agricultural products	(12.1%)	India	(2.1%)	China	(1.4%)	USA	(1.0%)
3	Textile products	(8.6%)	USA	(3.3%)	Germany	(0.5%)	Japan	(0.4%)
MALAYSIA (Total exports: 176 206 million US$)								
1	Electrical machinery	(29.3%)	Singapore	(5.6%)	USA	(5.3%)	China	(3.0%)
2	Machinery	(18.8%)	USA	(6.6%)	Singapore	(2.1%)	Netherlands	(1.5%)
3	Minerals	(14.5%)	Japan	(3.3%)	Singapore	(2.7%)	Korea	(2.0%)
PHILIPPINES (Total exports: 50 466 million US$)								
1	Electrical machinery	(22.9%)	Netherlands	(6.5%)	Hong Kong	(3.7%)	USA	(2.9%)
2	Machinery	(12.3%)	USA	(4.8%)	Japan	(2.8%)	China	(1.3%)
3	Metal products	(4.5%)	China	(0.9%)	Korea	(0.7%)	Japan	(0.5%)
SINGAPORE (Total exports: 299 297 million US$)								
1	Electrical machinery	(36.4%)	Malaysia	(5.7%)	Hong Kong	(5.6%)	China	(4.7%)
2	Machinery	(17.3%)	USA	(2.5%)	Indonesia	(2.1%)	Malaysia	(1.9%)
3	Minerals	(13.8%)	Hong Kong	(2.4%)	Indonesia	(2.3%)	Malaysia	(2.1%)
THAILAND (Total exports: 153 571 million US$)								
1	Machinery	(18.7%)	China	(2.7%)	USA	(2.6%)	Japan	(1.9%)
2	Electrical machinery	(16.8%)	Japan	(2.9%)	USA	(2.4%)	Hong Kong	(1.6%)
3	Transport equipment	(9.6%)	Australia	(1.5%)	Indonesia	(0.7%)	Singapore	(0.6%)

Note: 'Share' indicates the percentage ratios to total exports.

Sources: United Nations, UN comtrade database. Global Trade Information Services, World Trade Atlas (for Taiwan).

while other countries saw destinations divert from the USA to China during the same period. Note that such structural change in trade is consistent with the emergence of triangular trade in the region, as shown below.

To further investigate the shifting structure of trade in and around the Asian region, the trade flow is analysed by using different categories of commodities. Figures 1.3a to 1.5b illustrate the trade flows classified according to the main end-use of commodities.[2]

The trade flows between Asian countries, the USA and the EU experienced significant changes. First, from 2000 to 2007, the trade volumes of Asia with the USA and the EU increased by factors of 1.6 and 2.4 respectively, as can be observed from Figures 1.3a and 1.3b describing the trade flows of all commodities between Asia, the USA and the EU for 2000 and 2007. One aspect of the increased trade is the increase in the trade surplus of Asian countries against the other two regions from 2000 to 2007. Asia's exports to the USA and the EU were much larger than Asia's imports from these regions and the imbalance expanded from 2000 to 2007. Another important aspect is the rising share of China's exports to the USA and the EU. In 2007, China's exports accounted for more than half of total exports from Asia to other regions; 52 per cent to the USA and 53 per cent to the EU as shares, respectively, having increased significantly from the 2000 figures of 27 per cent (to the USA) and 28 per cent (to the EU). Second, intra-Asia trade also increased from 472 billion US$ to 1.1 trillion US$. A remarkable change can also be observed in intra-Asia trade. In 2000, the trade amount between China and ASEAN countries was very small. However, in 2007, China–ASEAN trade increased about fivefold. Interdependency within the Asian region is considered to have strengthened during this period.

As for the trade flows of 'Parts and accessories' for Asian countries and the EU, intra-regional trade expanded more rapidly than that with other regions from 2000 to 2007 (Figures 1.4a and 1.4b) by factors of 2.4 and 2.1 respectively. Within the Asian region, sizable trade imbalances existed and expanded, while exports to China from other Asian countries were much larger than imports of the latter from China. Similarly, the exports from Japan and Korea to ASEAN countries were much larger than their imports from ASEAN. These imbalances reflect the structure of the triangular trade, whereby China imports parts and accessories from other East Asian countries in order to assemble them for the final products. ASEAN countries may play a similar role to China with respect to Korea and Japan.

The trade flows of 'Consumer goods' show a striking contrast with the 'Parts and accessories' (Figures 1.5a and 1.5b). The exports of consumer

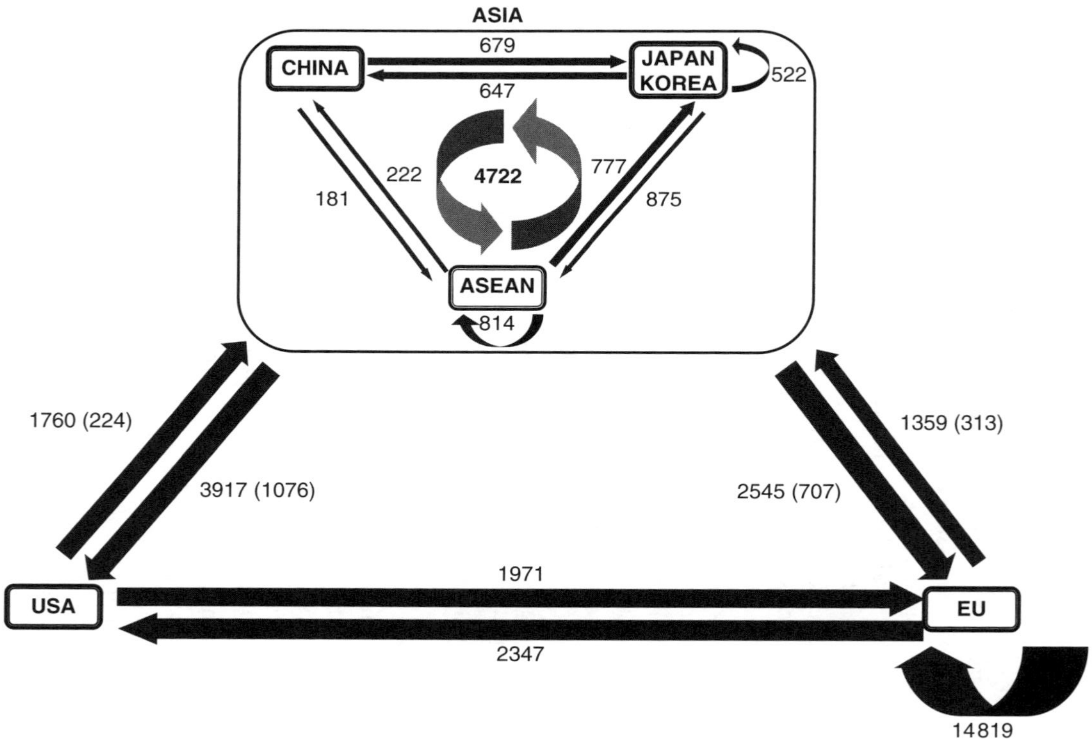

Note: Figures in parentheses indicate the amount of trade with China.

Source: United Nations, UN comtrade database.

Figure 1.3a Trade flows of all commodities (2000, 100 million US$)

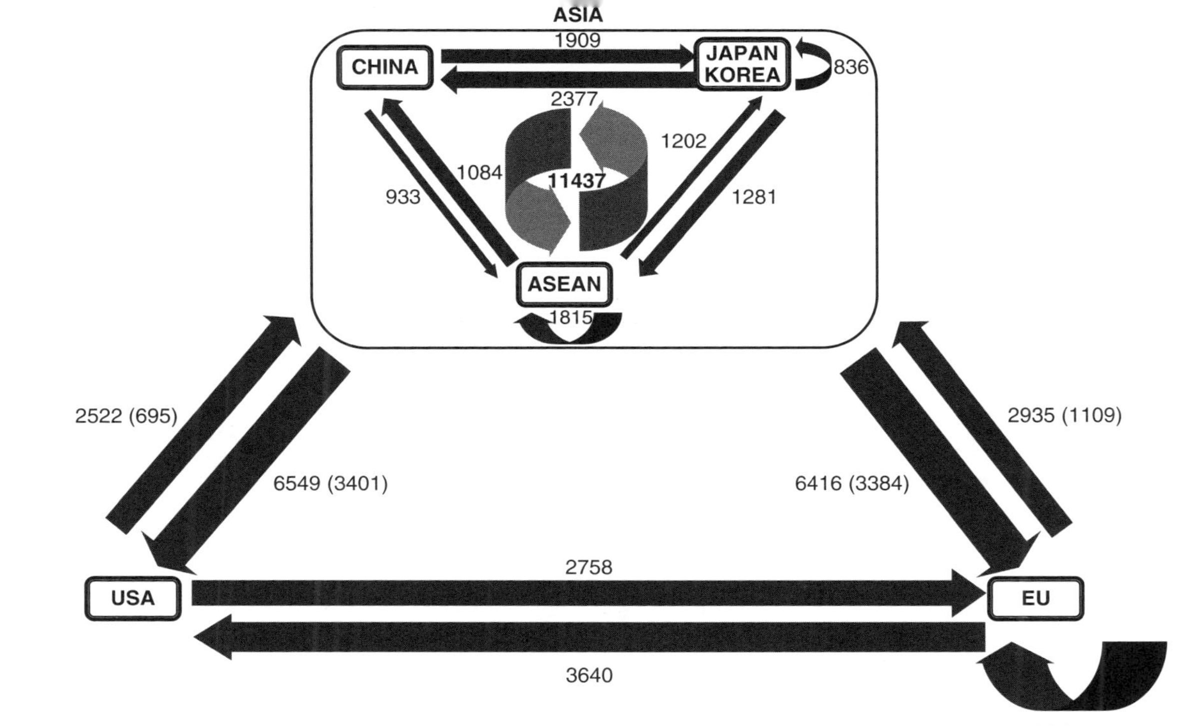

Note: Figures in parentheses indicate the amount of trade with China.

Source: United Nations, UN comtrade database.

Figure 1.3b Trade flows of all commodities (2007, 100 million US$)

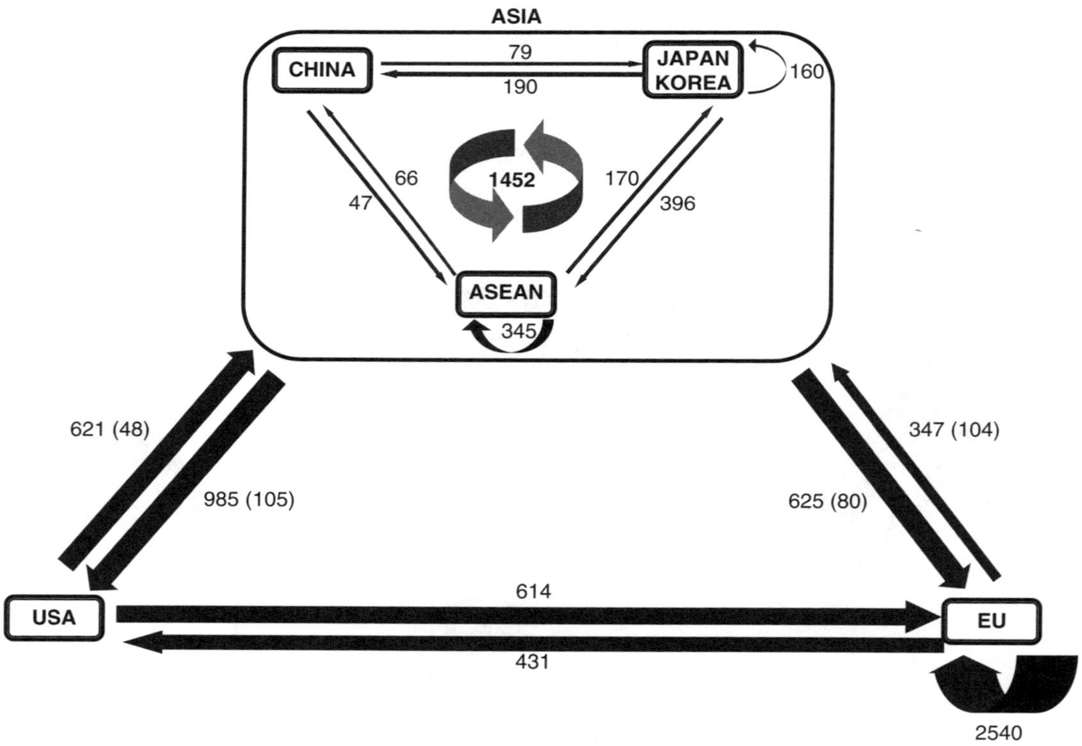

Note: Figures in parentheses indicate the amount of trade with China.

Source: United Nations, UN comtrade database.

Figure 1.4a Trade flows of parts and accessories (2000, 100 million US$)

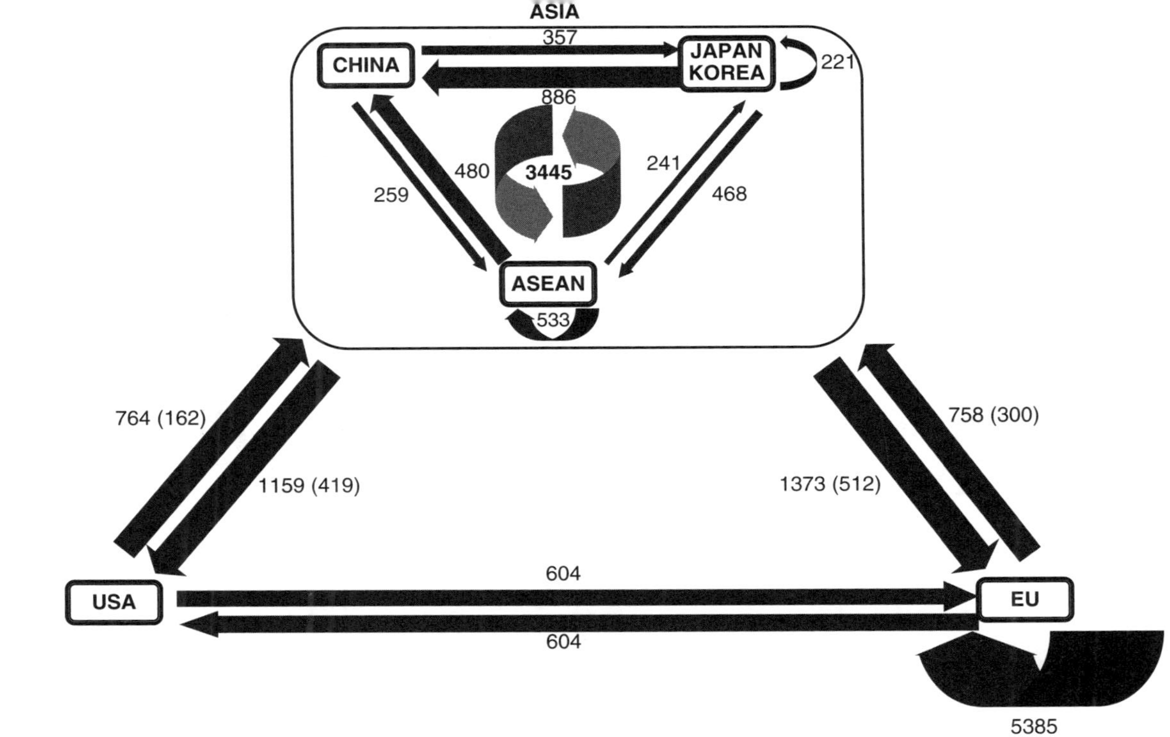

Note: Figures in parentheses indicate the amount of trade with China.

Source: United Nations, UN comtrade database.

Figure 1.4b Trade flows of parts and accessories (2007, 100 million US$)

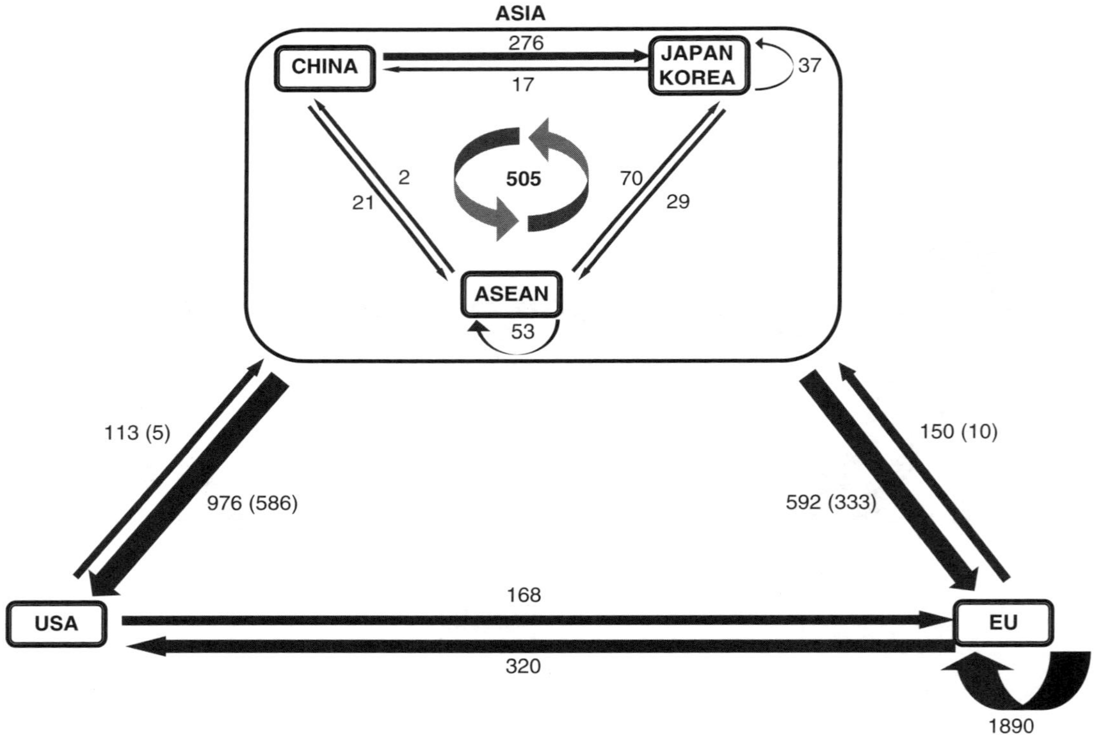

Note: Figures in parentheses indicate the amount of trade with China.

Source: United Nations, UN comtrade database.

Figure 1.5a Trade flows of consumer goods (2000, 100 million US$)

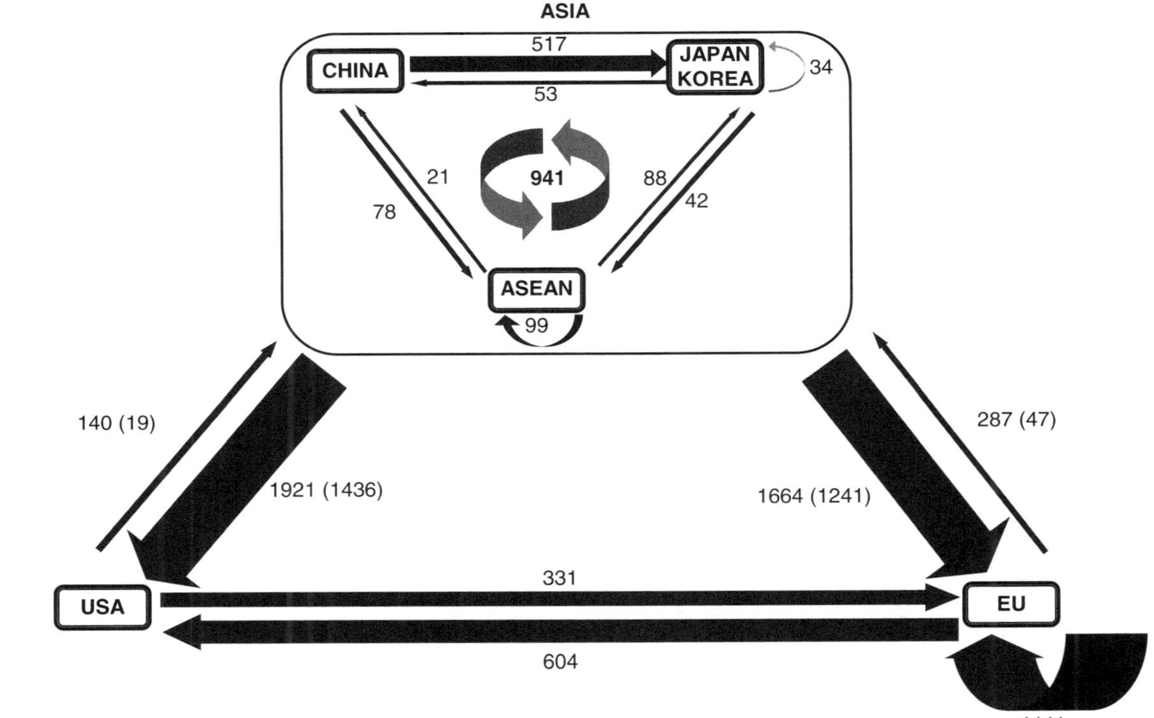

Note: Figures in parentheses indicate the amount of trade with China.

Source: United Nations, UN comtrade database.

Figure 1.5b Trade flows of consumer goods (2007, 100 million US$)

goods from the Asian region to the other two regions increased sharply while intra-regional trade did so only marginally, except for the trade flow from China to Japan and to Korea. Exports of consumer goods from Asia to the USA almost doubled from 2000 to 2007, while those to the EU almost tripled. Among the exports of consumer goods to other regions, those from China accounted for about 75 per cent of total exports, which indicates that the USA and EU became major markets for consumer goods produced in Asia, especially China, and that this structure has widened the trade imbalance to an unprecedented level.

The trade flows illustrated so far present a clear picture of the structure of trade in and around the Asia-Pacific region: that is, China imports significant amounts of parts and accessories from other Asian countries and then assembles and exports final products to the USA. The Asia-Pacific region has formed a 'triangular trade' structure during the observed period (2000–2007). Under such structure, any collapse in consumer demand in the USA will affect not only the direct exports of consumer goods to the US markets but also the indirect exports of parts and components to China from other Asian countries. This is an important transmission mechanism of the economic crisis in Asian countries, as will be further discussed in the next section.

3. IMPACTS OF THE ECONOMIC CRISIS ON INDUSTRIAL OUTPUT IN ASIA[3]

3.1 Trend of Exports to the USA

Figures 1.6a and 1.6b report trends of exports to the USA from nine Asian countries since the first quarter of 2005, when total exports to the USA from the entire world amounted to 380.6 billion US$.

Global exports to the USA continued to increase until the third quarter of 2008, with seasonal fluctuations. However, they subsequently plummeted after the Lehman shock which occurred in September 2008, and thus the strong influence of the crisis could be observed from the fourth quarter onwards. The declining trend in world exports continued until the first quarter of 2009, and it remains unclear when the trends will be reversed in the Asian region.[4]

Chinese exports grew significantly faster than world exports, but the impact of the financial crisis was very strong even for China; Chinese exports to the USA declined from 188.5 to 127.1 points during the period of the third quarter of 2008 to the first quarter of 2009 (first quarter 2005=100). It is notable that Indonesian exports performed relatively

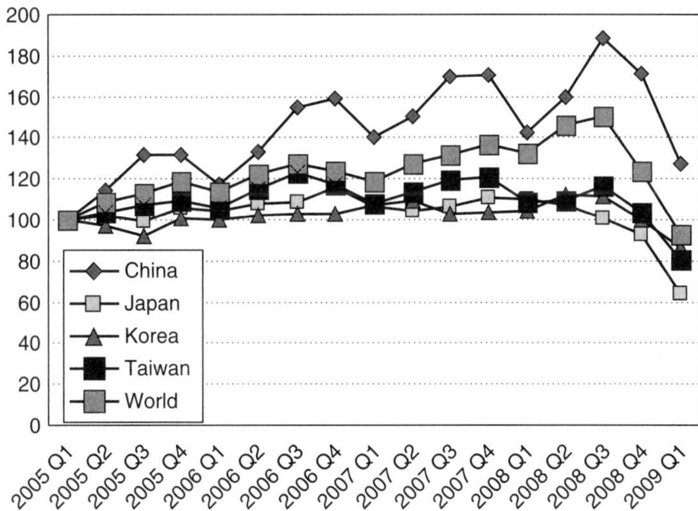

Source: Global Trade Information Services, World Trade Atlas.

Figure 1.6a Trend in exports to the USA (North-east Asia, 2005, Q1 = 100)

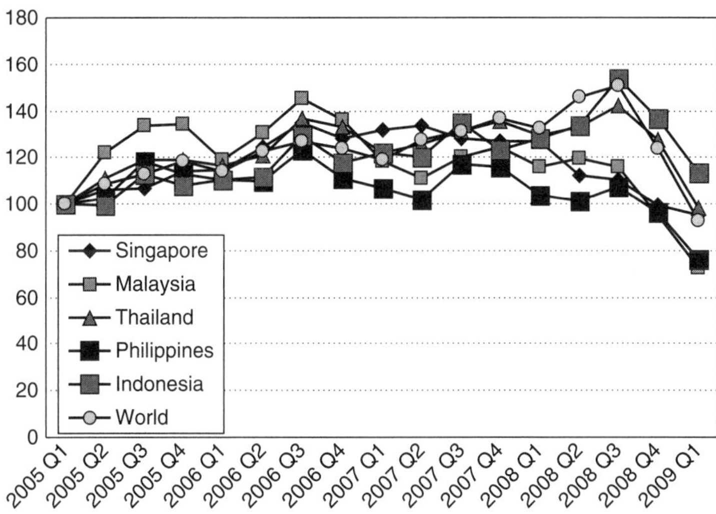

Source: Global Trade Information Services, World Trade Atlas.

Figure 1.6b Trend in exports to the USA (South-east Asia, 2005, Q1 = 100)

well during the same period – it seems that Indonesian exports were more affected by the trend of primary commodity prices. In contrast, exports of other Asian countries fell below the trend of global exports. In particular, those from Japan and Malaysia remained rather stagnant and started to decline before the Lehman shock, hitting rock bottom in the first quarter of 2009 at 64.2 and 72.9 points respectively.

As shown in Figures 1.6a and 1.6b, global exports to the USA peaked before the Lehman shock, but plummeted soon after. Such a rapid decline in exports was expected to affect Asian industries significantly. In the following section, the impact of the US financial crisis on Asian industries will be estimated.

3.2 From Trade Analysis to the International Input–Output Analysis

In this section onwards, we attempt to measure the impacts of the crisis by input–output analyses. In the national account framework, exports constitute a major demand item for national products. Their decline thus has a direct impact on a country's output. The decline in US demand for Korean cars, for example, causes a decrease of Korean car exports, and hence of car production in Korea.

Now, the decline in the output of cars triggers secondary repercussions on the production of other commodities. Apparently, it reduces the demand for car parts and components such as engines, tyres, bodies, handles, and so on. The decrease in production of these goods, however, further reduces the demand for, and hence the production of, their subparts and materials: ignitions, motors, cylinders, steel, rubber, glass . . . and so on.

This is called a (negative) multiplier effect. A change, or 'shock', that occurs in one industry (say, a drop in demand for cars) will be amplified throughout the complex production networks, and bring a larger and wider impact on the rest of the economy.

In the international context, the multiplier effect transcends national borders. The contraction in Korean car exports reduces its import demand for engine parts made in Thailand and bumpers made in China, which then reduces Thailand's import demand for steel and China's demand for chemicals from Japan. Over the last few decades, such cross-national production networks have developed extensively in the Asia-Pacific region, and the multiplier effect has become increasingly strong and complex.

In order to analyse the impact of the US financial crisis on Asian countries, we have to probe these complex production networks in the Asia-Pacific region, for which the Asian International Input–Output Tables (AIO tables) will be used, enabling us to capture every recursive impact,

Table 1.4 Multiplier of the US demand shock

	(1) Exports to the USA (3rd Qtr 2008)	(2) Exports to the USA (1st Qtr 2009)	(3) Decline of exports after the crisis =(2) − (1)	(4) Output loss caused by the export decline	Multiplier =(4)/(3)
China	96150	64810	−31339	−68987	**2.20**
Japan	34174	21768	−12406	−28175	**2.27**
Korea	12490	9665	−2824	−7176	**2.54**
Taiwan	9676	6669	−3006	−6738	**2.24**
Singapore	3915	3356	−559	−2007	**3.59**
Malaysia	7978	5016	−2962	−6130	**2.07**
Thailand	6281	4358	−1923	−3647	**1.90**
Philippines	2294	1630	−663	−2979	**4.49**
Indonesia	4402	3253	−1149	−2602	**2.26**

Sources: Calculated by the authors from the Asian International Input–Output Table (2008) and the US Department of Commerce, Bureau of Census.

through both direct and indirect channels, of the collapse in US import demand on each industrial output of Asian countries.[5]

The AIO table covers nine Asian countries and the USA, which are endogenously treated within the model. (In other words, their mutual transactions of goods and services are explicitly presented in the table. See the 'Explanatory notes' in Chapter 8 for a more detailed description of the data.) In this study, however, both the rows and columns of the USA are exogenized from the intermediate transactions matrix, and, in order to calculate the total impact of the US financial crisis, the extent of the decline in US imports from these nine Asian countries for the period from the third quarter of 2008 to the first quarter of 2009 are given as exogenous variables of the model.

The calculation of the impact reveals that in the Asia-Pacific region the negative multipliers of shock repercussion lie around the levels of two to three, with the exceptions of Singapore and the Philippines (Table 1.4).

Regarding the impact of the financial crisis, it is convenient to decompose it into three effects according to the channels of multipliers; namely, (1) the decrease in output induced by the domestic multiplier; (2) that induced by the triangular-trade multiplier through China; (3) that induced by other inter-country multipliers. The first effect, that of the domestic multiplier, is called 'domestic' in the sense that the repercussion process of an impact will start and end within the border of the country in question.[6] For example, the US demand shock directly reduces Korean exports to the USA, whereupon the repercussion starts and spills over to the entire Korean economy. The other two effects measure the cross-national transmission of shock repercussion. The US demand shock first reaches land somewhere outside Korea, where it triggers repercussions. Subsequently, via the direct trade channel between Korea and that country as well as the indirect trade channel via the third country,[7] the impact is finally transmitted to Korea for further repercussion within the Korean production system. Among these inter-country effects, effect (2) deals with the special case of our current interest, whereby the impact is transmitted through trade with China.[8]

Table 1.5a shows the result of our simulation for impact decomposition: the list of top 10 industries (in descending order) in North-east Asian countries, which are affected most significantly by the financial crisis. These industries suffer a serious decrease in outputs during the crisis period. The decline of output is then decomposed into the three effects, as described above. In addition, the elasticity of induced production (the percentage decrease in the output of each industrial sector divided by the percentage decrease in the total output) is calculated in order to compare the magnitude of the impact of the crisis for respective sectors.

The table shows that China's output fell by 68 987 million US$ during the third quarter of 2008 and the first quarter of 2009. China saw the largest decline, because it is the largest exporter to the USA, and its exports have been significantly affected by the crisis. Reflecting the export volumes, 'Textile and leather' declined most significantly (9953 million US$), followed by 'Computers and electronic equipment' (9498 million US$) and 'Other electrical equipment' (8772 million US$). It should be noted that the last two industries have also been significantly affected in other Asian countries. Similarly, material industries ('Metal products' and 'Chemical products') and services industries ('Trade and transport' and 'Services') have been significantly affected in many Asian countries.

The share of the other inter-country effects (that is effect (3) as listed above) is relatively low in China, with the exception of 'Computers and electronic equipment' (7.75 per cent). Indeed, a significant part of China's output (96.02 per cent) is reduced through the domestic multiplier effect (effect (1)).[9]

Japan's total output fell by 28 175 million US$, with the biggest decline in 'Transport equipment' (5859 million US$), followed by 'Services' (5645 million US$) and 'Computers and electronic equipment' (3732 million US$). The rapid decline of 'Transport equipment' reflects the trade structure of Japan whereby transport equipment, especially automobiles, has been Japan's largest export item for the US market. Moreover, since its output (as well as its exports to the USA per se) is highly elastic, its impact

Table 1.5a Decline of output (08Q3–09Q1) in North-east Asia

Rank	Industrial sector	Declines (Million US$)	Contribution of Decomposed Effects (%)				Elasticity
			Domestic multiplier effect	**Inter-country multiplier effect**	**Triangular-trade multiplier effect (thru. China)**	**Other inter-country multiplier effect**	
			Effect (1)	Effect (2) + (3)	Effect (2)	Effect (3)	
CHINA							
1	Textile and leather	9953	98.97	1.03	–	1.03	1.00
2	Computers and electronic equipment	9498	92.25	7.75	–	7.75	0.94
3	Other electrical equipment	8772	97.24	2.76	–	2.76	1.08
4	Other manufacturing products	7149	98.41	1.59	–	1.59	1.11
5	Metal products	6424	94.22	5.78	–	5.78	1.04
6	Chemical products	5721	96.07	3.93	–	3.93	0.95
7	Trade and transport	3272	92.45	7.55	–	7.55	1.00
8	Services	2388	96.23	3.77	–	3.77	0.97
9	Electricity, gas and water supply	2333	95.70	4.30	–	4.30	1.01
10	Pulp, paper and printing	1832	97.50	2.50	–	2.50	1.15
Total		**68987**	**96.02**	**3.98**	**–**	**3.98**	**1.00**
JAPAN							
1	Transport equipment	5859	99.00	1.00	0.46	0.54	1.26
2	Services	5645	93.67	6.33	3.47	2.86	1.20
3	Computers and electronic equipment	3732	68.25	31.75	18.09	13.66	0.97
4	Other electrical equipment	2404	88.73	11.27	5.56	5.72	1.06
5	General machinery	2131	92.19	7.81	3.44	4.37	0.77

Table 1.5a (continued)

Rank	Industrial sector	Declines (Million US$)	Contribution of Decomposed Effects (%)				Elasticity
			Domestic multiplier effect	**Inter-country multiplier effect**	**Triangular-trade multiplier effect (thru. China)**	**Other inter-country multiplier effect**	
			Effect (1)	Effect (2) + (3)	Effect (2)	Effect (3)	
6	Metal products	2102	71.84	28.16	13.57	14.59	0.86
7	Trade and transport	1917	75.86	24.14	13.20	10.93	0.96
8	Chemical products	1082	66.71	33.29	20.37	12.92	0.59
9	Other manufacturing products	905	86.03	13.97	8.27	5.70	0.88
10	Pulp, paper and printing	499	81.63	18.37	10.50	7.87	0.93
Total		**28175**	**85.82**	**14.18**	**7.75**	**6.44**	**1.00**
KOREA							
1	Computers and electronic equipment	1717	49.76	50.24	33.70	16.54	1.23
2	Metal products	917	66.26	33.74	21.05	12.68	1.10
3	Services	801	77.20	22.80	15.53	7.27	0.89
4	Other electrical equipment	618	73.08	26.92	16.68	10.24	0.55
5	Petroleum and petro products	578	82.65	17.35	13.29	4.06	1.84
6	Chemical products	563	47.78	52.22	41.06	11.16	1.11
7	Transport equipment	378	96.40	3.60	1.45	2.16	0.86
8	Trade and transport	355	54.78	45.22	30.70	14.52	0.98
9	Textile and leather	251	80.24	19.76	16.72	3.04	1.20
10	General machinery	250	84.86	15.14	7.19	7.95	0.75
Total		**7176**	**66.90**	**33.10**	**22.50**	**10.61**	**1.00**

Table 1.5a (continued)

Rank	Industrial sector	Declines (Million US$)	Contribution of Decomposed Effects (%)				Elasticity
			Domestic multiplier effect	**Inter-country multiplier effect**	**Triangular-trade multiplier effect (thru. China)**	**Other inter-country multiplier effect**	
			Effect (1)	Effect (2) + (3)	Effect (2)	Effect (3)	
TAIWAN							
1	Computers and electronic equipment	1747	56.51	43.49	30.05	13.43	1.03
2	Metal products	874	78.13	21.87	16.52	5.34	1.10
3	Services	837	81.90	18.10	13.11	4.99	1.14
4	Other electrical equipment	454	84.88	15.12	9.81	5.31	0.60
5	Trade and transport	442	56.22	43.78	31.69	12.09	0.98
6	Other manufacturing products	374	85.49	14.51	10.73	3.78	0.97
7	Textile and leather	370	87.85	12.15	10.52	1.63	1.21
8	General machinery	353	93.97	6.03	3.15	2.87	1.12
9	Chemical products	333	53.32	46.68	40.29	6.38	1.08
10	Petroleum and petro products	236	64.36	35.64	28.26	7.38	0.95
Total		**6738**	**73.10**	**26.90**	**19.51**	**7.39**	**1.00**

Note: 'Total' indicates the sum of all commodities.

Sources: Calculated from Asian International Input–Output Table (2008) and US Department of Commerce, Bureau of Census.

of the crisis is further magnified (see Table 1.5a).[10] Among the manufacturing industries, 'Computers and electronic equipment' are strongly affected due to the inter-country multipliers (31.75 per cent). Similarly, material industries, such as 'Chemical products' and 'Metal products', indicate relatively high shares of inter-country effects; in particular, the triangular-trade multiplier through China was overwhelmingly important for these industries. Note that these industries show a strong contrast with 'Transport equipment' where the share of the inter-country effects is extremely low (only 1.00 per cent).

The total output in Korea is reduced by 7176 million US$. 'Computers and electronic equipment' (1717 million US$) declines most significantly, followed by 'Metal products' (917 million US$) and 'Services' (801 million US$). It is astonishing that the share of the inter-country effects, especially the triangular-trade multiplier through China, is extremely high in such industries as 'Chemical products', 'Computers and electronic equipment', 'Trade and transport', and 'Metal products'. This implies that the intensive production networks were shaped in East Asia, where Korea supplies many electronic parts and components (as well as relevant materials and services) to China and then final products are exported from China to the USA. On the other hand, as in the case for Japan, the share of the inter-country multiplier effects in 'Transport equipment' is very small, and this implies that the rapid fall in Korea's (or Japan's) transport equipment production is principally induced through the domestic multiplier effect.

Total production in Taiwan fell by 6738 million US$ and showed great similarity with Korea. For example, like Korea, 'Computers and electronic equipment' (1747 million US$) declined most sharply, followed by 'Metal products' (874 million US$) and 'Services' (837 million US$). It is also notable that industries such as 'Chemical products', 'Trade and transport', and 'Computers and electronic equipment', have extremely high shares of the inter-country effects, especially the triangular-trade multiplier through China.

It is very clear that Korea and Taiwan are deeply involved in the triangular trade through China. In particular, close regional production networks have been formed in 'Computers and electronic products' and material industries such as 'Chemical products' and 'Metal products'.

Table 1.5b reports the results for South-east Asian countries for top eight industries. Except for Indonesia, the production of 'Computers and electronic equipment' presents the most significant decline in all four countries (Singapore, Malaysia, Thailand and the Philippines). Especially in Malaysia, this industrial sector accounts for more than half the total decline of industrial output caused by the drop in US import demand (54.11 per cent, 3317 million US$). Also, in Singapore and the Philippines, the category of 'Computers and electronic equipment' occupies significant shares (44.89 per cent and 42.46 per cent, respectively). Though not as significant as the former category, 'Other electronic products' also showed significant decline in these countries.

Indonesia reveals a different picture from the other four South-east

Table 1.5b Decline of output (08Q3–09Q1) in South-east Asia

Rank	Industrial sector	Declines (Million US$)	Contribution of Decomposed Effects (%)				Elasticity
			Domestic multiplier effect Effect (1)	Inter-country multiplier effect Effect (2) + (3)	Triangular-trade multiplier effect (thru. China) Effect (2)	Other inter-country multiplier effect Effect (3)	
SINGAPORE							
1	Computers and electronic equipment	901	61.82	38.18	14.42	23.75	1.81
2	Other electrical equipment	592	81.09	18.91	6.19	12.72	1.84
3	Services	301	69.11	30.89	11.97	18.92	1.10
4	General machinery	162	70.74	29.26	10.25	19.01	1.23
5	Trade and transport	156	27.81	72.19	28.02	44.18	0.88
6	Petroleum and petro products	133	−15.35	115.35	43.51	71.84	0.99
7	Metal products	96	47.35	52.65	16.76	35.88	1.26
8	Transport equipment	36	68.43	31.57	9.57	22.00	0.84
Total		**2007**	**46.71**	**53.29**	**20.05**	**33.24**	**1.00**
MALAYSIA							
1	Computers and electronic equipment	3317	85.02	14.98	9.53	5.45	1.10
2	Other electrical equipment	959	90.39	9.61	3.96	5.65	1.12
3	Trade and transport	493	80.49	19.51	10.85	8.66	1.01
4	Services	187	75.54	24.46	9.51	14.95	0.84
5	Metal products	181	79.82	20.18	8.06	12.12	0.99
6	Timber and wooden products	140	89.75	10.25	3.65	6.61	0.96
7	Food, beverage and tobacco	134	95.71	4.29	2.40	1.89	0.65
8	Textile and leather	116	95.21	4.79	1.84	2.95	0.93
Total		**6130**	**83.87**	**16.13**	**8.65**	**7.48**	**1.00**

Table 1.5b (continued)

Rank	Industrial sector	Declines (Million US$)	Contribution of Decomposed Effects (%)				Elasticity
			Domestic multiplier effect	Inter-country multiplier effect	Triangular-trade multiplier effect (thru. China)	Other inter-country multiplier effect	
			Effect (1)	Effect (2) + (3)	Effect (2)	Effect (3)	
THAILAND							
1	Computers and electronic equipment	811	61.21	38.79	26.89	11.90	1.00
2	Other electrical equipment	614	91.09	8.91	4.06	4.85	1.32
3	Trade and transport	278	70.64	29.36	16.44	12.93	1.01
4	Other manufacturing products	238	96.55	3.45	1.55	1.90	1.32
5	Services	197	86.65	13.35	6.98	6.37	1.11
6	Textile and leather	195	94.34	5.66	3.42	2.24	0.73
7	General machinery	171	75.93	24.07	6.88	17.18	0.75
8	Metal products	160	89.10	10.90	2.48	8.42	1.53
Total		**3647**	**80.67**	**19.33**	**10.92**	**8.41**	**1.00**
PHILIPPINES							
1	Computers and electronic equipment	1265	69.29	30.71	20.94	9.78	1.01
2	Trade and transport	316	67.27	32.73	19.01	13.72	1.04
3	Services	238	72.10	27.90	15.97	11.93	0.89
4	Other electrical equipment	203	94.20	5.80	3.06	2.75	0.88
5	Food, beverage and tobacco	184	94.63	5.37	2.80	2.57	1.31
6	Textile and leather	161	97.95	2.05	1.10	0.94	0.67
7	Transport equipment	98	92.70	7.30	0.50	6.80	1.89
8	Metal products	74	75.87	24.13	7.38	16.76	1.33
Total		**2979**	**77.16**	**22.84**	**14.05**	**8.79**	**1.00**

Table 1.5b (continued)

Rank	Industrial sector	Declines (Million US$)	Contribution of Decomposed Effects (%)				Elasticity
			Domestic multiplier effect	Inter-country multiplier effect	Triangular-trade multiplier effect (thru. China)	Other inter-country multiplier effect	
			Effect (1)	Effect (2) + (3)	Effect (2)	Effect (3)	
INDONESIA							
1	Crude petroleum and natural gas	431	73.24	26.76	7.23	19.53	1.68
2	Forestry	275	98.12	1.88	1.21	0.67	1.96
3	Trade and transport	223	69.16	30.84	11.06	19.78	1.00
4	Chemical products	192	85.37	14.63	6.12	8.51	1.34
5	Services	170	79.85	20.15	7.48	12.67	1.12
6	Metal products	144	65.94	34.06	6.36	27.70	1.64
7	Other electrical equipment	134	87.53	12.47	3.24	9.23	0.98
8	Other mining	116	20.97	79.03	34.80	44.23	1.18
Total		**2602**	**78.84**	**21.16**	**7.33**	**13.83**	**1.00**

Note: 'Total' indicates the sum of all commodities.

Sources: Calculated from Asian International Input–Output Table (2008) and US Department of Commerce, Bureau of Census.

Asian countries. In Indonesia, 'Crude petroleum and natural gas' declined most sharply (431 million US$), followed by 'Forestry' (275 million US$).

When examining the contribution of inter-country effects, it is remarkable that its share as a total decline of industrial outputs is extremely high in Singapore (53.29 per cent), because its industries are deeply involved in Asian production networks. In particular, industries such as 'Petroleum and petro products' (115.35 per cent),[11] 'Trade and transport' (72.19 per cent), and 'Metal products' (52.65 per cent) are significantly affected by the inter-country effects. In Malaysia, there are high shares in 'Services' (24.46 per cent), 'Metal products' (20.18 per cent) and 'Trade and transport' (19.51 per cent). In Thailand and the Philippines, shares are high in 'Computer and electronic equipment' and in 'Trade and transport', while in Indonesia, shares are relatively high in 'Metal products', 'Trade and transport', and 'Crude petroleum and natural gas'.

When focusing on the triangular-trade multiplier effect through China, it is obvious that in all countries a significant part of the inter-country effect is accounted for by trade through China: that is 20.05 per cent in Singapore, 8.65 per cent in Malaysia, 10.92 per cent in Thailand, 14.05 per cent in the Philippines, and 7.33 per cent in Indonesia respectively. At an industry level, there are several variations across countries. In Singapore, industries such as 'Petroleum and petro products', 'Trade and transport', 'Metal products' and 'Computers and electronic equipment' are significantly affected by the triangular trade through China. In Thailand and the Philippines, the ratio is high in 'Computers and electronic equipment' and 'Trade and transport'. In Indonesia, it is high in 'Other mining' (34.8 per cent), indicating that Indonesia is deeply involved in regional production networks as an important supplier of mining products.

It is also noticeable here that, as well as for North-east Asia, industries such as 'Computers and electronic equipment' and 'Other electrical equipment' were significantly affected by the US financial crisis and the impacts have been mainly transmitted through the triangular trade through China.

4. INFLUENCE OF THE TRIANGULAR TRADE THROUGH CHINA

As described above, Asian industries are significantly affected by the inter-country effects, especially the triangular-trade multiplier through China. Figure 1.7 shows the percentage shares of inter-country effects for all industrial sectors combined; here, the US import demands for 2000 and 2008 are given as exogenous variables, and then the percentage shares of the inter-country multiplier effects for total output, which is induced by inter-country effects through respective Asian countries, are indicated by each segment in the bar. It emerges that the percentage shares of triangular trade through China are not significantly high in 2000 (all below 5 per cent). However, these shares increase drastically in 2008; in particular, the shares of total industrial output for Korea and Taiwan are 15.9 per cent and 18.1 per cent, respectively. It is also notable that Japan – which was historically less dependent on the Asian countries – is now heavily involved in triangular trade through China (7.5 per cent). In South-east Asia, the Philippines have the highest share (12.4 per cent), reflecting the geographical proximity between China and the Philippines. Interestingly, close geographical proximity is also an important factor for determining the interdependency between Singapore and Malaysia. For example, the share of Singapore's total output in 2000 induced by trade through Malaysia was 10.5 per cent. In 2008, however, Singapore's dependency on

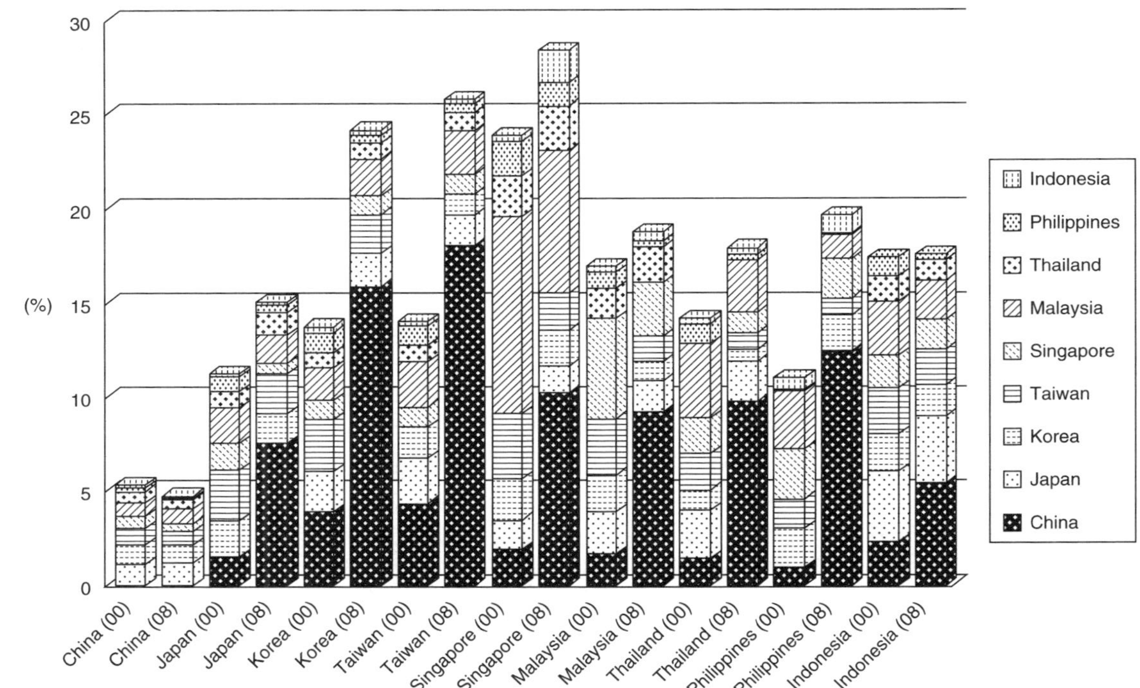

Source: Calculated by the authors from Asian international input–output tables.

Figure 1.7 Percentage shares of the inter-country multiplier effect (totals: 2000, 2008)

Malaysia declined and was overtaken by dependency on China (10.2 per cent).

The evidence for the increasing presence of triangular trade through China is more clearly indicated by Figure 1.8, which shows the percentage shares of the inter-country multiplier effects for the 'Computers and electronic equipment' industry. Note that this industrial sector is affected most strongly by the US financial crisis and its output is significantly influenced by the triangular trade (see Tables 1.5a and 1.5b). Figure 1.8 indicates that during the period 2000–2008 the shares of the inter-country multiplier effects increased sharply, especially in Korea (17.6→46.0 per cent) and Taiwan (16.9→42.2 per cent). In particular, the shares of the triangular multiplier effects through China increased drastically during this period (2.7→30.9 per cent in Korea and 3.0→29.1 per cent in Taiwan). In South-east Asia, meanwhile, shares notably increased in Thailand and the Philippines.

The above observation on the case of the 'Computers and electronic equipment' industry suggests that the geographical spread of production networks, which is reflected in the share of inter-country multiplier effects, is largely determined by the characteristics of the industry in question. For example, parts and accessories in the automotive industry are generally bulky and heavy. Therefore, automotive assemblers have strong incentives to save on transport costs by procuring parts and components from local suppliers. In addition, just-in-time production increases the need for local agglomeration of supporting industries, so that the share of inter-country multiplier effects of transport equipment (including automotive) is very small, as shown in Japan and Korea.

In contrast, the electronics industry lacks such strong agglomeration economies and is instead very active in production fragmentation, because its parts and accessories, especially high-tech products, are small and light with high value-added content. Moreover, since the electronics industry is highly export-oriented and given preferential treatment, such as unlimited access to imported inputs and exemption from import duties, it has little incentive to raise its share of local procurement (Kuroiwa, 2008, 2009). Such characteristics obviously encourage the industry to be involved in the inter-country production networks.

5. CONCLUSIONS

This chapter has analysed the impacts of the economic crisis by addressing two specific questions. First, what is the extent of the impact that the collapse of the US economy inflicted on Asian industries? Second, why was the impact so magnified when it reached Asian shores? By using AIO

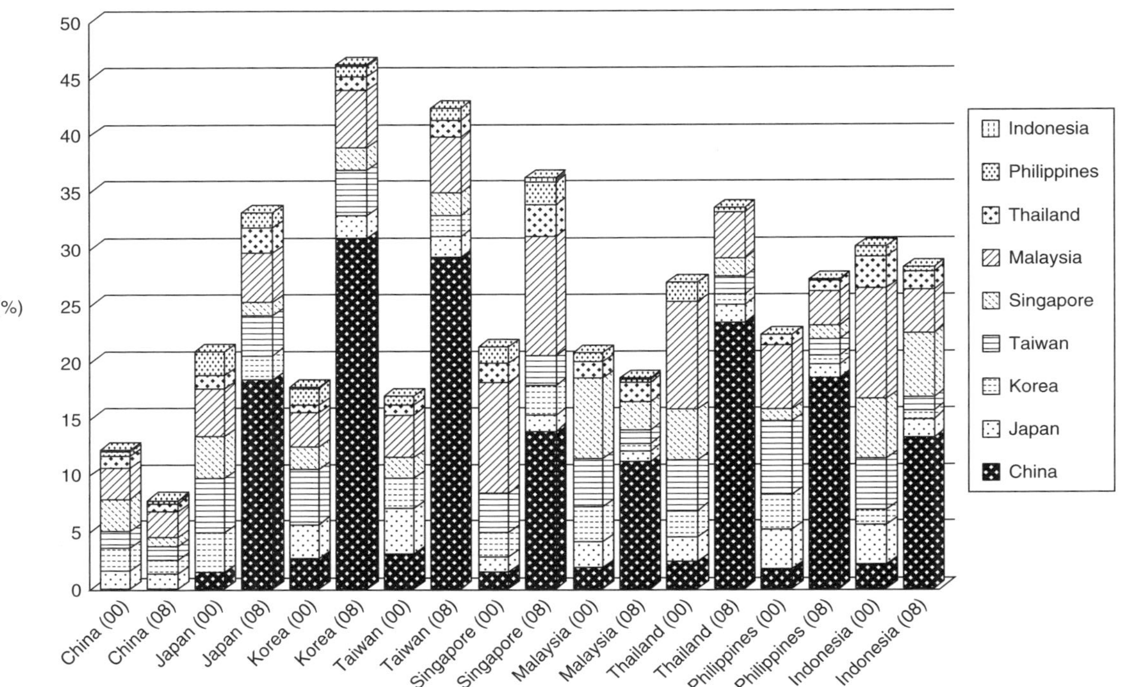

Source: Calculated by the authors from Asian international input–output tables.

Figure 1.8 Percentage shares of the inter-country multiplier effect (computers and electronic equipment: 2000, 2008)

tables and trade statistics as the main analytical tools, attempts have been made to answer these questions.

As for the first question, analyses using the AIO tables identified the quantitative impacts of the economic crisis on industrial production in Asian countries. It revealed that the production of Asian industries was severely damaged by the collapse in US import demand caused by the economic crisis after the Lehman shock. The quarterly industrial production in China and Japan is estimated to have been the most severely affected, falling by 68 987 million US$ and 28 175 million US$, respectively. Industries in other Asian countries were also hurt and their quarterly industrial output is estimated to have decreased within the range of 2007 million US$ (Singapore) and 7176 million US$ (Korea).

For the second question, analyses in this chapter revealed 'triangular trade through China' as one of the key factors explaining the amplification of the impact. Analyses using trade statistics clearly showed that the countries in the Asia-Pacific region formed a triangular trade structure: that is, Asian countries exporting parts and components to China, whereupon China exports final products to the US market after assembling the imported intermediate parts. Therefore, the impact of the collapse in US import demand is transmitted indirectly to Asian countries through the trade with China as well as through the direct channel from the US markets. International input–output analysis revealed that this triangular trade structure had a significant impact on the production of Asian industries. In particular, such impact is prominent in key industries such as electronics, which have developed extensive production networks in the Asia-Pacific region.

In the rest of the book, the 'triangular trade through China' as a principal shock transmission mechanism in the Asia-Pacific region is investigated from various perspectives. The next chapter examines the impact of the crisis on employment, which addresses a crucial issue for all the policy makers of the countries concerned.

NOTES

1. Throughout this book, the terms 'North-east Asia', 'South-east Asia', 'ASEAN', 'East Asia', and 'the EU' are used to indicate the following groups of countries (Taiwan is sometimes excluded due to the non-availability of trade data):

   (1) North-east Asia: China, Japan, Korea, Taiwan
   (2) South-east Asia: Indonesia, Malaysia, the Philippines, Singapore, Thailand
   (3) ASEAN: Brunei, Cambodia, Indonesia, Laos PDR, Malaysia, Myanmar, the Philippines, Singapore, Thailand, Vietnam (ASEAN10)
   (4) East Asia: China, Japan, Korea, Taiwan, ASEAN10

(5) The EU: Austria, Belgium, Bulgaria, Cyprus, the Czech Republic, Denmark, Estonia, Finland, France, Germany, Greece, Hungary, Ireland, Italy, Latvia, Lithuania, Luxembourg, Malta, the Netherlands, Poland, Portugal, Romania, Slovakia, Slovenia, Spain, Sweden, the United Kingdom (EU27)

2. The classification is based on the United Nations' Broad Economic Categories (BEC), which classify internationally-traded commodities according to their main end-use.
3. The authors would like to thank Yosuke Noda for his assistance in processing the trade data.
4. Figure 1.6a indicates that exports to the USA were tending to dip in the first quarter, even before the economic crisis. However, it is obvious that the decline in the first quarter 2009 was much larger than expected from seasonal fluctuation.
5. Although the latest version of the official AIO table is for the year 2000, the updated 2008 table was compiled specifically for this analytical purpose. See the 'Explanatory notes' in Chapter 8 for the updating method.
6. As shown in Miller and Blair (1985), the domestic multiplier effect is further decomposed into the intra-country effect and the feedback effect. See Appendix 1A.1 for technical details.
7. For example, if China's exports to the USA decline, this will directly affect China's intermediate import from Korea (direct trade channel). At the same time, it will also affect China's import demand from other East Asian countries, such as Japan and Taiwan, which will then affect the latter's import demand from Korea, finally impacting on Korea's production (indirect trade channel via the third country).
8. The multiplier effect is calculated as a column sum of the elements in sub-matrices of the Leontief Inverse constructed from the AIO table. It is categorized into domestic or inter-country effects, depending on which parts of the Leontief Inverse are observed. Viewing the image of the AIO table given in the 'Explanatory notes' in Chapter 8, if we point to the segment of the Leontief Inverse that corresponds to A^{KK}, for example, this gives us the domestic multiplier of Korea. If we look at the rest of the column, we are referring to the inter-country multipliers of Korea with respect to other countries. In particular, the sub-matrix A^{KC} corresponds to Korea's triangular-trade multiplier through China.
9. Note that China's exports of intermediate inputs to other Asian countries are relatively small compared to its counterpart imports (see Figure 1.4b), and likewise the contribution of the inter-country effects in China.
10. Note that many upstream industries in Tables 1.5a and 1.5b indicate relatively high elasticity in other Asian countries as well.
11. The figure, 115.35 per cent, exceeds 100 per cent. This occurred because the domestic multiplier effect of 'Petroleum and petro products' was negative (that is the output of this sector was increased due to the domestic multiplier effects; see Table 1.5b).

REFERENCES

Asian Development Bank (2009), *Asian Development Outlook 2009: Rebalancing Asia's Growth*, Asian Development Bank.

International Monetary Fund (2009), *World Economic Outlook April 2009: Crisis and Recovery*, International Monetary Fund.

Kuroiwa, I. (2008), 'Cross-border production networks in Southeast Asia: application of the international input–output analysis', in I. Kuroiwa and T.M. Heng (eds), *Production Networks and Industrial Clusters: Integrating Economies in Southeast Asia*, Singapore: Institute of Southeast Asian Studies, pp. 54–85.

Kuroiwa, I. (2009), 'Value content and production networks in Southeast Asia:

application of AFTA and ASEAN-Plus-One FTA formulas', *The Developing Economies*, **47** (2), 147–76.
Miller, R. and P.D. Blair (1985), *Input–Output Analysis: Foundations and Extensions*, Englewood Cliffs, NJ: Prentice-Hall.

APPENDIX 1A.1: MULTIPLIER DECOMPOSITION METHOD

This appendix explains the calculation methodology used to measure the impact of the decline of US import demand caused by the economic crisis.

Consider the AIO table that excludes the USA from the endogenous countries. In this augmented AIO table consisting of nine countries, we denote the member countries as C (China), I (Indonesia), J (Japan), K (Korea), M (Malaysia), N (Taiwan), P (Philippines), S (Singapore) and T (Thailand). Suppose further that in matrices (and vectors) appearing in the following equations, countries are arranged in the above (alphabetical) order.

From the macroeconomic accounting identity, the equilibrium between supply and demand in the augmented AIO table can be expressed as follows:

$$X = AX + F \tag{1.A1}$$

where

$X = \begin{bmatrix} X^C \\ \vdots \\ X^T \end{bmatrix}$: The vector of gross output (X^r is country r's $n \times 1$ vector of output)[1]

$A = \begin{bmatrix} A^{CC} & \cdots & A^{CT} \\ \vdots & \ddots & \vdots \\ A^{TC} & \cdots & A^{TT} \end{bmatrix}$: The input coefficient matrix (A^{rs} is an $n \times n$ matrix that describes the input structure from country r to country s)

$F = \begin{bmatrix} F^C \\ \vdots \\ F^T \end{bmatrix}$: The vector of final demand (F^r is country r's $n \times 1$ vector of final demand)

Solving equation (1.A1) for X yields:

$$X = (I - A)^{-1}F = LF \tag{1.A2}$$

where

$I = \begin{bmatrix} I_n & \cdots & 0_n \\ \vdots & \ddots & \vdots \\ 0_n & \cdots & I_n \end{bmatrix}$: Identity matrix ($I_n$ is $n \times n$ identity matrix and 0_n represents an $n \times n$ matrix of zeros)

$L = (I - A)^{-1}$

$$= \begin{bmatrix} L^{CC} & \cdots & L^{CT} \\ \vdots & \ddots & \vdots \\ L^{TC} & \cdots & L^{TT} \end{bmatrix} : \text{ The inverse matrix of } I - A$$

Equation (1.A2) can be decomposed as

$$X = LF = (L_1 + L_2 + L_3 + L_4)F \tag{1.A3}$$

where

$$L_1 = \begin{bmatrix} \tilde{L}^{CC} & \cdots & 0_n \\ \vdots & \ddots & \vdots \\ 0_n & \cdots & \tilde{L}^{TT} \end{bmatrix} : \text{ Intra-country multiplier } (\tilde{L}^{rr} = (I - A^{rr})^{-1})$$

$$L_2 = \begin{bmatrix} L^{CC} - \tilde{L}^{CC} & \cdots & 0_n \\ \vdots & \ddots & \vdots \\ 0_n & \cdots & L^{TT} - \tilde{L}^{TT} \end{bmatrix} : \text{ Feedback multiplier}$$

$$L_3 = \begin{bmatrix} 0_n & 0_n & \cdots & 0_n \\ L^{IC} & 0_n & \cdots & 0_n \\ \vdots & \vdots & \ddots & \vdots \\ L^{TC} & 0_n & \cdots & 0_n \end{bmatrix} : \text{ Triangular-trade multiplier through China}$$

$$L_4 = \begin{bmatrix} 0_n & L^{CI} & \cdots & L^{CT} \\ 0_n & 0_n & \cdots & L^{IT} \\ \vdots & \vdots & \ddots & \vdots \\ 0_n & L^{TI} & \cdots & 0_n \end{bmatrix} : \text{ Other inter-country multiplier}$$

Since $\tilde{L}^{rr}$ indicates the 'intra-country multiplier effect' of country r, the first term post-multiplied by the final demand vector in equation (1.A3) ($\tilde{L}^{rr}F^r$) represents the industrial output induced by its own country's (direct) exports to the USA (factor (1)). The diagonal matrix post-multiplied by the corresponding final demand vector $(L^{rr} - \tilde{L}^{rr})F^r$ indicates the 'feedback effect' of country r (factor (2)), while $L^{rC}F^C + \cdots + L^{r(r-1)}F^{(r-1)} + L^{r(r+1)}F^{(r+1)} + \cdots + L^{rT}F^T$ indicates the magnitude of the 'inter-country multiplier effect' of country r (factors (3) and (4)). Moreover, if only $L^{rC}F^C$ is extracted, the magnitude of the 'triangular-trade multiplier effect through China' can be obtained (factor (3)). To get an intuition, the decomposition of induced outputs of Korea (K) is presented below, as an example:

Effect (1)	Factor (1)	$\tilde{L}^{KK}F^{K}$	Korea's industrial output induced by the 'intra-country multiplier effect'
	Factor (2)	$(L^{KK} - \tilde{L}^{KK})F^{K}$	Korea's industrial output induced by the 'feedback effect'
Effect (2)	Factor (3)	$L^{KC}F^{C}$	Korea's industrial output induced by the 'triangular-trade multiplier effect through China'
Effect (3)	Factor (4)	$L^{KI}F^{I} + L^{KJ}F^{J} + L^{KM}F^{M} + L^{KN}F^{N} + L^{KP}F^{P} + L^{KS}F^{S} + L^{KT}F^{T}$	Korea's industrial output induced by the 'other inter-country multiplier effect'

As shown above, in this chapter, factors (1) and (2) are not separated and are measured as the 'domestic multiplier effect' (effect (1)), for simplicity.

Analogously, the impact of the Lehman shock can be calculated and decomposed as follows:

$$\Delta X = (L_1 + L_2 + L_3 + L_4)\Delta F \tag{1.A4}$$

where

$$\Delta F = \begin{bmatrix} \Delta F^{C} \\ \vdots \\ \Delta F^{T} \end{bmatrix}$$

is the difference (drop) in the US import demand between the time before and after the Lehman shock.

The factor decomposition described above can be illustrated as shown in Figure 1A.1.

Note

1. r, s (= $C, I, J, K, M, N, P, S, T$) denote member countries in the augmented Asian tables and n (=1, 2, . . ., 25) stands for the number of industrial sectors.

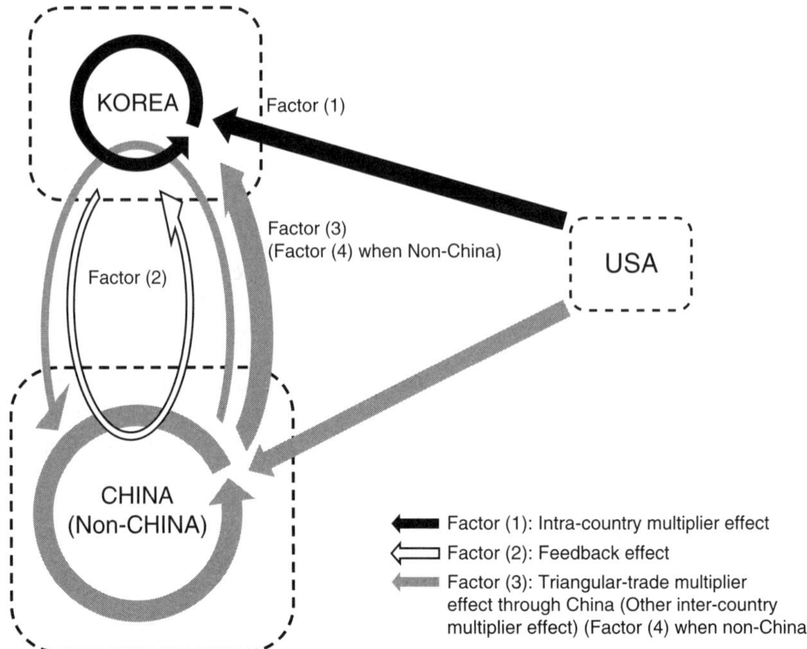

Note: Arrows indicate the directions of repercussion effects (i.e. backward linkage effects induced by US import demand, as a source of final demand).

Source: Drawn by authors.

Figure 1A.1 Decomposition of cross-border linkage effects induced by US import demand (case for Korea)

2. Impact of the global economic crisis on employment in the Asia-Pacific region

Bo Meng and Satoshi Inomata[1]

1. INTRODUCTION

The recent economic crisis is considered 'the most serious financial crisis' since the Great Depression, as seen in the significant decline in many economic indicators, especially those that are employment-related. According to a recent report[2] by the International Labour Office (ILO), the crisis could cause the loss of an estimated 18–30 million job opportunities. Juan Somavia, the ILO Director-General, stated 'this is not simply a crisis on Wall Street, this is a crisis on all streets'. A more pressing concern is that without prompt government action to contain rising unemployment, it may lead to social or political upheaval in the worst hit countries. To take appropriate employment measures, policy makers should have a clear understanding of the depth and extent of the crisis from a global perspective.

In this field of research, the following three economic models are probably most frequently used: macro-econometric models, Computable General Equilibrium (CGE) models, and input–output (I–O) models. For the impact analysis of the crisis on employment, which is most suitable? Considering the analytical purpose of the chapter and data availability, the I–O model is adopted here for the following reasons. On the one hand, compared to macro-econometric models, the I–O models are considered preferable for analysing structural change, especially when such change is caused by external economic shocks. On the other hand, compared to CGE models, I–O models guarantee high cost–performance since there is no need to calibrate many unknown parameters, which is always resource-intensive. Also, I–O models can estimate indirect impacts step by step, and thus ensure explicit consideration of the production networks.

The purpose of this chapter is to estimate the impact of the crisis on employment in the Asia-Pacific region, using internationally harmonized data of the Asian International Input–Output Tables (AIO tables). The questions to be considered are: (1) what kind of structural change took place in the labour markets of the Asia-Pacific region in the last decade? (2) How did the crisis damage these labour markets, and how much more unemployment could result thereafter? (3) How did countries in the Asia-Pacific region affect each other during the crisis through inter-country production networks?

The chapter proceeds as follows. Section 2 describes the analytical model for estimating the impact of the crisis on employment, with reference to the orthodox international I–O techniques. Section 3 gives a brief description of the data sources. Section 4 applies the model introduced in section 2 to the Asia-Pacific region, and discusses the simulation results. Concluding remarks are given in section 5.

2. MODEL

The model used in this chapter is an orthodox, demand-driven I–O model. As shown in Figure 2.1, the reduction of final demand caused by the crisis is considered to be an external shock coming from the demand side. Such a shock affects the supply side (output side) through inter-country, inter-industrial production networks, which, in turn, impacts on the demand for factor inputs such as labour.

Here we consider an international I–O model with two countries (*r* and *s*) and two industries (1 and 2) to illustrate how the impacts of the crisis on employment can be measured by cross-national input–output relations in the production system.

The international I–O model for employment analyses can be given as follows:

$$\Delta EMP = \hat{W} \cdot \Delta X = \hat{W} \cdot (I - A)^{-1} \cdot \Delta F = \hat{W} \cdot L \cdot \Delta F = E \cdot \Delta F \quad (2.1)$$

where

EMP: Employment vector

$\hat{W}$: A diagonal matrix that consists of labour input coefficients (i.e. the number of workers required in an industry in order to produce one unit of its product) for its diagonal elements

X: Output vector

A: International input coefficient matrix

F: Final demand vector

L: International Leontief inverse matrix

E: Employment-cum international Leontief inverse matrix

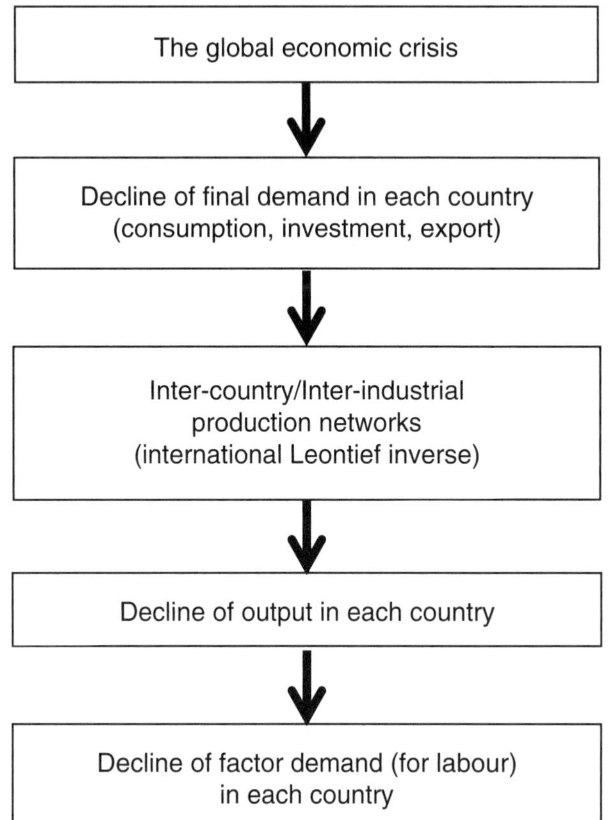

Figure 2.1 Flowchart of the I–O model for employment analysis

and

$$EMP = \begin{pmatrix} EMP^r \\ EMP^s \end{pmatrix}, \hat{W} = \begin{pmatrix} W^r & 0 \\ 0 & W^s \end{pmatrix}, X = \begin{pmatrix} X^r \\ X^s \end{pmatrix}, A = \begin{pmatrix} A^{rr} & A^{rs} \\ A^{sr} & A^{ss} \end{pmatrix},$$

$$F = \begin{pmatrix} F^r \\ F^s \end{pmatrix}, L = \begin{pmatrix} L^{rr} & L^{rs} \\ L^{sr} & L^{ss} \end{pmatrix}, E = \begin{pmatrix} E^{rr} & E^{rs} \\ E^{sr} & E^{ss} \end{pmatrix},$$

$$EMP^r = \begin{pmatrix} EMP_1^r \\ EMP_2^r \end{pmatrix}, W^r = \begin{pmatrix} w_1^r & 0 \\ 0 & w_2^r \end{pmatrix}, X^r = \begin{pmatrix} x_1^r \\ x_2^r \end{pmatrix}, F^r = \begin{pmatrix} f_1^r \\ f_2^r \end{pmatrix},$$

$$A^{rs} = \begin{pmatrix} a_{11}^{rs} & a_{12}^{rs} \\ a_{21}^{rs} & a_{22}^{rs} \end{pmatrix}, L^{rs} = \begin{pmatrix} l_{11}^{rs} & l_{12}^{rs} \\ l_{21}^{rs} & l_{22}^{rs} \end{pmatrix}, E^{rs} = \begin{pmatrix} e_{11}^{rs} & e_{12}^{rs} \\ e_{21}^{rs} & e_{22}^{rs} \end{pmatrix}.$$

Within a conventional I–O framework, it is easy to understand that e_{12}^{rs} represents the amount of employment created/lost in industry 1 of country r if there is one unit increase/decrease in the demand for goods produced by industry 2 in country s. Therefore, recalling the multiplier decomposition analysis conducted in Chapter 1, the elements in the diagonal sub-matrices (E^{rr} and E^{ss}) and those in the non-diagonal sub-matrices (E^{rs} and E^{sr}) of matrix E are respectively defined as the domestic and inter-country employment multipliers for one unit change of final demand in each country. The basic concept of multipliers is exactly the same as for those used in Chapter 1. They measure the magnitude of every recursive impact of the external shock, through both direct and indirect channels, on each industry in the Asia-Pacific region. The only difference here is that the model is extended beyond the measurement of output changes, to also capture the impact on employment of all countries concerned.

Since the AIO tables explicitly present inter-country trade of final demand, F can be given in the following form:

$$F = \begin{pmatrix} F^r \\ F^s \end{pmatrix} = \begin{pmatrix} F_C^{rr} \\ F_C^{sr} \end{pmatrix} + \begin{pmatrix} F_I^{rr} \\ F_I^{sr} \end{pmatrix} + \begin{pmatrix} F_C^{rs} \\ F_C^{ss} \end{pmatrix} + \begin{pmatrix} F_I^{rs} \\ F_I^{ss} \end{pmatrix} + \begin{pmatrix} EX^{rw} \\ EX^{sw} \end{pmatrix}. \quad (2.2)$$

For simplicity, we assume that domestic final demand just consists of consumption expenditure items and investment items (= fixed capital formation). In equation (2.2), $F_C^{rs} = (f_{1C}^{rs}, f_{2C}^{rs})'$, $F_I^{rs} = (f_{1I}^{rs}, f_{2I}^{rs})'$ represent the domestic consumption and investment of country s for goods (1 & 2) produced in country r, while $EX^{rw} = (ex_1^{rw}, ex_2^{rw})'$ represents the export demand of the rest of the world for the goods produced in country r. Using the above two equations (2.1) and (2.2), the impact of final demand shock by different expenditure categories can be estimated in detail.

3. DATA

The main data sources are the 1985, 2000 and 2008 AIO tables. The AIO tables cover 10 countries: China (C), Indonesia (I), Japan (J), Korea (K), Malaysia (M), Taiwan (N), the Philippines (P), Singapore (S), Thailand (T) and the United States (U) and 76 industrial sectors, which accounted for about 45 per cent of the world's GDP and 35 per cent of the world's population in the year 2000. The 1985 and 2000 tables are survey-based international I–O tables, in which information concerning inter-country and inter-industrial transactions is constructed, not only from each country's own international trade statistics but also from special surveys on the use of imported goods. These surveys provide important information on which domestic industry uses which kind of imported goods and to what extent. In contrast, the 2008 table is an updated table. The domestic input structure of the table is mainly estimated using information from the 2000 table, but the control totals and international trade structure are based on the latest national statistics as well as the trade data from the World Trade Atlas (see the 'Explanatory notes' in Chapter 8 for the updating method). The 2008 table reflects the adjusted international trade structure, which is used to estimate the impacts of the crisis for the year 2009. The employment data for labour input coefficients is taken from the 2000 employment matrix, appended to the 2000 AIO table. The other related data used here are from the OECD and national statistical offices of the target countries.

4. SIMULATION RESULTS

4.1 Structural Change in Labour Markets of the Asia-Pacific Region

Let us first get a quick picture on the sensitivity of the labour market to a change in domestic demand, by assuming a flat 1 per cent increase in the domestic final demand of each country. The simulation result (Table 2.1) shows that the demand increase induced the creation of approximately 9.25 million employment opportunities in 1985, 9.83 million in 2000 and 10.18 million in 2008. When economic globalization and regional integration were still at their early stages (the year 1985), the impact on labour markets mainly results from the domestic multiplier effect, which accounts for about 96 per cent of the total effect, in comparison to 4.3 per cent from the inter-country multiplier effect. With deepening economic interdependency among countries (the year 2000), the contribution rate of the inter-country effect rises to 8.2 per cent. The increasing tendency of the inter-country effect was, however, reversed in 2008, when global trade

Table 2.1 Sensitivity of the labour market to a 1 per cent increase in final demand (person, %)

	Total effect	Domestic multiplier effect	Inter-country multiplier effect
1985	9 249 109 (100.00)	8 854 416 (95.73)	394 693 (4.27)
2000	9 827 073 (100.00)	9 018 821 (91.78)	808 252 (8.22)
2008	10 180 594 (100.00)	9 520 973 (93.52)	659 620 (6.48)

Source: Calculated by the authors.

stumbled due to the economic crisis: the inter-country multiplier effect drops back to 6.5 per cent.

Table 2.2 presents a matrix of cross-national transfer of employment opportunities by origins and destinations, for the years 2000 and 2008, based on the same assumption as in Table 2.1; namely a flat 1 per cent increase in the final domestic demand of each country. For example, in 2000, the value in the cell at the intersection of China's row and the US column is 225989, which indicates that a 1 per cent increase in US final demand could have created about 226000 job opportunities in China in 2000. Moving down the column, one sees multiplier effects for other countries including the USA itself (domestic effect). The sum, about 1.7 million, represents the total employment effect that the USA exerts on the Asia-Pacific region as a whole, while the sub-total of the US inter-country multiplier effect indicates that in 2000 the USA would have been able to create about 360000 jobs elsewhere in the Asia-Pacific region. We call this the 'employment give-out potential' of the USA.

Similarly, the row total of China (6219506) represents the total employment opportunities that China receives from the whole region. Again, disregarding the domestic multiplier effect, the sum of inter-country effects for China is 509545, which can be called the 'employment gain potential' of China from other countries of the region.

In order to illustrate the development of the 'employment trade' structure from 2000 through to 2008, the above two potentials of each country are normalized by using deviations from the average. The normalized indices are plotted in Figure 2.2.

Even at a quick glance, the position of China catches our immediate attention. China, with its huge population and highly labour-intensive industrial structure, is the largest beneficiary of employment opportunities in the region. At the opposite end of the diagram lies the USA, which purchases a massive amount of goods and services from the region, generating a significant number of jobs in Asian countries. Japan also works in the same way, though to a lesser extent than the USA.

Looking at the movement of each country, the United States slightly enhanced its position from 2000 to 2008 as a provider of jobs. Japan moved sharply in the opposite direction, but increased its employment-gain potential.

The movement of China is particularly interesting. It moved in a south-easterly direction, indicating that the country has less employment-gain potential but is more capable of providing jobs to the region. This is an important aspect of the structural change in the Asia-Pacific region. China, which had been a mere 'gainer' of employment opportunities in the year 2000, became one of the main providers of jobs during the next

Table 2.2 Cross-national transfer of employment opportunities

2000 Origin / Destination	C	I	J	K	M	N	P	S	T	U	Total	Domestic multiplier effect	Inter-country multiplier effect	Employment gain index
China (C)	5 709 961	4 551	205 435	37 842	8 677	9 838	3 327	6 223	7 661	225 989	6 219 506	5 709 961	509 545	6.30
Indonesia (I)	8 336	756 251	32 057	4 838	4 563	4 655	1 640	3 349	2 727	44 984	833 399	726 251	107 148	1.33
Japan (J)	3 574	571	615 634	2 182	1 001	2 520	407	761	1 033	17 062	644 745	615 634	29 11	0.36
Korea (K)	2 454	238	3 195	126 657	219	638	172	166	202	6 520	140 460	126 657	13 803	0.17
Malaysia (M)	1 586	496	4 955	832	45 595	838	379	2 412	601	8 893	66 587	45 595	20 992	0.26
Taiwan (N)	3 186	215	3 090	481	373	61 767	174	172	332	7 098	76 888	61 767	15 121	0.19
Philippines (P)	1 769	292	11 110	1 517	522	1 036	200 028	277	593	22 164	239 308	200 028	39 280	0.49
Singapore (S)	266	85	467	155	254	154	84	10 691	132	1 394	13 683	10 691	2 991	0.04
Thailand (T)	2 981	1 805	17 270	1 761	2 589	2 399	694	1 547	211 916	22 003	264 964	211 916	53 048	0.66
USA (U)	2 224	355	8 301	2 147	571	2 199	304	612	498	1 310 320	1 327 533	1 310 320	17 212	0.21
Total	5 736 339	734 859	901 513	178 412	64 365	86 045	207 209	26 209	225 695	1 666 428	9 827 073	9 018 821	808 252	
Domestic multiplier	5 709 961	726 251	615 634	126 657	45 595	61 767	200 028	10 691	211 916	1 310 320	9 018 821	0	0	
Inter-country multiplier	26 378	8 608	285 879	51 756	18 770	24 278	7 180	15 518	13 779	356 107	808 252	0	0	
Employment give-out index	0.33	0.11	3.54	0.64	0.23	0.30	0.09	0.19	0.17	4.41				

Table 2.2 (continued)

2000 Origin / Destination	C	I	J	K	M	N	P	S	T	U	Total	Domestic multiplier effect	Inter-country multiplier effect	Employment gain index
China (C)	6 030 515	10 246	101 289	29 881	6 897	9 701	2 155	6 773	8 442	214 515	6 420 415	6 030 515	389 900	5.91
Indonesia (I)	11 531	818 758	13 460	3 597	6 351	2 006	953	3 813	2 773	21 203	884 444	818 758	65 686	1.00
Japan (J)	11 499	1 361	604 595	3 271	1 075	2 509	390	841	1 747	13 477	640 765	604 595	36 170	0.55
Korea (K)	6 586	443	2 282	130 388	326	487	121	445	355	4 731	146 163	130 388	15 775	0.24
Malaysia (M)	4 413	1 122	3 548	847	53 940	566	233	1 986	924	6 296	73 874	53 940	19 934	0.30
Taiwan (N)	8 205	402	2 340	703	446	63 307	193	446	466	5 558	82 066	63 307	18 759	0.28
Philippines (P)	7 626	618	7 156	1 638	649	602	209 274	749	1 111	8 855	238 279	209 274	29 005	0.44
Singapore (S)	510	372	227	144	216	66	65	8 531	124	590	10 843	8 531	2 313	0.04
Thailand (T)	10 032	3 894	17 163	2 816	4 413	2 134	2 012	2 056	263 226	21 165	328 912	263 226	65 686	1.00
USA (U)	4 885	610	5 492	1 837	614	1 188	258	978	530	1 338 440	1 354 833	2 704 781	16 393	0.25
Total	6 095 801	837 826	757 553	175 122	74 925	82 567	215 653	26 617	279 700	1 634 830	10 180 594	10 887 314	659 620	
Domestic multiplier	6 030 515	818 758	604 595	130 388	53 940	63 307	209 274	8 531	263 226	1 338 440	9 520 973			
Inter-country multiplier	65 286	19 068	152 958	44 735	20 986	19 259	6 379	18 087	16 473	296 390	659 620			
Employment give-out index	0.99	0.29	2.32	0.68	0.32	0.29	0.10	0.27	0.25	4.49				

Source: Calculated by the authors.

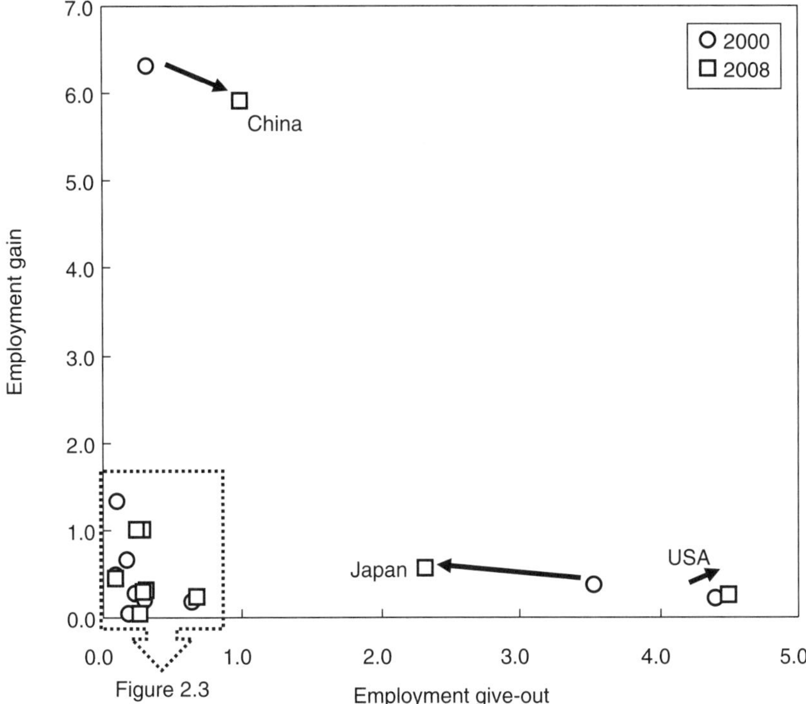

Figure 2.2 Development of 'employment trade', 2000–2008, the whole region

decade. The backdrop to this observation can be found in the analysis in Chapter 1, namely, the development of 'triangular trade' through China. On the one hand, China still exports a massive amount of its final products to the USA, the major customer of the region, and thus enjoys the domestic employment opportunities created thereby. On the other hand, in order to produce the goods exported to the United States, the country imports a large amount of parts and materials from neighbouring Asian countries, which promoted its position as a provider of jobs to the region.

Other Asian countries are less significant players in terms of the contribution to the 'employment trade' structure in the Asia-Pacific region. If we zoom in on the details of movement (Figure 2.3), however, it turns out that most of them have increased their employment give-out potentials, indicating that they became more involved in the regional production networks during the decade. Despite some variations for the direction of changes in employment gain potentials, it is considered that these

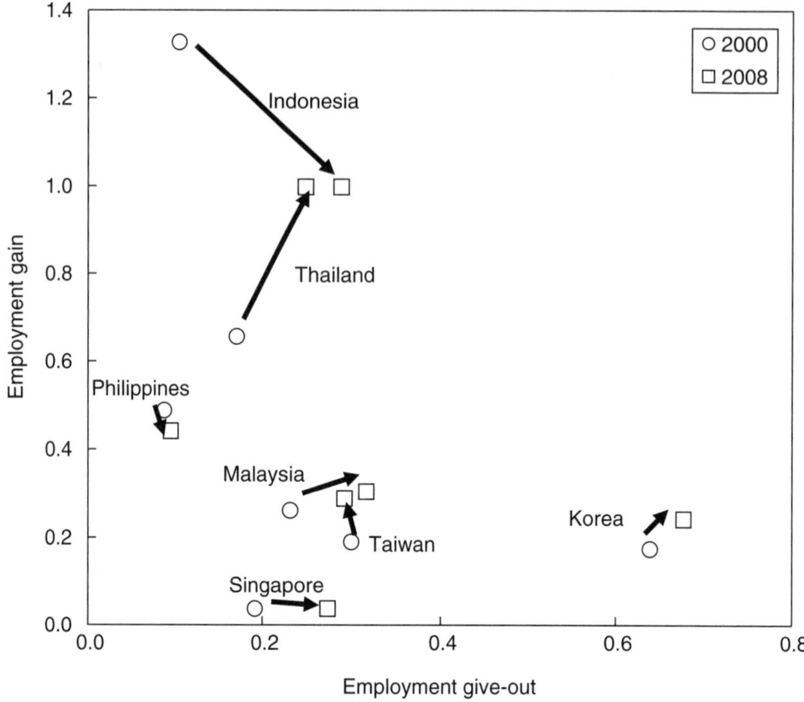

Figure 2.3 Development of 'employment trade', 2000–2008, selected countries

emerging economies as a group now have a significant influence on the employment situation of the region.

The structural change that took place in the last decade has a significant consequence when we consider the impact of the crisis on employment in the Asia-Pacific region, which is further investigated in the following section.

4.2 Impacts of the Crisis on Employment

In the previous section, a flat and simultaneous 1 per cent change of all the final demand items was imposed. This is appropriate as the simulation is designed for structural analysis, in which the main analytical purpose is to draw a 'skeleton' of the flow of employment opportunities between the countries.

In this section, however, we are more concerned about simulating the possible number of job losses in each country, so that a more plausible

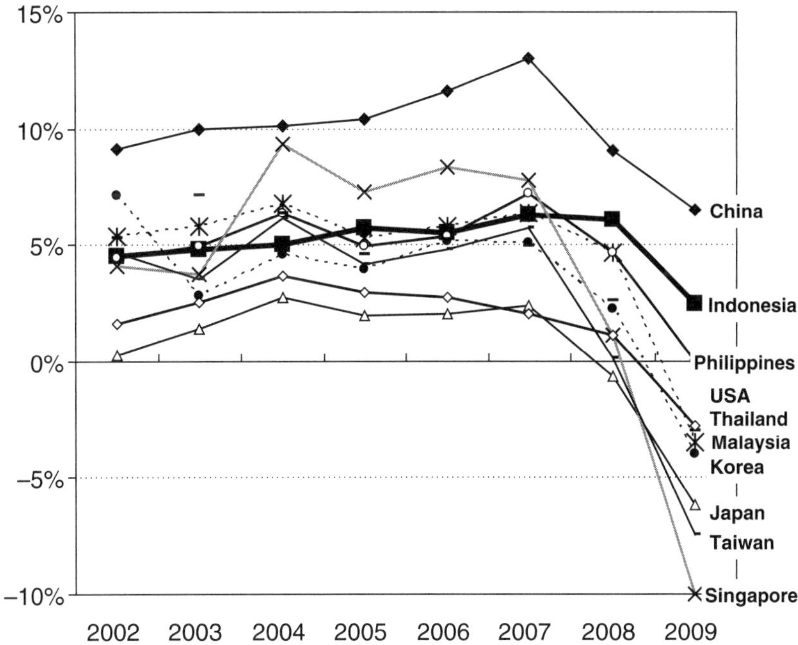

Note: The rate of the year 2009 is based on the IMF estimate.

Figure 2.4 GDP growth rates of the countries in the AIO table

setting for the basic scenario (that is the likely percentage changes in final demand) has to be tailored, rather than simply giving a flat rate across all countries and industries.

Figure 2.4 shows the recent GDP growth rates of the countries covered in the AIO table. It shows that every country was significantly affected by the crisis, though the magnitude of the impact varies across countries. Countries with relatively developed financial markets and larger dependence on international trade, such as Singapore, Taiwan, Japan and Korea, seem to be more heavily affected. On the other hand, although the GDP growth rates of China and Indonesia decreased, they still maintained positive growth.

In order to capture the different magnitudes of demand shocks caused by the crisis in a relative scale, a new concept, 'forgone GDP growth rate', is introduced in our analysis, as defined as follows:

Forgone growth rate = Hypothetical growth rate (in the absence of the crisis) − Actual growth rate (in the presence of the crisis)

Table 2.3 Forgone GDP growth rates in 2008 and 2009 (%)

	2008			2009		
	(1) Estimates in Oct. 2007	(2) Realized growth rate	Growth rate forgone (2)−(1)	(3) Estimates in Apr. 2008	(4) Estimates in Apr. 2009	Growth rate forgone (4)−(3)
China	10.0	9.0	−1.0	9.5	6.5	−2.9
Indonesia	6.1	6.1	0.0	6.3	2.5	−3.8
Japan	1.7	−0.6	−2.3	1.5	−6.2	−7.7
Korea	4.6	2.2	−2.4	4.4	−4.0	−8.4
Malaysia	5.6	4.6	−1.0	5.3	−3.5	−8.7
Taiwan	5.8	4.6	−1.2	5.8	0.0	−5.8
Philippines	5.8	1.1	−4.7	4.5	−10.0	−14.5
Singapore	3.8	0.1	−3.7	4.1	−7.5	−11.6
Thailand	4.5	2.6	−1.9	5.6	−3.0	−8.6
USA	1.9	1.1	−0.8	0.6	−2.8	−3.3

Source: Calculated by the authors.

where

(For the year 2008)

- Hypothetical growth rate: the growth rate of 2008, which had been estimated and publicly announced before the crisis happened.
- Actual growth rate: the realized growth rate of 2008.

(For the year 2009)

- Hypothetical growth rate: the growth rate of 2009, which had been estimated and announced before the crisis happened.
- Actual growth rate: the growth rate of 2009, which was estimated after the crisis.

The GDP growth rate of 2008 that was estimated before the crisis reflects the country's expectation regarding growth for that year, which might have been achieved if the crisis had not happened. So, the 'forgone GDP growth rate' is considered as an index for the relative scale of divergence from the economy's stationary path, caused by the onset of the crisis. Table 2.3 shows the estimated forgone GDP growth rates of 2008 and 2009. Compared to the situation in 2008, things seem to be worsening in the year 2009. This particularly applies to small open economies such as the Philippines, Singapore, Malaysia, Thailand and Korea, which are heavily affected.

Since the value of gross GDP measured from the expenditure side is merely the aggregation of final demand items, the inclusion of the above index should be able to offer more appropriate settings for measuring the magnitude of demand contraction across the countries.

In addition to the inclusion of the 'forgone GDP growth rate', we also take account of the differences in the responsiveness to the crisis of each final demand item, in order to further shape up the appropriate setting for the basic scenario of the simulation. Table 2.4 shows the quarter-to-quarter percentage change of the final demand items of each country. As clearly shown, different demand items have different reactions to the crisis. Exports and imports are the most sensitive items that have been critically damaged. In the case of Japan, the decline in exports was about 37 per cent in the first quarter of 2009, significantly higher than that of imports (16 per cent). For China, however, a different pattern can be observed, with a larger fall in imports than exports. The contraction of domestic production and hence demand for imported intermediate parts and materials (as well as the rise of protectionism following the crisis) are considered as the main reasons behind the large decline in imports.

Compared to the movement of private and government consumption, the investment item (=fixed capital formation) shows a more remarkable reaction. Investment incentives, and hence demand for capital goods, seems to be highly sensitive to the change in the business environment. Note that China's investment shows a large positive percentage increase. This is simply accounted for by the recent large-scale fiscal commitment of the Chinese government to tackle the crisis shock. (See Chapter 6 for the evaluation of the policy effects.)

Now, from the statistics prepared in Tables 2.3 and 2.4, we construct a set of exogenous variables (basic scenario) to the employment model formulated in section 2, in order to simulate the impact of the crisis on employment.[3] Table 2.5 shows the simulation results for the latest years, 2008 and 2009.

In 2008, a short-run impact of the crisis may cause a loss of about 9.2 million employment opportunities in the Asia-Pacific region as a whole, of which the inter-country multiplier effect accounts for a share of almost 8.4 per cent (a fall of 775 000 persons) of the total effect. In 2009, unemployment may further increase by 13.5 million persons, in which the inter-country effect contributes about 12.5 per cent (–1.7 million persons).

Note that the shares of the inter-country multiplier effect differ significantly between countries. There seems to be a close correlation between the magnitude of an inter-country effect and the sensitivity of trade volumes to external shocks, which can be confirmed by a cross-reference between Tables 2.4 and 2.5; generally speaking, the higher the sensitivity of trade volumes, the larger the inter-country effect on the employment of the country concerned.

Table 2.4 Quarter-to-quarter percentage change of final demand items (unit: %, national currency base)

Q4, 2008	Private consumption	Government consumption	Fixed capital formation	Exports	Imports
China	–	–	–	4.30	−8.80
Indonesia	1.70	25.60	0.80	−5.50	−11.70
Japan	−0.20	0.10	−7.80	−12.90	2.60
Korea	−3.80	4.80	−7.90	−6.90	−11.40
Malaysia	5.30	12.70	−10.20	−13.30	−10.20
Taiwan	−1.69	2.17	−22.62	−19.24	−21.40
Philippines	4.50	4.70	−9.00	−7.50	−1.20
Singapore	−1.20	2.70	−9.90	−9.60	−5.80
Thailand	2.12	10.99	−3.29	−6.53	1.02
USA	−1.80	3.10	−7.50	−3.40	−6.80
EU	−0.60	2.60	−5.30	−5.80	−4.30
Q1, 2009	**Private consumption**	**Government consumption**	**Fixed capital formation**	**Exports**	**Imports**
China	–	–	30.23	−20.68	−32.43
Indonesia	6.00	19.20	3.40	−18.70	−26.00
Japan	−2.70	0.60	−14.10	−36.30	−15.30
Korea	−4.40	7.40	−6.80	−10.80	−18.20
Malaysia	−0.70	2.10	−10.80	−15.20	−23.50
Taiwan	−1.22	3.22	−29.40	−23.66	−26.88
Philippines	0.75	3.56	−15.47	−17.07	−18.00
Singapore	−4.20	−1.70	−15.10	−21.10	−18.50
Thailand	−2.60	2.83	−15.79	−16.45	−31.41
USA	−1.50	1.90	−15.30	−11.60	−16.20
EU	−1.90	1.90	−11.20	−15.60	−13.60
Q2, 2009	**Private consumption**	**Government consumption**	**Fixed capital formation**	**Exports**	**Imports**
China	–	–	35.70	−21.80	−25.40
Indonesia	4.80	17.00	2.70	−15.70	−23.90
Japan	−1.00	0.90	−14.70	−29.30	−17.10
Korea	−1.00	7.00	−4.10	−3.40	−13.60
Malaysia	–	–	–	–	–
Taiwan	0.36	1.49	−23.67	−18.36	−19.44
Philippines	–	–	–	–	–
Singapore	−3.70	6.30	−7.20	−15.70	−16.70
Thailand	–	–	–	–	–
USA	−1.80	2.50	−16.90	−15.20	−18.60
EU	−1.70	1.20	−11.60	−16.40	−15.30

Sources: Data for Japan, Korea, USA and EU is from the OECD, data for other countries is from their National Statistical Offices.

Table 2.5 Impacts of the crisis on employment: 2008 and 2009

2008 Origin Destination	C	I	J	K	M	N	P	S	T	U	Total effect	Inter-country multiplier effect	Share of Inter-country effect
China (C)	−3 340 759	−11 154	−115 468	−76 291	−11 062	−10 705	−7 027	−13 341	−12 117	−228 791	−3 826 715	−485 956	12.7%
Indonesia (I)	−4 055	−870 341	−12 204	−8 973	−6 611	−1 639	−2 613	−4 989	−2 869	−13 163	−927 457	−57 116	6.2%
Japan (J)	−8 815	−1 510	−739 690	−8 479	−1 783	−2 818	−1 274	−1 807	−2 514	−14 554	−783 244	−43 554	5.6%
Korea (K)	−3 867	−424	−2 255	−476 857	−475	−454	−402	−859	−461	−4 144	−490 198	−13 341	2.7%
Malaysia (M)	−2 691	−1 155	−3 803	−2 205	−121 907	−545	−739	−3 416	−1 183	−5 538	−143 182	−21 275	14.9%
Taiwan (N)	−4 502	−391	−2 293	−1 572	−661	−72 804	−684	−887	−597	−4 859	−89 250	−16 446	18.4%
Philippines (P)	−4 730	−613	−7 246	−3 786	−969	−592	−864 258	−1 429	−1 374	−7 843	−892 840	−28 582	3.2%
Singapore (S)	−537	−611	−353	−417	−495	−106	−240	−24 940	−246	−869	−28 814	−3 874	13.4%
Thailand (N)	−9 077	−4 854	−22 495	−7 036	−7 765	−2 776	−5 080	−3 895	−470 638	−25 570	−559 186	−88 548	15.8%
USA (U)	−2 566	−545	−4 751	−3 668	−804	−897	−822	−1 782	−644	−1 429 949	−1 446 428	−16 479	1.1%
Total	−3 381 599	−891 598	−910 558	−589 284	−152 532	−93 336	−883 139	−57 345	−492 643	−1 735 280	−9 187 314	−775 171	8.4%

Table 2.5 (continued)

2009 Origin Destination	C	I	J	K	M	N	P	S	T	U	Total effect	Inter-country multiplier effect	Share of Inter-country effect
China (C)	−4 683 659	−24 415	−256 644	−130 214	−22 563	−23 856	−10 970	−24 937	−24 551	−515 580	−5 717 389	−1 033 730	18.1%
Indonesia (I)	−17 451	−1 218 896	−25 201	−15 089	−16 667	−3 772	−4 356	−11 546	−6 662	−39 425	−1 359 065	−140 169	10.3%
Japan (J)	−23 731	−3 655	−1 036 298	−15 212	−3 861	−7 481	−2 052	−3 345	−5 685	−37 171	−1 138 491	−102 193	9.0%
Korea (K)	−7 921	−825	−4 261	−667 729	−866	−893	−596	−1 418	−834	−8 579	−693 922	−26 193	3.8%
Malaysia (M)	−8 712	−2 563	−8 008	−3 873	−170 820	−1 414	−1 204	−7 546	−2 781	−16 039	−222 960	−52 140	23.4%
Taiwan (N)	−11 143	−876	−5 039	−2 844	−1 347	−102 024	−1 020	−1 587	−1 230	−11 616	−138 726	−36 702	26.5%
Philippines (P)	−12 169	−1 431	−15 538	−6 679	−1 990	−1 337	−1 209 983	−2 629	−2 973	−19 996	−1 274 725	−64 742	5.1%
Singapore (S)	−1 088	−1 182	−693	−732	−914	−208	−367	−34 937	−458	−1 724	−42 303	−7 366	17.4%
Thailand (T)	−20 741	−10 377	−46 998	−12 435	−15 536	−6 345	−9 227	−7 916	−659 114	−53 007	−841 696	−182 582	21.7%
USA (U)	−6 596	−1 186	−10 174	−6 456	−1 613	−2 206	−1 246	−3 106	−1 263	−2 002 881	−2 036 727	−33 846	1.7%
Total	−4 793 211	−1 265 406	−1 408 854	−861 263	−236 177	−149 536	−1 241 021	−98 967	−705 551	−2 706 018	−13 466 004	−1 679 663	12.5%

Note: Shaded sections indicate the domestic multiplier effect of the respective countries.

Source: Calculated by the authors.

The decline of the US economy naturally inflicts the greatest damage on its own labour market (the domestic multiplier effect), with 1.4 million and 2.0 million job losses in 2008 and 2009, respectively. Yet it has also caused China, one of its biggest trade partners, to lose 230 000 and 520 000 jobs in 2008 and 2009, respectively. Furthermore, the transmission of unemployment from China to other Asian countries is also significant. Table 2.6 shows that, with the exception of Indonesia, Asian countries in 2008 rank China highly as a transmission hub of unemployment within the region. The situation is even more prominent in 2009; China ranks first for half of the countries and second for all the others.

This is a clear reflection of the 'triangular trade' discussed in Chapter 1 and in line with the structural analysis of the previous section. The transmission of negative impacts on industrial outputs through the trade channel with China is precisely echoed in the labour market.

Table 2.7 shows the impacts of a decrease in US final demand on employment by industry in the Asia-Pacific region. It emerges that the distributional structures of the impact of the crisis among countries/industries are quite similar in both years, yet the magnitudes of the impacts are much larger in 2009 than in 2008.

In the United States, the worst-hit industrial sectors include 'Construction' and 'Other services'. This is not so surprising since the bursting of the US housing bubbles and the consequent financial meltdown was one of the main triggers of the recent crisis. For Japan, Korea and Taiwan, the negative impacts are concentrated in high-technology manufacturing industries, such as 'Computers and electronic equipment', 'Other electrical equipment' and 'Transport equipment'. Due to the development of 'triangular trade' in the Asia-Pacific region, China and ASEAN countries see that the induced unemployment is not only concentrated in traditional labour-intensive and export-oriented industries such as 'Agriculture', 'Pulp etc.' and 'Textile etc.', but is also prevalent in 'Other electrical equipment' and 'Other manufacturing products'.

5. CONCLUSIONS

The recent economic crisis has led to serious employment crises in many countries. It is important for national policy makers to understand how many people will be affected, in what way countries will affect each other, and how the impact of the crisis will be delivered and propagated across industries. This chapter focused on estimating the crisis impact on employment in the Asia-Pacific region. The simulation result shows that: (1) an important structural change took place in the 'employment trade' of the

Table 2.6 Transmission of unemployment in the Asian region: 2008 and 2009

2008	Asian inter-country multiplier effects										China's ranking
Destination / Origin	C	I	J	K	M	N	P	S	T	Total	
China (C)	–	4.3%	44.9%	29.7%	4.3%	4.2%	2.7%	5.2%	4.7%	100.0%	–
Indonesia (I)	9.2%	–	27.8%	20.4%	15.0%	3.7%	5.9%	11.4%	6.5%	100.0%	5
Japan (J)	30.4%	5.2%	–	29.2%	6.1%	9.7%	4.4%	6.2%	8.7%	100.0%	1
Korea (K)	42.0%	4.6%	24.5%	–	5.2%	4.9%	4.4%	9.3%	5.0%	100.0%	1
Malaysia (M)	17.1%	7.3%	24.2%	14.0%	–	3.5%	4.7%	21.7%	7.5%	100.0%	3
Taiwan (N)	38.9%	3.4%	19.8%	13.6%	5.7%	–	5.9%	7.7%	5.2%	100.0%	1
Philippines (P)	22.8%	3.0%	34.9%	18.3%	4.7%	2.9%	–	6.9%	6.6%	100.0%	2
Singapore (S)	17.9%	20.3%	11.7%	13.9%	16.5%	3.5%	8.0%	–	8.2%	100.0%	2
Thailand (T)	14.4%	7.7%	35.7%	11.2%	12.3%	4.4%	8.1%	6.2%	–	100.0%	2

2009	Asian inter-country multiplier effects										China's ranking
Destination / Origin	C	I	J	K	M	N	P	S	T	Total	
China (C)	–	4.7%	49.5%	25.1%	4.4%	4.6%	2.1%	4.8%	4.7%	100.0%	–
Indonesia (I)	17.3%	–	25.0%	15.0%	16.5%	3.7%	4.3%	11.5%	6.6%	100.0%	2
Japan (J)	36.5%	5.6%	–	23.4%	5.9%	11.5%	3.2%	5.1%	8.7%	100.0%	1
Korea (K)	45.0%	4.7%	24.2%	–	4.9%	5.1%	3.4%	8.1%	4.7%	100.0%	1
Malaysia (M)	24.1%	7.1%	22.2%	10.7%	–	3.9%	3.3%	20.9%	7.7%	100.0%	1
Taiwan (N)	44.4%	3.5%	20.1%	11.3%	5.4%	–	4.1%	6.3%	4.9%	100.0%	1
Philippines (P)	27.2%	3.2%	34.7%	14.9%	4.4%	3.0%	–	5.9%	6.6%	100.0%	2
Singapore (S)	19.3%	21.0%	12.3%	13.0%	16.2%	3.7%	6.5%	–	8.1%	100.0%	2
Thailand (T)	16.0%	8.0%	36.3%	9.6%	12.0%	4.9%	7.1%	6.1%	–	100.0%	2

Source: Calculated by the authors.

Table 2.7 Impacts of the decline of the US economy on regional employment by industrial sector (unit: number of employed people)

2008	China	Indonesia	Japan	Korea	Malaysia	Taiwan	Philip.	Singap.	Thailand	USA
Agriculture	−65 091	−3 302	−190	−145	−396	−68	−1 371	−1	−9 141	−16 625
Crude petroleum and natural gas	−857	−905	−3	−7	−39	−6	−25	0	−248	−1 392
Other mining	−888	−466	−45	−12	−82	−17	−202	−5	−6 985	−83
Food, beverage and tobacco	−319	−19	−1	0	−4	−1	0	0	−29	−3 855
Textile, leather, and the products	−4 630	−172	−16	−11	−6	−4	−30	0	−7	−2 102
Wooden furniture and other wood products	−795	−124	−49	−18	−87	−10	−91	−6	−561	−21 096
Pulp, paper and printing	−23 969	−1 202	−145	−142	−176	−187	−738	−14	−811	−12 014
Chemical products	−9 008	−726	−46	−16	−288	−123	−82	−2	−317	−12 255
Petroleum and petro products	−3 226	−92	−237	−86	−51	−77	−30	−11	−109	−21 463
Rubber products	−4 897	−171	−345	−90	−33	−80	−29	−30	−105	−7 956
Non-metallic mineral products	−362	−6	−9	−11	−4	−7	−2	−1	−6	−1 383
Metals and metal products	−810	−16	−146	−78	−80	−67	−28	−2	−233	−1 876
Industrial machinery	−2 996	−198	−138	−39	−27	−43	−23	−4	−110	−5 749
Computers and electronic equipment	−7 427	−53	−919	−308	−139	−645	−121	−19	−248	−22 800
Other electrical equipment	−20 835	−171	−3 356	−913	−1 615	−1 043	−178	−164	−1 300	−35 669
Transport equipment	−1 851	−15	−1 842	−214	−53	−78	−69	−18	−115	−42 535
Other manufacturing products	−20 490	−176	−718	−174	−80	−365	−138	−27	−552	−15 798
Electricity, gas and water supply	−2 704	−11	−78	−19	−25	−12	−36	−2	−88	−10 354
Construction	−120	−56	−153	−13	−64	−69	−181	−36	−9	−99 580
Trade and transport	−43 862	−4 329	−4 004	−1 097	−1 532	−1 195	−3 140	−262	−3 129	−276 544
Other services	−11 699	−941	−1 781	−620	−365	−676	−1 192	−253	−1 274	−774 370
Public administration	−1 954	−11	−335	−133	−397	−87	−135	−12	−194	−44 449
Total	−228 790	−13 162	−14 556	−4 146	−5 537	−4 860	−7 841	−869	−25 571	−1 429 948

Table 2.7 (continued)

2009	China	Indonesia	Japan	Korea	Malaysia	Taiwan	Philip.	Singap.	Thailand	USA
Agriculture	−153 776	−10 551	−477	−297	−1 197	−181	−3 613	−2	−20 142	−23 294
Crude petroleum and natural gas	−1 763	−1 404	−7	−14	−84	−11	−56	0	−421	−1 950
Other mining	−1 698	−997	−96	−22	−184	−35	−417	−8	−12 877	−117
Food, beverage and tobacco	−674	−42	−1	0	−8	−1	0	0	−48	−5 400
Textile, leather, and the products	−9 415	−352	−36	20	−12	−8	−66	0	−13	−2 949
Wooden furniture and other wood products	−1 903	−473	−129	−38	−307	−30	−246	−13	−1 268	−29 539
Pulp, paper and printing	−60 365	−6 592	−395	−319	−638	−567	−2 119	−30	−1 890	−16 828
Chemical products	−17 594	−1 682	−113	−31	−694	−261	−184	−3	−613	−17 161
Petroleum and petro products	−6 478	−199	−573	−159	−121	−165	−70	−21	−210	−30 067
Rubber products	−10 690	−473	−801	−183	−80	−181	−70	−57	−226	−11 172
Non-metallic mineral products	−771	−15	−20	−21	−10	−15	−6	−2	−12	−1 937
Metals and metal products	−1 680	−40	−347	−143	−182	−143	−65	−4	−461	−2 630
Industrial machinery	−5 539	−349	−306	−76	−61	−85	−47	−7	−190	−8 055
Computers and electronic equipment	−14 338	−111	−2 070	−577	−323	−1 223	−252	−39	−436	−31 999
Other electrical equipment	−46 721	−494	−8 347	−1 892	−4 305	−2 482	−406	−328	−2 750	−50 178
Transport equipment	−4 487	−46	−5 332	−471	−160	−243	−194	−37	−268	−59 593
Other manufacturing products	−43 315	−473	−1 744	−344	−212	−843	−316	−53	−1 106	−22 144
Electricity, gas and water supply	−5 738	−34	−195	−38	−67	−28	−90	−3	−188	−14 500
Construction	−268	−126	−388	−28	−168	−167	−464	−71	−20	−139 419
Trade and transport	−96 538	−12 290	−10 043	−2 238	−4 059	−2 847	−7 745	−520	−6 558	−387 413
Other services	−25 763	−2 506	−4 525	−1 283	−948	−1 646	−3 036	−501	−2 797	−1 084 306
Public administration	−6 068	−175	−1 224	−384	−2 218	−450	−534	−24	−514	−62 229
Total	−515 582	−39 424	−37 169	−8 578	−16 038	−11 612	−19 996	−1 723	−53 008	−2 002 880

Source: Calculated by the authors.

Asia-Pacific region as China turned its position from a pure beneficiary of employment opportunities to the double-role of beneficiary/provider of jobs for the region. This is in line with the development of 'triangular trade' as discussed in Chapter 1; (2) The increasing trend of inter-country multiplier effects was immediately reversed after the crisis. It shows that the configuration of international trade is highly sensitive to external shocks; (3) The sectoral impact of the recent crisis on employment varies across countries. In the USA, the worst-hit industries are concentrated in the services and construction sectors. In the Asian region, traditional labour-intensive industries are severely damaged in China and South-east Asia, while in North-east Asian countries high-technology manufacturing industries incurred the largest impact. This is partly attributed to the difference in industrial structure among countries, but also reflects the different roles that each country plays in the 'triangular trade' structure in the Asia-Pacific region.

As seen above, the expansion of domestic demand and promotion of labour-intensive industries should be the principal policies for averting the spread of unemployment. A swift and comprehensive countermeasure is called for in an internationally concerted manner, as the employment shock may otherwise develop into a more serious, long-lasting social crisis across all countries.

NOTES

1. We are thankful to Colin Webb and Norihiko Yamano of the OECD for their very constructive comments and kind support regarding this chapter.
2. *Global Employment Trends*, January 2009, ILO.
3. Sensitivity of final demand may also vary according to the type of commodity, yet the time series data of final demand by commodity is not available, so that the sensitivity parameter by commodity is mainly estimated from the 2000 and 2008 AIO tables.

REFERENCES

Escaith, H. and F. Gonguet (2009), 'International trade and real transmission channels of financial shocks in globalized production networks', *WTO Staff Working Paper ERSD*.

He, D., Z. Zhang and W. Zhang (2009), 'How large will be the effect of China's fiscal-stimulus package on output and employment?', *Working Papers* 0905, Hong Kong Monetary Authority.

Isard, W., (1951), 'Interregional and regional input–output analysis: a model of a space economy', *Review of Economics and Statistics*, **33** (4), 318–28.

Lahr, M.L. and E. Dietzenbacher (2001), *Input–Output Analysis: Frontiers and Extensions*, London: Palgrave Macmillan.

Leontief, W., (1947), 'Introduction to a theory of the internal structure of functional relationships', *Econometrica*, **15**, 361–73.

Miller, R. and P.D. Blair (1985), *Input–Output Analysis: Foundations and Extensions*, Englewood Cliffs, NJ: Prentice-Hall.

Moses, L.N. (1955), 'The stability of interregional trade patterns and input–output analysis', *American Economic Review*, **45** (5), 803–32.

Oosterhaven, J., D. Stelder and S. Inomata (2007), 'Evaluation of non-survey international IO construction methods with the Asian-Pacific input-output table', *IDE Discussion Paper*, **114**.

Round, J.I. (1985), 'Decomposing multipliers for economic systems involving regional and world trade', *Economic Journal*, **95**, 383–99.

Sasaki, K., M. Shinmei and S. Kunihisa (1987), 'Multi-regional model with endogenous price system for evaluating road construction projects', *Environment and Planning A*, **19**, 1093–114.

3. International trade and real transmission channels of financial shocks in global production networks: an Asian–USA perspective

Hubert Escaith and Fabien Gonguet[1]

1. INTRODUCTION

For the past 20 years, globalization has implied not only the expansion of international trade and finance, but also the geographical fragmentation of the production processes within networks of firms associated through contractual arrangements or belonging to multinational enterprises. Nowadays, specific industrial operations, from the conception to the assembly of final products, are no longer undertaken by a single establishment but increasingly outsourced within these global supply chains, leading to what is known as 'trade in tasks' (Baldwin, 2006).

It is becoming common practice for firms to process unfinished goods through affiliate or non-affiliate firms. Sometimes the goods are manufactured by firms within the domestic economy; sometimes the material is sent abroad. This process is very common among industries such as chemical, electronic and metallic manufacturing. Indeed, most of the enormous growth in trade recorded in the last 20 years consisted in relatively similar goods (manufactures) between relatively similar countries; moreover, this feature is robust to the level of disaggregation: no matter how finely industries are defined, a high proportion of trade takes place within industries rather than between them (Neary, 2009). In 2007, almost half of the world trade in merchandise, excluding oil, was attributed to intermediate goods. This proportion (relative to imported goods) rose to 68 per cent for Malaysia and 61 per cent for China.[2]

However, the greater interconnection has also provided greater and faster channels of propagation of adverse external shocks. Because production is internationally diversified, adverse external shocks can affect firms not only through final demand (a sudden decline in exports), but also through a rupture in the flow of inputs received from their suppliers. Indeed, the large drop in trade registered since the end of 2008 is attributed to the leverage effect induced by the geographical fragmentation of production (Tanaka, 2009; Yi, 2009), albeit the estimation of trade elasticities in times of crisis is a complex matter (Escaith et al., 2010).

While the financial and macroeconomic channels of transmissions have received much attention, the role of industrial linkages as vectors of contagion is yet to be thoroughly investigated. The disruptive potential of a failure in the international supply chain is becoming larger with time: trade in manufactures represented a quarter of the world industrial output in 2000; this proportion doubled in only five years. Almost 30 per cent of this trade relates to the exchange of intermediate inputs and goods for processing, either traded between establishments pertaining to the same multinational enterprise, or exported to contracting parties for processing, then re-exported.

The objective of the chapter is to focus on the real transmission channels of financial shocks and apply the model to the USA and a selection of Asian countries. More precisely, the study analyses how monetary restrictions – for example a credit crunch initiating in a particular country – can disrupt a series of productive activities, affect worldwide production processes and lead to self-sustained debt deflation. To do so, the chapter develops an approach that builds on two concepts: international input–output (I–O) analysis and the monetary circuit. By combining these two concepts, we will describe and model the sequence of financial and productive interactions along the international supply chain. Because firms rely on suppliers in carrying out part of the production process (outsourcing or offshoring), and/or because they sell their production to other firms, the smooth realization of production plans from initial investment to final sales depends on the availability of credit at all stages of the production chain. An initial exogenous monetary shock, for example when a bank shuts down an existing line of credit, will, therefore, replicate through the production chain. Through this 'real transmission channel', the initial financial shock will propagate itself along the chain, affecting all firms in the supply network. Modelling how these supply-driven impulses propagate through open economies and feed back into the monetary circuit are the main objectives of the chapter. An application is made on the US–Asian case in 2000 and 2008, using international I–O data developed for China, Japan, Malaysia, Thailand and the USA. A section of conclusions presents the main findings and the shortcomings of the proposed methodology.

2. MEASURING THE TRANSMITTED IMPACT

2.1 The Model

Since the intermediate goods produced are not commodities, but are specific to the client's need, it is not easy – and it is certainly costly – to shift to another supplier. As a corollary, the failure of any single supplier will affect the entire production chain in the short and medium term. At best, as a result of this supply shock, the client-firm will suffer an increase in costs of production when shifting to an alternative supplier; at worst, it will have to stop its production.[3]

International I–O tables allow us to model the real transmission channels of such a financial shock occurring at any stage of the production chains across the countries. While the Leontief model is demand-driven and simulates the transmission of demand shocks through backward linkages, the supply-driven shocks are simulated through forward linkages, with I–O tables adapted into what is known as the Ghosh matrix (see Appendix 3A.2).

The 'real channel impact' from a country of origin to a country of destination will therefore be proportional to (i) the foreign final demand for exported consumer goods and services, and (ii) the sum of Ghosh inverse coefficients linking industries of both countries. The second part, which measures the real impact through the supply chain, is larger than a simple measure based on the value of imported intermediate goods from the country of origin, because the Ghosh inverse considers both direct and indirect impacts.

Ignoring final demand effects (the usual 'Leontief approach' based on backward linkages), the intensity of inter-country transmission of financial shocks following a credit crunch affecting the industrial sectors will differ according to the degree of vertical integration, as measured by the strength and depth of forward industrial linkages. Ignoring also quantitative disruption effects that would prevail when no substitution among inputs is possible, the Imported Real Supply-driven Impact Coefficient (IRSIC) is proportional to the import content of domestic production; that is,

$$\text{IRSIC} = \%\Delta P/P = \Delta X(I - B)^{-1} \cdot 1/X \tag{3.1}$$

where

X: a row vector of initial sectoral output,

ΔX: a row vector of supply-driven shocks,

$\%\Delta P/P$: a vector of price shocks in percentage,

$(I - B)^{-1}$: The Ghosh inverse matrix, and
'$\cdot$' denotes the Hadamard product.[4]

It should be clear that, because of the inherent limitations of the Ghosh inverse matrix, only one type of supply-driven shock – translating into an increase in production prices – will be captured at macroeconomic level. Being non-disruptive, these supply-driven shocks initiating from a supplier's default imply that client firms are always able to find a substitute supplier instantly, but at a higher cost. The price shock hypothesis is obviously well-suited for segmented markets, with semi-monopolistic characteristics, but is also compatible with standard neoclassical hypotheses, as long as marginal costs are increasing in the short term. The Ghosh multipliers computed on international I–O tables simulate the transmission of the higher production costs caused by the initial shock through the entire supply chain. By factoring-in the direct and indirect cost effects, it provides the analyst with an adequate 'tracking methodology' which incorporates transnational impacts.

The additional production costs are related to the elasticity of technical substitution in production, including elasticity of substitution between domestic and imported inputs (Armington elasticity).[5] When Armington elasticities are low, large price changes are required to accommodate small changes in quantities. This is typically the case when manufactured intermediate inputs are differentiated and client-specific (for example, automobile components), unlike standard commodities such as oil and minerals. Substitution in a supply-constrained situation is difficult and takes time in the long run; in the short-run framework of this chapter, it takes money and has a big impact on supply chain management: buying critical components on the spot market, paying premium air or sea fare rates to get materials, and extra production wages for subcontractors (Stadtler and Kilger, 2008).

Dealing only with price effects tracked by the Ghosh matrix may be seen as a limitation. Severe shocks that translate into critical disruption of the production chain, creating bottlenecks and a decline in the volume of production, are excluded. Even a moderate negative supply-driven shock, but close enough to the initial demand impulse (final demand), may impede the normal implementation of the initial production project if the producers cannot easily redeploy their demand for intermediate goods to other suppliers.[6]

Nevertheless, in open economies with large numbers of suppliers, systemic disruptive shocks are not common, except perhaps when the supply restriction affects strategic commodities like oil. In addition, it should be noted that the distance of the initial shock to the final demand is taken into account, because the Ghosh matrix ponders the suite of technical coefficients according to the proximity of each round to the initial demand. The closer the shock, the larger the impact.[7]

2.2 The Data

International I–O tables are necessary to measure IRSIC. Building these tables from national I–O data is a painstaking exercise, requiring the harmonization of national formats and classifications, the inclusion of additional information such as disaggregating imports into sectoral intermediates and final goods and, finally, the compilation of all national tables into a single I–O matrix. We build our case study on a series of interlinked economies, China, Japan, Malaysia, Thailand and the USA, which are all key international and regional traders at different stages of industrial development and with strong specificities in terms of their insertion in the global economy.

We use a subset of the Asian International Input–Output Tables (AIO tables) developed by the Institute of Developing Economies, JETRO.[8] The original AIO tables are available for year 2000 in 1000US$, and are disaggregated into 76 sectors of activity. Inter-industrial flows based on year 2000 are nevertheless inadequate to analyse the present state of interdependence between those economies, considering in particular that China joined the WTO only in 2001. More recent results are derived from the estimated I–O matrices produced by IDE-JETRO, incorporating updated information on multilateral trade and national accounts aggregates in current US$ for 2008. The 2008 estimates are available only at a higher degree of aggregation (26 industrial sectors), and we used the sectoral definition of 24 industrial sectors for both 2000 and 2008 tables. Results obtained have been regrouped in 11 primary, secondary and tertiary sectors, to facilitate their presentation, but all intermediary calculations are done at the level of 24 sectors.

2.3 Calculation Results

Supply-driven shocks occurring in the regional sourcing network, like those which would result from a sudden disruption of trade due to lack of trade finance, are modelled as price shocks emanating from one of the five economies linked in the international I–O table. An arbitrary value of 30 per cent will be used for all sectors.[9] In our simulation, all manufacturing sectors ('Agroindustries', 'Textile and clothing', 'Industrial machinery', 'Transport equipment' and 'Other manufactured products') are shocked using the 24-sector disaggregation. The simulation computes the domestic impacts and its transmission to the other regional partners through the

Imported Real Supply-driven Impact Coefficient (IRSIC) as previously described. As IRSIC uses the Ghosh inverse matrix, the sectoral impacts include primary and secondary effects (that is, the real transmission channel follows both direct and indirect forward linkages). The initial calculations dealt with all ten countries encompassed by the AIO tables, while results presented below are restricted to China, Japan, Malaysia, Thailand and the USA; it should be noted that the end results are sensitive to sectoral and country disaggregation. Finally, 2000 and 2008 results are not directly comparable because of changes in the composition of trade with the rest of the world that occurred between these two years; in addition, 2008 is based on an estimate. Nevertheless, the evolution of the IRSIC values provides relevant information on the direction of changes.

As seen in Table 3.1, the largest secondary impacts from a price shock are felt domestically. The relative effect on the domestic economy depends negatively on its degree of openness and on the relative size of the originating sector in relation to the rest of the economy. As expected, manufacturing industries are more sensitive to imported shocks originating from foreign manufacturers, especially transport equipment. Using a more disaggregated sectoral decomposition available only for the 2000 production structure, the 'Electronics' sector appears also much more internationally integrated than the 'Transport equipment' and 'Textiles' sectors, with an IRSIC (excluding domestic effects) twice as high (Escaith and Gonguet, 2009). With the exception of Malaysia, the national impact of a shock originating in the domestic manufacturing sector tends to decrease between 2000 and 2008, indicating a greater openness to imported inputs and/or a greater participation of non-manufacture domestic inputs in the domestic content of manufacturing sectors.

Table 3.2 presents a summary of the results obtained for shocks initiating from, and imported by, the manufacturing sectors, which are more integrated in international supply chains. Imported and exported price shocks are expressed as a weighted average of the national increase in sectoral production costs resulting from an initial 30 per cent price shock on the manufacturing sectors. They are based on the existing intra- and inter-industrial linkages, in 2000 and 2008. Over the two periods, Japan is the largest potential exporter of price shocks (2.9 per cent and 2.0 per cent, respectively). Nevertheless, its dominant position as supplier of intermediate inputs has been eroded from 2000 to 2008 due to the rise of other competitors (from the region or from the rest of the world). Malaysia and Thailand, on the other hand, are the largest importers of such shocks, because of the high degree of integration of their manufacturing sectors and reliance on imported inputs from the other partners. In contrast, the low domestic impact of a local price shock observed for Malaysia and

Table 3.1 Transmission of an initial 30 per cent price shock from manufacturing sectors, 2000 and 2008[a] (percentage)

Origin of the shock, year	From all manufacturing sectors, 2000[b]					From all manufacturing sectors, 2008[b]				
From China to:	China	Japan	Malaysia	Thailand	USA	China	Japan	Malaysia	Thailand	USA
Agriculture	13.1	0.1	0.3	0.3	0.1	4.6	0.4	0.6	0.8	0.4
Mining	13.9	0.1	0.2	0.1	0.1	4.6	0.6	1.0	0.2	0.3
Agroindustries	44.8	0.2	0.7	0.4	0.1	38.2	0.5	1.0	0.7	0.5
Textile and clothing	60.8	0.9	2.2	1.6	0.6	55.2	4.4	3.1	1.2	2.8
Industrial machinery	61.6	0.4	1.6	2.2	0.4	53.8	2.0	4.9	4.6	1.8
Transport equipment	70.0	0.3	0.9	0.9	0.4	56.0	1.8	2.3	3.2	1.5
Other products	54.7	0.3	0.8	0.6	0.2	45.2	0.8	1.8	0.8	0.8
Utilities	16.7	0.1	0.2	0.1	0.1	6.7	0.1	0.7	0.1	0.2
Construction	30.2	0.2	0.8	0.8	0.3	19.3	1.0	2.2	1.9	1.1
Trade and transport serv.	17.8	0.0	0.2	0.2	0.1	8.8	0.2	0.5	0.3	0.3
Other services	15.6	0.1	0.3	0.3	0.1	7.7	0.3	0.7	0.5	0.3
Total sectors[c]	38.5	0.2	0.8	0.7	0.1	30.4	0.7	2.2	1.6	0.6
From Japan to:	China	Japan	Malaysia	Thailand	USA	China	Japan	Malaysia	Thailand	USA
Agriculture	0.3	9.8	1.2	0.7	0.2	0.1	7.7	0.6	1.2	0.2
Mining	0.7	12.9	0.8	0.6	0.2	0.2	10.3	0.9	0.4	0.1
Agroindustries	0.4	41.4	1.2	1.4	0.2	0.2	39.8	0.9	1.0	0.2
Textile and clothing	1.2	48.0	3.7	1.8	0.4	0.5	44.2	1.6	1.0	0.3
Industrial machinery	2.0	50.6	7.1	6.5	1.2	2.1	48.5	3.9	5.8	0.6
Transport equipment	2.1	65.4	9.2	10.7	1.7	1.4	60.9	3.8	5.6	1.0
Other products	1.1	46.3	3.6	2.4	0.4	0.7	43.4	2.1	1.1	0.3
Utilities	0.8	6.3	1.0	0.4	0.1	0.4	1.4	0.7	0.1	0.1
Construction	1.2	14.8	3.9	3.4	0.3	0.9	12.0	2.6	2.3	0.3
Trade and transport serv.	0.7	4.4	0.7	0.9	0.2	0.4	3.6	0.6	0.5	0.1
Other services	1.1	21.3	3.6	2.5	0.3	0.4	4.2	0.7	0.6	0.1
Total sectors[c]	1.1	21.3	3.6	2.5	0.3	0.8	19.4	2.0	2.1	0.2
From Malaysia to:	China	Japan	Malaysia	Thailand	USA	China	Japan	Malaysia	Thailand	USA
Agriculture	0.0	0.0	8.3	0.2	0.0	0.0	0.0	4.3	0.3	0.0
Mining	0.1	0.0	1.4	0.1	0.0	0.0	0.1	2.5	0.1	0.0

Table 3.1 (continued)

Origin of the shock, year	From all manufacturing sectors, 2000[b]					From all manufacturing sectors, 2008[b]				
Agroindustries	0.1	0.0	51.9	0.3	0.0	0.0	0.0	40.9	0.3	0.0
Textile and clothing	0.1	0.1	41.3	0.2	0.1	0.1	0.1	46.3	0.3	0.1
Industrial machinery	0.3	0.2	35.2	1.4	0.2	0.5	0.2	44.9	1.5	0.2
Transport equipment	0.1	0.1	40.7	0.5	0.1	0.1	0.1	41.0	0.9	0.1
Other products	0.1	0.1	38.5	0.4	0.0	0.1	0.1	37.3	0.3	0.1
Utilities	0.1	0.0	4.8	0.1	0.0	0.1	0.1	3.2	0.0	0.0
Construction	0.1	0.1	12.1	0.5	0.0	0.1	0.1	10.7	0.6	0.1
Trade and transport serv.	0.1	0.0	3.2	0.1	0.0	0.1	0.0	3.1	0.1	0.0
Other services	0.1	0.0	3.8	0.1	0.0	0.1	0.0	3.1	0.2	0.0
Total sectors[c]	0.1	0.1	23.5	0.4	0.0	0.2	0.1	24.2	0.5	0.1
From Thailand to:	China	Japan	Malaysia	Thailand	USA	China	Japan	Malaysia	Thailand	USA
Agriculture	0.0	0.0	0.2	7.0	0.0	0.0	0.1	0.4	8.6	0.0
Mining	0.0	0.0	0.1	5.4	0.0	0.0	0.1	0.3	2.3	0.0
Agroindustries	0.0	0.1	0.6	39.2	0.0	0.0	0.1	0.9	44.0	0.0
Textile and clothing	0.1	0.1	0.8	47.7	0.2	0.1	0.1	0.7	42.4	0.1
Industrial machinery	0.2	0.1	1.3	36.7	0.1	0.5	0.2	1.0	44.5	0.1
Transport equipment	0.1	0.2	0.5	40.5	0.1	0.1	0.2	1.3	45.6	0.1
Other products	0.1	0.0	0.5	36.2	0.0	0.1	0.1	0.7	34.3	0.0
Utilities	0.1	0.0	0.1	4.3	0.0	0.1	0.0	0.2	0.5	0.0
Construction	0.1	0.0	0.4	11.3	0.0	0.1	0.1	0.6	6.7	0.1
Trade and transport serv.	0.1	0.0	0.1	6.6	0.0	0.1	0.0	0.2	3.5	0.0
Other services	0.1	0.0	0.2	7.1	0.0	0.1	0.0	0.2	5.4	0.0
Total sectors[c]	0.1	0.0	0.6	22.6	0.0	0.1	0.1	0.6	24.3	0.0
From USA to:	China	Japan	Malaysia	Thailand	USA	China	Japan	Malaysia	Thailand	USA
Agriculture	0.2	0.2	0.5	0.4	9.4	0.1	0.3	0.4	0.4	8.8
Mining	0.3	0.2	0.4	0.2	4.8	0.1	0.3	0.6	0.1	3.3
Agroindustries	0.3	0.5	0.9	0.7	42.4	0.1	0.3	0.8	0.5	42.1
Textile and clothing	0.4	0.5	1.7	0.8	47.0	0.2	0.4	1.1	0.4	43.4
Industrial machinery	0.9	0.8	5.1	3.1	42.1	0.8	0.6	3.3	1.6	42.5
Transport equipment	0.6	0.8	1.5	1.5	48.6	0.5	0.9	1.4	1.2	49.8

Table 3.1 (continued)

Origin of the shock, year	From all manufacturing sectors, 2000[b]					From all manufacturing sectors, 2008[b]				
Other products	0.5	0.4	1.5	0.9	43.0	0.3	0.4	0.9	0.4	42.1
Utilities	0.3	0.1	0.5	0.2	3.2	0.1	0.1	0.4	0.0	2.1
Construction	0.4	0.2	1.3	0.7	12.3	0.3	0.3	0.9	0.5	11.4
Trade and transport serv.	0.3	0.1	0.4	0.3	3.8	0.1	0.1	0.3	0.1	3.7
Other services	0.4	0.1	0.7	0.4	3.9	0.2	0.1	0.4	0.2	3.8
Total sectors[c]	0.5	0.3	2.1	1.0	14.5	0.3	0.3	1.4	0.6	14.3

Notes:
a. Impact of an increase in 30 per cent of the cost of inputs originating from the manufacturing sectors on the respective sectoral production costs.
b. The manufacturing sectors from where price shocks originate are: 'Agroindustries', 'Textile and clothing', 'Industrial machinery', 'Transport equipment' and 'Other products'; 'Industrial machinery' includes computers and other electric and electronic equipment.
c. Weighted average.

Source: Authors' calculations.

Thailand in 2000 (diagonal of the table) is related to their openness and high reliance on imported inputs. On these criteria, all countries are more homogeneous in 2008.

Despite its relative inward-oriented economy (that is, sourcing inputs from and selling them to domestic agents), a price shock originating from the US manufacturing sectors also has a moderate domestic impact, because the US manufacturing sector also incorporates a significant share of intermediate services. As in other cases, in 2008 China overtook Japan as the main source of potential supply-driven shocks.

Indeed, China registered a notable increase in its forward inter-country linkages. China's overall relative influence as an exporter of shocks between 2000 and 2008 has almost tripled, and in 2008 China's impact is even slightly higher than Japan's, while its vulnerability to an imported shock from one of its four partners has somewhat diminished.

2.4 Further Implications for the Real-channel Transmission of Financial Shocks

One should remember that IRSIC only captures part of the shock transmission. First, it measures the non-disruptive supply impact, maintaining

Table 3.2 Imported and exported shocks from/to the manufacturing sectors, 2000 and 2008

2000 To:[a] / From:	China	Japan	Malaysia	Thailand	USA	Exported shocks[b]
China	57.5	0.4	1.2	1.2	0.3	0.8
Japan	1.4	50.2	5.4	4.0	0.8	2.9
Malaysia	0.2	0.1	38.5	0.7	0.1	0.3
Thailand	0.1	0.1	0.9	38.9	0.1	0.3
USA	0.6	0.6	3.3	1.6	43.8	1.5
Imported shocks[b]	0.6	0.3	2.7	1.9	0.3	1.1
2008 To: / From:	China	Japan	Malaysia	Thailand	USA	Exported shocks[b]
China	49.2	1.4	3.4	2.5	1.2	2.1
Japan	1.1	47.4	2.9	3.3	0.5	2.0
Malaysia	0.2	0.1	42.2	0.8	0.1	0.3
Thailand	0.2	0.1	0.9	41.8	0.1	0.3
USA	0.4	0.5	2.2	0.9	43.6	1.0
Imported shocks[b]	0.5	0.6	2.3	1.9	0.5	1.2

Notes:
a. Weighted averages of domestic sectoral shocks on all manufacturing sectors.
b. Simple average of country shocks, excluding those from or to the rest of the world.

Source: Calculations based on Table 3.1.

constant production levels. Second, it ignores the secondary demand-driven impacts resulting from lower activity levels.

The previous simulation was based on non-disruptive supply-driven shocks translating into a standard initial 30 per cent price increase for the intermediate goods that were directly affected. The flat 30 per cent rate is a strong hypothesis, because the countries analysed in the case study differ widely in their level of development. The technologies used (and technical coefficients) differ in relation to their respective technological capacity, and the previous sections showed large differences in the domestic product content of production.

These characteristics have two implications for the intensity of an imported supply-driven shock:

- For the relatively less developed countries, if the shock originates from an industrialized country, it might become disruptive in case the affected firm cannot shift to another supplier, since it does not have the technological capacity to substitute the inputs, at any price.

- For the most advanced industrialized countries, while there is always the possibility of substituting domestically an intermediate input produced in a less developed country, the increase in production costs may be much higher than the standard 30 per cent used in the simulation, due to, *inter alia*, the difference in the cost of factorial services.

As discussed in Appendix 3A.2, the input–output framework is inappropriate to measure the first type of disruptive shocks because the combination of strict complementarities of inputs and forward linkages would progressively bring the economy to an almost complete halt. In a more realistic scenario, one can consider that most of the export-oriented activities would stop, generating a severe macroeconomic shock to the economy.

For Japan and the USA, the induced rise in domestic prices due to a shutdown of their Asian suppliers of intermediate manufacture goods is significant when differences in production costs are imputed. This is the case especially for the textile and clothing industries (see Appendix 3A.3 for details on the calculation). The disruption of supply chains in the manufacturing sectors of the three developing Asian countries would lead to a 5 per cent increase in the average price of manufacture outputs in Japan, and 4 per cent in the USA. Textile and clothing are particularly vulnerable, suffering an increase in production cost of 13 per cent in Japan and 9 per cent in the USA.

Considering that only a minority of firms engage in offshoring, this average sectoral impact will fall disproportionately on a few firms – probably the most dynamic ones – with potentially large disruptive microeconomic impact as their production costs will rise by a multiple of the average rate. Incidentally, the results of this simulation also show the potential gains and competitive advantage those vertically integrated firms were able to obtain in the first place, when outsourcing part of their production to emerging Asia.

3. MONETARY CIRCUIT AND INTER-INDUSTRY SUPPLY CHAINS

The September turmoil that led to the 2008–2009 trade collapse was initially a financial crisis. Modelling the parallel transmission of real and financial shocks along inter-industry channels is important to understand the nature of the crisis. This section is devoted to the conceptual building of the monetary aspects of the model. The basic concepts behind the monetary circuit are simple and closely match the economy's production process. This process is divided into a finite number of stages, so that the output of one stage constitutes the input of the next – with the final stage yielding consumable output. All firms depend on credit to finance the current production costs (wages, intermediate consumption and use of capital goods). The monetary model starts with a request for credit by a productive firm to a bank in order to start a production process, and ends when the loan is reimbursed. The '*temps du circuit*', the elapsed time between money creation and its destruction, is closely related to the production time.[10]

In a globalized production network, the financial and productive establishments constituting this interlinked network need not be localized in the same country. As mentioned, the current centrifugal forces that characterize the geographical distribution of the productive activities mean that the individual links will be distributed among different countries, most probably at different levels of development, in order to capture the opportunities offered by the different relative costs of labour *vis-à-vis* the costs of capital. A corollary is that the participating economies may be at a different phase of their business cycles and that macroeconomic risks also include an exposure to exchange rate fluctuations. In addition, the quality of the available information on the financial credentials of the overseas suppliers and clients is lower than in the case of other domestic counterparts. Thus, firms engaged in import or export operations will need to request special lines of credit (or guarantees) from the banking sector or specialized financial institutions in order to realize their international operations.

Considering that on average the time needed for production will be longer when international operations are involved, because of higher transaction costs (communication and transport, in particular), any production network involving overseas operators will require more credit than a pure domestic one (particularly, see Table 3.3). Because business cycles and the capital adequacy ratio may differ from country to country and will also fluctuate rather independently, the probability of facing credit rationing at any point of the production chain is greatly increased.

Finally, the model relates mainly to the manufacturing sector. Even if the service sector is also increasingly engaged in international operations and is spreading across different countries, the specificities of services (for example, prevalence of wages in the cost structure, low technical coefficients and stock requirements, coincidence of production and consumption) imply that their credit requirement by unit of output is lower than in the more traditional manufacturing sector. But the international provision

Table 3.3 Costs of exporting merchandise, 2007 or most recent survey period

Grouping or region	**Time for export (days)**	**Cost to export (US$ per container)**[a]
World (country average)	26.1	1230
North and South-east Asia & Pacific	24.5	885
Eastern Europe & Central Asia	29.3	1393
Latin America & Caribbean	22.2	1108
Middle East & North Africa	24.8	992
OECD	9.8	905
South Asia	32.5	1180
Sub-Saharan Africa	35.6	1660

Note: [a] Cost is recorded as the fees levied on a 20-foot container, excluding tariffs or trade taxes.

Source: World Bank 'Doing Business Project'.

of transportation and business services is rising, and plays an increasing role in smoothing the operation of the production chain. Indirectly, the share of domestic service content of exports is also high in industrialized countries (Daudin et al., 2009). Thus any adverse shock affecting a key service provider may also disrupt the production chain.

3.1 The Basic Model of the Monetary Circuit

A canonical version of the monetary model starts with a request for credit by a firm to a bank in order to start a production process. In order to simplify the model without modifying the reasoning, it will be assumed that all profits made by the firm are redistributed to owners, so that there is no retained earnings and that all the value-added created in the production process goes back to households as wages or distributed profits.[11]

The bank's decision to grant the loan rests on (i) a microeconomic component proper to its evaluation of the firm's capacity to manage the project properly and reimburse its debt; (ii) a sectoral evaluation of the market prospects; (iii) the macroeconomic perception of the systemic risk attached to the business cycle; and (iv) the status of its capital adequacy ratio, reflecting its previous loan activity (a stock variable) in relation to capital requirements set by the prudential or regulatory authorities.

Using the borrowed money, the firm purchases inputs and pays workers to produce the merchandise. The goods produced are sold to consumers or to other firms (if the firm produces investment or intermediate goods).

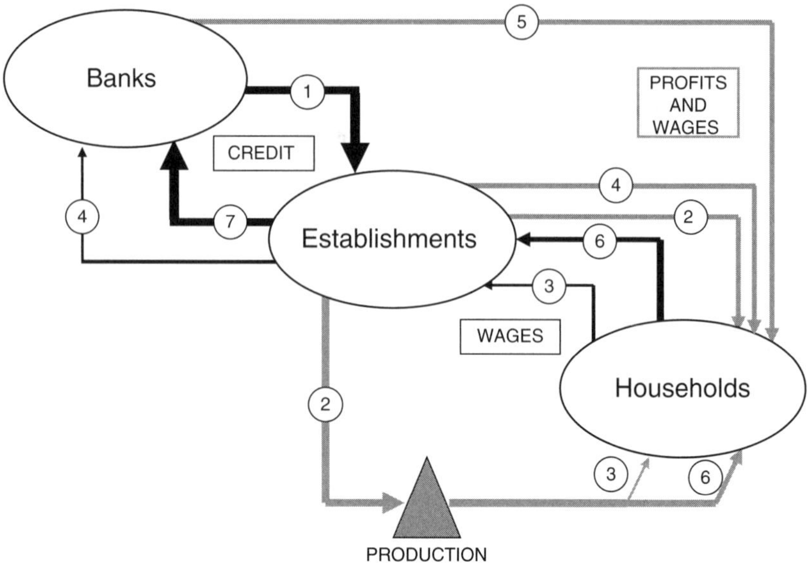

Note: Arrow numbers correspond to the flows described in Table 3.4.

Figure 3.1 A schematic presentation of the monetary circuit

When the firm is paid, it uses the money resulting from the sale to repay its debt to the bank (plus interest rate), and its own suppliers if they had extended payment facilities.[12]

The repayment of outstanding loans not only 'destroys money', but also allows the bank to extend new credit within the limit of the prudential loans/assets ratio. Since this is credit money, any money injected in the circuit is balanced by a debt obligation. The record of debt and its ratio with respect to the bank's assets (gold in the Physiocrats' perspective, or any asset considered as secure by the regulatory authorities in a contemporary context) is a key feature of our model.[13] As we will see, it acts as a bridge between flows and stocks, between real and monetary shocks, and between micro and macro effects.

Because the price of the asset is also linked to the macroeconomic conjuncture (business cycle), the regulatory process is pro-cyclical: in phases of boom, asset prices go up, increasing the lending capacity of banks; when the business cycle is downward oriented, asset prices go down and banks have to cut down on their credits in order to respect the prudential ratio.[14]

In a dynamic perspective, the monetary circuit can be presented in a graphical and a tabular format as shown in Figure 3.1 and Table 3.4. The

Table 3.4 Simple monetary circuit in a closed economy

Time	Capital adequacy ratio	Flow of funds		
		Bank account	Firm account	Households
0. Initial situation	A	0	0	0
1. Credit	$A/\alpha L$	0	L	0
2. Production	$A/\alpha L$	0	$L - W$	W
3. First round of sales	$A/\alpha L$	0	$L - W + X(1)$	$W - X(1)$
4. Firm pays interest and distributes profit	$A/\alpha L$	rL	$L+X(1) - W - rL - \pi X$	$W - X(1) + \pi X$
5. Bank pays employees and distributes profits	$A/\alpha L$	0	$L+X(1) - W - rL - \pi X$	$W - X(1) + \pi X + rL$
6. Second round of sales	$A/\alpha L$	0	$L+X - W - rL - \pi X$	$W - X + \pi X + rL$
7. Firm repays loan	A	0	$X - W - rL - \pi X$	$W - X + \pi X + rL$

Notes:
A: initial assets of the bank.
L: Loan from the bank to the firm to finance the production costs.
α: risk weight attached to the loan (credit rating).
W: wages needed to produce X.
X: value of merchandise produced by the project; $X(1)$ is the value sold during the first round (corresponding to wages paid by firms), $X(2)$ is the amount that is sold later after profits are distributed and employees from the financial sector are paid. There are no savings, all profits are distributed and
$X = X(1) + X(2)$.
r: interest rate.
π: rate of profit after wages and operating costs.

first column in Table 3.4 is simply a book entry that tracks the net asset situation of the banking system, because the bank does not actually loan money out of its capital. Each loan weighs on the adequacy ratio according to the risk attached to the loan. In turn, this risk, while specific to each firm (its own financial situation and that of its clients and key suppliers), depends also on the macroeconomic situation and the particular sensitivity of the sector to downturns.

Credit money is created *ex nihilo* when a loan is granted to the firm and its account is credited with a sum (L) that the firm will be able to use in order to pay for the goods and services it needs. The system is sustainable as long as (i) the production plan pays its costs and remunerates the stakeholders (salaries and distributed profits), that is $(X - W - rL - \pi X)$

is positive or nil, and (ii) the banking system does not exceed its adequacy ratio.

Because all profit is distributed to households and all income is consumed, the last position (No. 7) is equivalent to the initial one (0), closing the circuit from a dynamic perspective. All credit money has been destroyed when the loan is repaid in full, and net flows sum up to zero. For money to be destroyed, all real transactions should take place as planned, that is there are no unsold final or intermediary goods. This characteristic of the monetary circuit provides an insight into an important property of the system: any stock of goods remaining in the 'real' system (and reported as investment in national accounts) has a counterpart in outstanding credit money in the financial circuit.

Outstanding stocks can be voluntary, or 'desired', when firms wish to smooth production and sales (that is, to protect themselves from disruption in their production chain, or to be able to face a surge in demand). But stocks can be undesired when they correspond to major negative shocks or when production plans based on ex ante previsions prove to be too optimistic when confronted with the ex post situation. Any accumulation of stocks, either desired or undesired, must be financed out of retained profits or bank credit. In practice, because firms have a structural saving gap, any increase in their stocks (assimilated to gross investment in national accounts) will increase their net demand for credit.

This very simple model grossly underestimates the complexity of the actual circuit.[15] In reality, a multiplicity of simultaneous production plans are in place and the closure of the system (the sale of the production) does not depend on the wages and profits distributed by the producer, but on a stream of activities going on in the rest of the economy. In the same way, firms are not homogeneous: some produce final goods, others investment or intermediate goods. As seen before, even within the same sector of activity, the productive process can be fragmented among various establishments. Indeed, banks themselves pay wages and distribute profits, consume goods and services produced by other firms or pay an interest rate on time deposits from households and firms. Therefore the productive and monetary circuit are longer, and the elapsed time between initial and final positions (the '*temps du circuit*') is increased. The longer the circuit, the larger the number of individual firms participating in the supply chain, the higher the probability of outstanding credit money.

Because of the complexity and intricacy of the simultaneous production plans existing at any moment in an economy, there is always a large amount of outstanding credit money. Since this outstanding credit money has a counterpart in the capital adequacy ratio of banks, a limit may be reached (either because 'too much' credit has already been extended – in relation to banks' assets – or because the underlying quality of the borrowing firms has deteriorated, or because the value of assets went down), constraining the supply of new loans and the renewal of existing lines of credit. In their most severe forms, the binding constraints may cause a 'credit crunch'.

The procyclical nature of prudential ratios is a central feature of the model, and the object of much debate. In many reports on the implications of minimum capital-requirements, the potential restrictions are often qualified by mentioning that most banks hold capital in excess of the regulatory minima or are able to circumvent the binding constraints. According to Repullo and Suarez (2008), this 'benign neglect' of the potential pro-cyclical effect is due to a series of misconceptions. Indeed, the crisis of 2008/2009 showed that larger than expected market swings, with deteriorating balance-sheet quality, severely limit the access to equity and financial markets. As mentioned by Krugman (2008), in time of crisis, the core problem is capital rather than liquidity.

3.2 The Open Model of the Monetary Circuit

When the economy is open to international trade, domestic production competes with imports, but it can also be exported. Additionally, domestic production of final goods may include imported intermediate inputs, increasing the complexity of the process and the length of the circuit. As complexity increases, so does the probability of facing problems. Disregarding any differences in exchange and interest rates, a very simplified circuit involving two firms and two countries (a firm in a home country producing a final good, and its supplier located in a foreign country) would look as in Table 3.5.

When the system is open to the rest of the world, a series of complications arises. Part of the purchasing power created during the production process is distributed in the foreign country, while the final goods are sold in the home country. If X is not exported to the rest of the world, then the quantity produced will be greater than the quantity sold ($X > X(1) + X(2)$) even if there are no savings in the home country and all profits are distributed. Unless these final goods are exported, undesired stocks of finished products ($X - [X(1) + X(2)]$) will accumulate in the home country, associated with outstanding credit, while foreign households will accumulate savings for the amount of wages and profits created when processing the intermediate goods ($W^w + rL^w$).Contrary to the case of a closed economy, the situation described by the final row in the table is not identical to the initial one. In terms of national accounts, this appears as a trade deficit in the balance of payments of the home country (and a surplus for the rest of the world).[16]

Table 3.5 *Simple monetary circuit in an open economy*

Time index	Home country				Rest of the world			
	Capital adequacy ratio	Bank account	Firm account	Households	Capital adequacy ratio	Bank account	Firm account	Households
0. Initial situation	A^d	0	0	0	A^w	0	0	0
1. Credit production in home country	$A^d/(\alpha^d L^d)$	0	L^d	0	A^w	0	0	0
2. Credit intermediate inputs in RofW	$A^d/(\alpha^d L^d)$	0	L^d	0	$A^w/(\alpha^w L^w)$	0	L^w	0
3. Production intermediate inputs M	$A^d/(\alpha^d L^d)$	0	L^d	0	$A^w/(\alpha^w L^w)$	0	$L^w - W^w$	W^w
4. Import of inputs and production of X	$A^d/(\alpha^d L^d)$	0	$L^d - W^d - M$	W^d	$A^w/(\alpha^w L^w)$	0	$L^w + M - W^w$	W^w

5. First round: sales of $X(1)$	$A^d/(\alpha^d L^d)$	0	$L^d + X(1) - W^d - M$	$W^d - X(1)$	$A^w/(\alpha^w L^w)$	0	$L^w + M - W^w$	W^w
6. Firms pay interest and distribute profit	$A^d/(\alpha^d L^d)$	rL^d	$L^d + X(1) - rL^d - W^d - M - \pi X$	$W^d + \pi X - X(1)$	$A^w/(\alpha^w L^w)$	rL^w	$L^w + M - rL^w - W^w - \pi M$	$W^w + \pi M$
7. Banks pay employees and distribute profits	$A^d/(\alpha^d L^d)$	0	$L^d + X(1) - W^d - rL^d - M - \pi X$	$W^d + \pi X + rL^d - X(1)$	$A^w/(\alpha^w L^w)$	0	$L_i^w + M - rL^w - W^w - \pi M$	$W^w + \pi M + rL^w$
8. Second round of sales $X(2)$	$A^d/(\alpha^d L^d)$	0	$L^d + X - W^d - rL^d - M - \pi X$	$W^d + \pi X + rL^d - X$	$A^w/(\alpha^w L^w)$	0	$L^w + M - rL^w - W^w - \pi M$	$W^w + \pi M + rL^w$
9. Firms reimburse loans	A^d	0	$X - W^d - rL^d - M - \pi X$	$W^d + \pi X + rL^d - X$	A^w	0	$M - rL^w - W^w - \pi M$	$W^w + \pi M + rL^w$

Notes:
Same notation as Table 3.4, except: α: risk adjusted weights.
Superscripts: *d*: domestic; *w*: rest of the world.
M: intermediate goods produced in the rest of the world.

The funds borrowed to finance production are used to purchase intermediate goods and services from other firms that may be located in different countries. In the same way, the production process depends on the capacity of the respective supplier firms to obtain credit from their own banks and in time deliver their intermediate inputs.

4. UNIFYING THE TWO CIRCUITS: BANK'S ASSESSMENT OF BUSINESS RISKS

The previous two sections presented sequentially, from supply chain then monetary perspectives, the linkages that exist within and between globalized industrial systems. The following section will formalize the connections between both financial and real circuits, through the modelling of the 'α' parameter in the capital adequacy ratio which appears originally as a simple accounting device in the monetary circuit (see Table 3.4 and Table 3.5). This institutional ratio constrains the total amount of credit that a bank may issue. As mentioned, international standards, issued by the Bank for International Settlements (BIS), set an 8 per cent threshold for total risk-weighted assets.

We saw that the monetary circuit starts with a request for credit by a firm to a bank in order to finance a production process. The bank's decision regarding granting the loan is based on a mix of (i) microeconomic considerations, directly related to the financial situation of the firm and the quality of its management; (ii) sectoral specificities, such as the cyclical nature of the business in which the firm operates; (iii) macroeconomic considerations, such as the probability of expansion or recession; and (iv) the institutional capacity of the bank to extend new credit within the limit of its loans/assets ratio.

The microeconomic component of the bank's decision-making process is based, *inter alia*, on the direct supply-use connections of the firm requesting a loan. In a vertically integrated production chain, the default of a client can cause distress to its suppliers, and the difficulties of a key supplier can jeopardize the viability of a production plan. Some industrial sectors (like construction or automobiles) are more 'pro-cyclical' than others. According to the strength of its backward and forward linkage, the creditworthiness of a pro-cyclical firm will reflect, through the microeconomic channel, on its direct clients and suppliers, even when they do not operate in the same sector.

Also, because risks and the market value of assets are strongly related, the position in the business cycle has a greatly inflated pro-cyclical effect on the banks' propensity to extend new loans. Indeed, when a downward phase develops into a recession (when risks materialize), the price of assets may drop below a critical value, forcing banks to stop any new credit activity, and to cancel existing credit arrangements to reduce risk exposure irrespective of the merit of investment projects and firms' creditworthiness. This situation defines what is called a 'credit crunch'. Obviously, when a firm's request for credit is turned down, this must scale down production; this affects in turn its suppliers and even its clients through the supply chain, and influences final demand through lower household income (wages and profits).

For the most vulnerable sectors, which are both vertically and cyclically integrated, the conjunction of two waves of shocks, supply- and demand-driven, can lead to a resonance effect. The total effect of the shock is then a multiple of each component taken in isolation. Second, according to the monetary circuit described in Table 3.5, the shock will affect both flow variables (additional demand for credit money to cope with the shock) and stock variables (the credit rating of individual firms requesting additional loans, and the capital adequacy ratio of the banks extending loans). In a recessive cycle, the conjunction of real supply and demand shocks, on the one hand, and of stock–flow financial shocks, on the other hand, may have large systemic effects, even when the initial shocks are rather limited in scope.

Thus, even if initially a financial shock is exogenous, its effects on the industrial chain will cause this shock to reverberate through the real circuit, affecting in turn the monetary circuit through the default risks, as perceived by the financial sector. The size of the multiplier effect depends on the initial balance sheets of the financial intermediaries. Actually, modelling the weights 'α_i' (the financial rating of productive sectors) in the capital adequacy ratio ($A/\Sigma L_i \alpha_i$) synthesizes most of the real-monetary dynamics embedded in the present approach, including stock–flow interactions:

- From a 'flow' perspective, the 'α_i' are the result of a credit rating process that considers both financial and productive aspects, associated with (i) the firm itself and its management (what we called the microeconomic dimension); (ii) its mode of insertion in the productive economy and the related risks of supply-driven shocks transmitted through the supply chain; and (iii) its exposure to the macroeconomic business cycle, as captured by the demand-driven shocks.
- From a 'stock' perspective, the real shocks translate into the accumulation of undesired stocks and extend the life expectancy of credit money, with the related accumulation of liquidity, because loans

are not reimbursed in full.[17] Not only is money not destroyed as expected, but on the financial side, the accumulation of bad debts deteriorates the bank's balance sheet (loss provisions) and its capital adequacy ratio ($A/\Sigma L_i\alpha_i$).

The 'stock' effect on the capital adequacy ratio is not limited to the domestic industries. In a globalized economy such as that described in our model, the national financial sectors are also closely integrated and all economies now share 'leveraged common creditors'. In such a context, balance sheet contagion becomes pervasive (Krugman, 2008).

So, the chain of causalities is as follows:[18]

a. The shock initiates in the monetary circuit (for example, an existing line of credit is unexpectedly shut down), and it affects the production plans of a firm that is inserted at some point in a larger production chain; because both its clients and suppliers cannot shift to other producers immediately and at no cost, the discontinuity in the production flow will reverberate through higher costs across the system represented by the international I–O matrix. The real shock, once it has fully reverberated through the entire supply chains across industries and across countries, is proportional to the Ghosh coefficients that factor-in the sum of direct and indirect forward effects.
b. Exogenous supply-driven shocks also affect demand because increases in production costs are reflected in higher prices and lead to lower demand. As previously mentioned, the resulting negative demand-driven secondary shocks can be modelled individually using the traditional Leontief model (final demand impulses), or by capturing the backward (demand) sectoral effects of supply-driven multipliers (Papadas and Dahl, 1999).
c. The real shock, then, feeds back into the monetary circuit through (i) the building-up of undesired stocks of finished and intermediate goods through the supply chain, leading to the accumulation of outstanding credit-money in the circuit; and (ii) the contagion of financial risks affecting the rating of firms. Because the capacity of banks to create new money is limited by their capital adequacy ratio, the latter reduces in turn the capacity of banks to extend new credit, initiating a vicious circle. This obviously affects the most vulnerable firms (those more closely connected to the sector of activity affected by the initial shock), but has a systemic impact that reduces the banks' systemic capacity to extend new credit, regardless of the individual merits of the investment programmes.[19]

In sum, this reduced model of contagion through the supply chain only requires two variables to simulate and track the systemic implications of an exogenous financial shock: one variable of flow (the Imported Real Supply-driven Impact Coefficient, IRSIC, constructed on the real circuit, and possibly augmented for secondary demand-driven effects) and one of stock (capital adequacy ratio, derived from the monetary circuit). Because the stock-variable is partially dependent on the flow-variable, the only strategic variable to be measured in order to evaluate the risk of contagion is IRSIC, as has been implemented in the preceding section.

5. CONCLUSIONS

The global financial crisis that started in 2008 could possibly replicate, but on a much larger international scale, many patterns of Japan's lost decade, in particular the negative transmission mechanisms between the financial sectors and the real economy. In this context, the aim of the present study was to analyse the role of international supply chains as transmission channels of a financial shock from the monetary circuit into the real economy.

As the initial monetary shock reverberates through the production chains and affects final demand, more and more firms will face difficulties in completing their production plans or selling their output. These disruptions occurring in the real economy feed back into the monetary circuit. The disruption of the production chain and the building-up of undesired stocks impede the expected destruction of money and determine the accumulation of outstanding loans as well as a further downgrading of the exposed firms. Since the downgrading of an indebted individual firm affects the capital adequacy ratio of its banker, both flows and stocks are affected in the monetary circuit, and all firms see their access to credit potentially restricted.

If banks were originally operating at the limit of their institutional capacity, defined by the capital adequacy ratio, and if assets are priced to market, then a resonance effect amplifies the back and forth transmission between real and monetary circuits, leading to strongly non-linear results. The chaotic behaviour of the international financial system at the end of 2008, and its dire consequences on the real economy observed in 2009, are examples of such resonance and amplification. In that light, the recent crisis should provide an opportunity to address problems of macro-prudential pro-cyclicality to minimize the risks of boom and bust cycles initiating from the financial sector.

In this respect, the chapter illustrated the proposed methodology by devising and computing IRSIC, an indicator of supply-driven shocks based on forward linkages. Because individual firms are interdependent and rely on each other, either as suppliers of intermediate goods or clients for their own production, an exogenous financial shock affecting a single firm – such as the termination of a line of credit – reverberates through the production chain. The transmission of the shock through real channels can be tracked, at macroeconomic level, by modelling input–output interactions. Using an international version of the input–output matrices, the chapter conducted the calculation of IRSIC on five interconnected economies of different characteristics: China, Japan, Malaysia, Thailand and the United States. Calculations are based on the Asian International Input–Output Tables prepared on the basis of 2000 data, and on an estimate for 2008.

Results indicate that the real transmission effects through the international supply chain linking firms among these economies were heterogeneous across industries and across countries. The largest impacts, as expected, are felt domestically. The relative size of the shock on the domestic economy depends on its degree of openness, and also on the relative size of the originating industry in relation to the rest of the economy. Based on the existing inter- and intra-industrial linkages, Japan was the largest exporter of potential price shocks, while Malaysia and Thailand were the most vulnerable to such shocks, because of the high degree of vertical integration of their manufacturing sector. Between 2000 and 2008, China registered a notable increase in both inter-country forward linkages and domestic backward linkages, which increased its influence as an exporter of price shocks while its vulnerability to an imported shock remained relatively stable. Indeed, the Chinese manufacturing sectors are relying more and more on domestic suppliers for their industrial inputs.

The methodology used to estimate real transmission effects is fairly easy to implement. The Leontief and Ghosh models defined in an international context are very valuable statistical tools, which allowed us to obtain interpretable results quickly. The main weakness, however, is on the normative side. This partial modelling approach remains eclectic and does not easily provide for a simultaneous and integrated modelling of both physical and financial flows. The Ghosh methodology is intended only as a tracking device, and does not provide information on economic implications or welfare changes. The chapter also identifies the macroeconomic and sectoral determinants of the credit-migration matrices, but falls short of integrating them into the monetary circuit. Incorporating the various microeconomic, sectoral and macroeconomic dimensions into computable general equilibrium models would be an option, but these models have limitations in their financial components. In particular, the reductive assumption of exogenous money, typical of CGEs, would have to be abandoned for the endogenous approach characterizing monetary circuits.

NOTES

1. This is an updated version of WTO Staff Working Paper ERSD-2009-06. The views expressed in this chapter are those of the authors and do not represent a position, official or unofficial, of the WTO Secretariat or WTO Members.
2. Under the new System of National Accounts (2008 SNA), only goods for processing actually sold to non-resident firms will be considered as merchandise exports; 1993 SNA was more comprehensive and covered all supply chain transactions, irrespective of change of ownership.
3. In times of crisis, the firms with a greater market power (and financial capacities) will help their key suppliers in resolving their cash-flow problems, even when it means worsening their own cash-flow situation. See Appendix 3A.1 for an example on the automobile industry.
4. Entrywise product: $A \cdot B = (a_1 . b_1, a_2 . b_{2, \ldots,} a_n . b_n)$ similar to a Kronecker product on two matrices or vectors of same dimensions.
5. While I–O models suppose perfect inter-sectoral complementarities of inputs (zero technical substitution), they do not restrain intra-sectoral substitution between domestic and foreign inputs. The estimation of these elasticities, in particular through the Armington specification, plays a central role in the flourishing CGE literature.
6. It takes at least a year to redeploy the production of critical parts in the automotive industry, according to *Automotive News Europe* (see Appendix 3A.1).
7. Because technical coefficients are normalized and less than unity, a^n (the impact of initial demands at the nth stage of the production chain) rapidly tends to 0 when n increases.
8. See IDE-JETRO (2006) for details on the I–O coverage and the statistical treatments.
9. This conservative option may underestimate the price impact of a supply shock for developed countries, as it is more probable that the alternative suppliers will have to be found in the domestic market, for a relatively much higher cost (see Appendix 3A.3 for alternative parameters).
10. In a modern industrial system, firms cannot finance investment and production costs using their accumulated assets (initial capital plus retained earnings) and have to attract funding. National accounts present the productive sector with net borrowing requirements. For most firms, funding comes from loans rather than by issuing bonds or equities. Due to imperfect and asymmetric information, the Modigliani–Miller theorem does not hold, and when firms are denied bank credit, they usually do not wish, nor are they able, to raise capital by issuing new equity (Stiglitz and Greenwald, 2003, p. 34).
11. In a complete model, value-added is also used to pay taxes and finance reserves. The payment of interest to the banking sector is treated, under the System of National Accounts (2008 SNA), as intermediate consumption of services.
12. Because firms are structurally indebted, from a systemic perspective intra-firm quasi-credits increase the liquidity in the circuit.
13. Keen (2007) presents a monetary accounting matrix with a similar distinction between assets and liabilities, albeit within a different framework.
14. Under Basel II, banks determine the required capital of lending by applying the risk weight that corresponds to the borrower's rating and then by multiplying the risk weight by the (usually 8 per cent) minimum requirement of capital. Because risks and the market value of assets are strongly (and negatively) correlated, the position in the business cycle has a strong pro-cyclical effect on the banks' propensity to extend new loans. In practice, however, there are ways of circumventing the regulations through,

inter alia, off-balance-sheet operations. Tenants of the pure endogenous money theory doubt the actual binding effect of these requirements, and consider that banks that are willing to extend credit can always do so. Others maintain that Basel II is probably pro-cyclical (Repullo and Suarez, 2008). Accounting practices are also pro-cyclical (fair-value accounting, provisioning for expected losses on loans, and so on).

15. Godley and Lavoie (2007) offer a detailed presentation of a complete stock-flow representation of the circuit. Albeit their approach is clearly built from a post-Keynesian perspective regarding the capacity of banks to modulate their supply of credit, their description can be adapted to many other non-Walrasian theoretical settings, such as the loanable funds theory that competed with Keynesian theory after the 1930s or the Austrian school. Indeed, it is the flexibility of the monetary circuit in adapting to a number of theoretical settings that makes it very attractive from the practitioner's perspective.
16. Opening the monetary circuit to cover balance of payments operations involves a series of complex interactions that are not treated in this very simple model. See Godley and Lavoie (2007) for an example.
17. As mentioned, the core problem in the recent 2008/2009 financial crisis is capital, not liquidity.
18. Because our main objective is not to build a complete stock-flow model but to track the contagion of a shock initiating in the monetary sphere, a simplifying option is chosen. It starts from a hypothetical steady state in which all stocks and all flows are held constant, and explores what happens when sector-specific international supply chains suffer an exogenous shock, such as a 'credit crunch', typical of the 2008/2009 international conjuncture.
19. When the adequacy ratio is reaching a critical limit, the banking sector turns down most requests for new loans and invests in risk-free assets such as good quality government bonds, especially US bonds. The flight to quality that followed the 2008 sub-prime crisis and the subsequent melting down of the international banking system illustrate this point and explain why the dollar appreciated despite the fact that the US economy was at the core of the crisis.

REFERENCES

Baldwin R. (2006), 'Globalisation: the great unbundling(s)', Economic Council of Finland, 20 September.

Bloomfield, A.I. (1938), 'The foreign-trade doctrines of the physiocrats', *American Economic Review*, **28**(4), 716–35.

Daudin, G., C. Rifflart and D. Schweisguth (2009), 'Who produces what for whom in the world economy?', working paper, OFCE.

Escaith, H. and F. Gonguet (2009), 'International trade and real transmission channels of financial shocks in globalized production networks', *WTO Staff Working Papers*, May.

Escaith, H., N. Lindenberg and S. Miroudot (2010), 'International supply chains and trade elasticity in times of global crisis', *WTO Staff Working Papers*, February.

Godley, W. and M. Lavoie (2007), *Monetary Economics: An Integrated Approach to Credit, Money, Income, Production and Wealth*, London: Palgrave Macmillan.

Hummels, D., J. Ishii and K. Yi (2001), 'The nature and growth of vertical specialization in world trade', *Journal of International Economics*, **54**, 75–96.

Inomata, S. (2008), 'A new measurement for international fragmentation of the production process: an international input-output approach', *IDE Discussion Papers* No.175.

Institute of Developing Economies-JETRO (2006), 'How to make Asian Input–Output Tables', in *Asian International Input–Output Table 2000*, IDE Statistical Data Series No. 89.
Keen, S. (2007), 'A simple approach to modelling endogenous money', ICAPE.
Krugman, P. (2008), 'The international finance multiplier', mimeo.
de Mesnard, L. (2007), 'About the Ghosh model: clarifications', *Laboratoire d'Economie et de Gestion, Economy Series, Working Papar* 2007-06.
Neary, P. (2009), 'Putting the "new" into new trade theory: Paul Krugman's Nobel Memorial Prize in Economics', *University of Oxford and CEPR Discussion Paper Series*, No. 423.
Papadas, C. and D. Dahl (1999), 'Supply-driven input–output multipliers', *Journal of Agricultural Economics*, **50**(2), 269–85.
Pula, G. and T.A. Peltonen (2009), 'Has emerging Asia decoupled? An analysis of production and trade linkages using the Asian international input–output table', *European Central Bank WPS* No. 993.
Repullo, R. and J. Suarez (2008), 'The procyclical effects of Basel II', paper presented at the 9th Jacques Polack Annual Research Conference, IMF.
Saito, M. (2004), 'Armington elasticities in intermediate inputs trade: a problem in using multilateral trade data', IMF Working Paper WP/04/22.
Stadtler, H. and C. Kilger (2008), *Supply Chain Management and Advanced Planning: Concepts, Models, Software and Case Studies*, 4th edn, Berlin: Springler-Verlag.
Stiglitz, J. and B. Greenwald (2003), *Towards a New Paradigm in Monetary Economics*, Cambridge: Cambridge University Press.
Tanaka, K. (2009), 'Trade collapse and international supply chains: evidence from Japan', available at www.voxEU.org.
Yi, K. (2009), 'The collapse of global trade: the role of vertical specialisation', in R. Baldwin and S. Evenett (eds), *The Collapse of Global Trade, Murky Protectionism, and the Crisis: Recommendations for the G20*, available at www.voxEU.org.

APPENDIX 3A.1: FINANCING SUPPLIERS IN TIMES OF CRISIS: AUTOMAKER'S AID

According to the Head of the European suppliers' organization, CLEPA, it takes time to change one supplier for another. The changeover can take six months to a year, depending on how complicated the part is to produce, and a customer has to protect the weaker supplier until a stronger one learns how to produce the inputs according to the automaker's requirements.

Thus, many automakers have undertaken specific actions to help the suppliers they want to protect from the 2008 credit crunch. According to the reference article,[1] here is a sample of actions taken by some leading automakers to protect their key suppliers during the credit crunch:

- BMW: Encourage stronger suppliers to take over weaker ones; pay in advance for parts; speed up payments; temporarily pay higher price for parts;
- Ford: Give loans; speed up payments;
- Daimler: Temporarily pay higher price for parts; provide advice on how to cut cost; provide advice on how to improve efficiency;
- Porsche: Help finance production tooling;
- PSA: Speed up payments; pay in advance for parts; buy raw materials for them; help them find financing; advise on possible alliances, mergers;
- Renault: Speed up payments;
- VW group: Form special team in purchase department to prevent suppliers collapsing.

Note

1. *Automotive News Europe*, 8 December, 2008, available at http://www.autonews.com/apps/pbcs.dll/article?AID=/20081208/ANE03/812079905/1179.

APPENDIX 3A.2: DEMAND-DRIVEN AND SUPPLY-DRIVEN INPUT–OUTPUT MODELS

The well-known 'demand-driven' model was developed by Wassily Leontief in the 1930s; two decades later, Ambica Ghosh adapted the I–O model to analyse supply shocks. I–O models assume that all inputs are complementary (the production function is such that inputs should be used in a fixed proportion, with no substitution at least in the short run), and the demand impulses are transmitted primarily through backward linkages. When the final demand for a product '*i*' is altered exogenously, the primary impact is felt on the demand for those sectoral outputs and commodities that are used as inputs for the production of the product '*i*'. The backward linkages trigger a series of secondary demand effects that progressively die down and are captured by the Leontief inverse matrix $(I - A)^{-1}$.

The Ghosh approach states that each intermediate output is sold to a series of industrial sectors in fixed proportions. When the production of an intermediate product '*i*' is exogenously altered, the primary effect is felt by those sectors that need '*i*' as input. This will trigger forward effects, either direct (to the sectors requiring '*i*' as input for their production) or secondary (sectors depending on intermediate goods that had required '*i*' as input). As in the Leontief case, the iterative process dies down to reach another equilibrium.

The accumulation of impacts can be measured by the Ghosh inverse $(I - B)^{-1}$. As in the Leontief case, the matrix B is built using the inter-sectoral transaction matrix, but the allocation coefficients are normalized in rows (destination of output) by the value of production, and not in columns as for technical coefficients (origin of productive factors used in the production).

The Leontief logic for backward linkage is based on standard economics: sectors do respond to changes in demand, they increase their production when demand is higher and reduce it when demand is lower. The Ghoshian approach is much weaker, and its theoretical aspects are somewhat contentious. In absence of a change in effective demand, pushing up production through additional supply of inputs would have the same effect as pushing on a string. Indeed, the theoretical reservations about the Ghosh model led to its relative demise as a macroeconomic modelling tool in the quantity space.

Nevertheless, the Ghosh approach is still useful in the price space, and can be used, within certain limits, to model the transmission of shocks to the costs of production (de Mesnard, 2007). It is particularly true for short-term analysis, when firms have limited capacity for substituting the disrupted input by shifting to alternative and more expensive suppliers. The mechanism is as follows: a quantity restriction on any single intermediate good forces the client-firm to shift to other suppliers (foreign or domestic). While this is always possible in our model, it has a cost, as alternative suppliers will supply the needed quantities at a higher price. It should be noted that the dual of the Leontief model can also be used to model price effects, especially when the shocks originate in primary inputs (for example, wages).

The final impact on production costs depends on a conjunction of quantitative and qualitative factors. The quantitative factor is proportional to the contribution of the disrupted input in the production function and is captured by the allocation coefficients of the I–O matrix. The qualitative factor is microeconomic in nature, and is determined by the particular market structure for this product, in particular by the possibility of substitution. The supply elasticity is usually determined by the time frame allowed for substitution, by the spare production capacity available to alternative suppliers and their level of stocks, and by their technical capabilities (including the ownership of critical patents). The stronger the constraint (for example when the initial supplier had a de facto monopoly), the higher the potential rise in production cost. At the limit, when no substitution exists, then all the adjustments along the supply chain have to be done in the quantity space, proportionally to the bottleneck.

The elasticity of substitution between similar inputs, from various countries of origin, are known as Armington elasticities. Estimating these elasticities has generated large collection of literature, especially in areas linked with international trade literature and computable general equilibrium models. A review of existing results shows that the elasticities (estimated using multilateral trade data) for the intermediate inputs industries tend to be higher than those for the final consumption goods industries (Saito, 2004).

In practice, one should expect a mixture of price and quantity effects, as demand for higher priced products – intermediate input or the resulting final good – will go down. The modelling of the sectoral reactions to changes in relative input prices and the related structural interactions would ideally have to be realized using computable general equilibrium models.

APPENDIX 3A.3: SIMULATING A DISRUPTIVE SUPPLY-DRIVEN SHOCK IN THE ASIAN–US SUB-REGION

IRSIC reflects the possibility and cost of (imperfect) substitution between domestic and imported inputs for all participants in the supply chain. Nevertheless, for a country at an earlier stage of industrialization, a shock originating from an industrialized country might prove disruptive if the domestic firm is totally dependent on the international productive network or when alternative suppliers do not have the technological capacity to substitute the inputs, at any price.

Table 3A.1 Ratio of PPP conversion factor to market exchange rate, 2005

Ratio of PPP conversion factor to market exchange rate, 2005	Based on US dollar	Based on Japanese Yen
USA	1.00	0.85
Japan	1.18	1.00
China	0.42	0.36
Malaysia	0.46	0.39
Thailand	0.40	0.34

Source: International Comparison Program: 'New purchasing power parity estimates from the 2005 International Comparison Program', World Bank.

The disruptive shock created by a brutal disruption of manufactured inputs imported from Japan and the USA would probably slam on the brakes of the productive sectors in developing countries relying on these inputs; in particular, it could shut down most of their export-oriented manufacturing activities. As discussed above, the input–output framework defined by the Ghosh matrix is inappropriate to measure such disruptive shocks in the quantity space, because of the strict complementarities of inputs (corresponding to a null Armington elasticity of substitution between imported and domestic inputs).

Because of the existence of forward sectoral linkages, an economy based on strictly complementary production factors (Leontief technologies) would slow down to a complete stop as the supply constraints progressively extend to all sectors. A more realistic scenario is one where only the export-oriented activities stop when the required inputs for processing are no more available.

For the most advanced industrialized countries, there is always the technological possibility of domestically substituting an intermediate input produced in a less developed country. But the increase in production costs may be much higher than the standard 30 per cent used in the simulation, due to, *inter alia*, the difference in the cost of factorial services, especially labour.

Our back-of-the-envelope calculation of the potential increase in sectoral production cost is based on a single international price for tradable goods and a pricing of non-traded factorial services based on the equivalence of purchasing power parity. The purchasing power parity ratio between developed and developing countries is about 0.40; in other words, factorial services are 150 per cent more expensive in the USA and Japan than in the developing Asian countries (Table 3A.1).

Table 3A.2 Combined disruptive shock from the manufacturing sectors of Asian developing countries, 2008 (percentage)

From China, Malaysia and Thailand to:	Japan	USA
Agriculture	1.5	1.4
Mining	2.3	0.8
Agroindustries	1.8	1.9
Textile and clothing	13.2	8.8
Industrial machinery and other manufacture	7.0	6.1
Transport equipment	6.1	4.8
Other products	2.9	2.6
Utilities (water, gas, elect.)	0.7	0.6
Construction	3.4	3.5
Trade and transport services	0.8	0.9
Other services	1.0	1.0
Total sectors	2.5	1.9
Sub-total manufacturing sectors	4.9	4.1

Note: Expected increase in sectoral cost of production following a disruptive shock from China, Malaysia and Thailand manufacturing sectors, forcing a substitution of imported inputs for domestic ones.

Sources: Authors' calculations.

On the other hand, the direct share of domestic value-added (the remuneration of factorial services) in the value of production in Japan and the USA was about 58 per cent in 2008. Thus the expected increase in input prices, when shifting production from a typical developing Asian country supplier to a domestic (Japanese or the USA) supplier should be 87 per cent (0.58 × 150 per cent). This shock is applied simultaneously to the cost of all manufactured inputs previously imported from China, Malaysia and Thailand by Japan and the USA (Table 3A.2).

The induced rise in average output prices is significant, especially in the industrial sectors of 'Textile and clothing', where the disruption of supply chains in the manufacturing sectors of the three developing Asian countries would lead to a 13 per cent increase in the average price of the sector's outputs in Japan and about 9 per cent in the USA.

Japan is more affected than the USA in all sectors, showing its greater reliance on imported inputs and fragmented production. The average cost-push on all manufacturing sectors would be close to 5 per cent for Japan, and slightly over 4 per cent for the USA. The microeconomic impact is probably much higher considering that the average increase in costs registered at sectoral level will be caused by a minority of outward-oriented firms that decided to outsource and internationalize their supply chains in the first place. The resulting loss of competitiveness may well price them out of their market, or drastically reduce their profitability and investments.

4. Vertical specialization at the time of economic crisis

Yoko Uchida and Satoshi Inomata

1. INTRODUCTION

One of the key factors behind global trade growth in recent decades is the development of vertical production networks (Feenstra, 1998 and Krugman, 1995). Manufacturing goods are no longer produced in a single country. Production processes are subdivided into several stages, in which respective countries specialize according to their own comparative advantages. Many countries are involved in vertical production networks of producing just a single final good to consumers. In particular, as Pitigala (2009) points out, emerging economies considerably benefited from the development of vertical production networks since the network enabled them to install an appropriate portion of the production stages according to their levels of production technology. These countries enjoyed rapid trade growth through extensive participation in global production networks.

This chapter examines how the global economic crisis has changed the nature of production networks in the Asia-Pacific region, and, in so doing, aims to envisage a possible direction for a sustainable production system in the post-crisis 'Factory Asia' (Baldwin, 2006).

2. VERTICAL SPECIALIZATION: CONCEPT AND CALCULATION METHOD

Figure 4.1 illustrates an image of vertical production chains involving four countries. Intermediate goods, final goods and factor inputs are represented by circles, rectangles and triangles, respectively. Country 1 produces intermediate inputs that are exported. Country 2 combines imported intermediate inputs, domestic intermediate inputs, and capital/labour to produce new products. Some portion of country 2's output is consumed in the domestic market, while the rest is exported as intermediate or final goods to country 3.

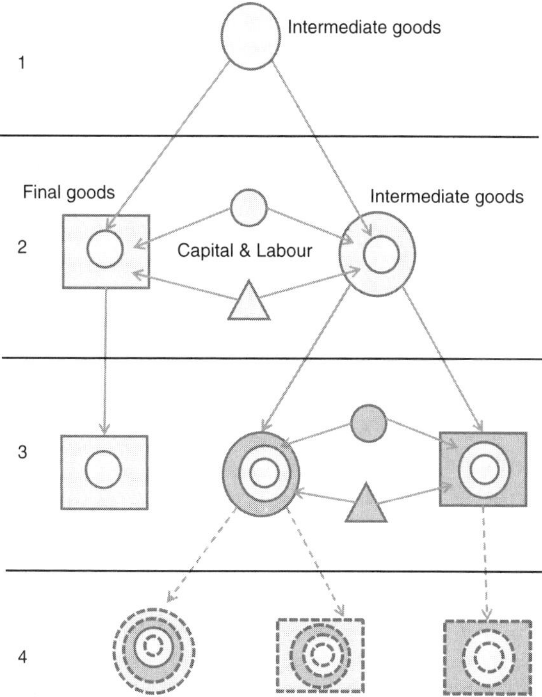

Figure 4.1 A schematic image of vertical production networks

Hummels et al. (2001) devised an index called 'vertical specialization' (VS) as a measurement of a country's degree of participation in vertical production networks. The VS index captures one aspect of a country's involvement in the cross-national production system, by calculating the amount of 'imported inputs used for producing a product that is subsequently exported', as formulated below.

$$\text{VS} = (\text{imported intermediate inputs / total output}) * \text{exports} \quad (4.1)$$

The first term of the right-hand side of equation (4.1) is the ratio of imported inputs in producing one unit of a product. By multiplying this ratio by the export value, we obtain the dollar value of the import contents of export. The VS value is zero if the country does not export any products using imported intermediate inputs. The aggregate VS value is obtained by summing up all the VS values of each industrial sector. Since we are interested in the VS composition, VS values are then normalized with respect to the total export of the country in question.

$$\text{Normalized VS: } \frac{VS}{EX} = \frac{\sum_i VS_i}{\sum_i EX_i}, \tag{4.2}$$

where EX and i denote the export value and industrial sector, respectively. To implement this calculation using an input–output table, we use the following matrix-form equation:

$$VS/EX = (\underline{u}M\underline{EX})/EX, \tag{4.3}$$

where $\underline{u}$ is a $1 \times n$ vector of 1's (a summation vector), M is an $n \times n$ import coefficient matrix, and $\underline{EX}$ is an $n \times 1$ export vector.

Input–output tables have a special property to capture both direct and indirect usage of inputs. We employ this property for our VS formulation in order to calculate the whole input amount in the production system that is required to produce country's exports. Equation (4.4) calculates normalized VS, taking account of both the direct and indirect input requirement.

$$VS'/EX = [\underline{u}M(I - A)^{-1}\underline{EX}]/EX, \tag{4.4}$$

where I is an $n \times n$ identity matrix, A is an $n \times n$ domestic input coefficient matrix, and $(I - A)^{-1}$ is the Leontief inverse matrix, respectively.

Now, it is known that the Leontief inverse matrix can be expanded as:

$$(I - A)^{-1} = I + A + A^2 + A^3 + \cdots. \tag{4.5}$$

Post-multiplying equation (4.5) by $\underline{EX}$, we obtain

$$(I - A)^{-1}\underline{EX} = (I + A + A^2 + A^3 + \cdots)\underline{EX} = \underline{EX} + A\underline{EX} + A^2\underline{EX} + A^3\underline{EX} + \cdots. \tag{4.6}$$

The first term of the right-hand side of equation (4.6) is a given export demand itself, while the second term shows a direct input requirement for producing output to meet this export demand. The third term shows the second-round input requirement to meet a set of demand for domestic goods and services given by the first term . . . and so on. So, the inclusion of the Leontief inverse matrix in the formula enables us to capture the total input requirement of every production stage in a vertical production chain.[1]

To calculate the VS index, Hummels et al. (2001) use conventional national I–O data for each country in question. Here, however, we employ the data of the Asian International Input–Output Tables (AIO table), which report cross-national transactions of both intermediate and final goods within the Asia-Pacific region.

While the method of Hummels et al. (2001) only picks up a country's immediate linkages, the use of AIO tables enables us to draw a more comprehensive picture of the vertical network participation of the countries concerned. As shown in the schematic image in the 'Explanatory notes' (see Chapter 8), the AIO table provides two-dimensional information concerning the 'destination' and 'usage' of each product. This dual information helps identify the product usage of exported goods, that is whether the product is exported for intermediate use or for final consumption overseas. This is a unique feature of the AIO table, which cannot be offered by trade statistics or by conventional national I–O tables.

From the viewpoint of vertical production chains, whether a country is mainly exporting intermediate goods or final consumption goods is directly related to the country's technological profile in the international division of labour. It is generally considered that the required level of technology and intricacy of production systems differ significantly between the 'production stage' and the 'assembly stage' of parts and components. The production of parts and components, especially those for high-end consumer goods, requires sophisticated technology with qualified logistic management for just-in-time delivery. The assembly of components to complete the final consumption goods, in contrast, needs relatively simple routines with low work skills.[2]

Therefore, by comparing the relative degree of commitment in the 'production stage' and that in the 'assembly stage' of the vertical production process, the technological development of the countries of interest can be profiled. In our study, this is done by splitting the VS index into two parts: VS_i and VS_f.

VS_i is the VS index of exports for intermediate usage in foreign countries, which shows the level of participation in the production of parts and components. VS_f, conversely, is the VS index of exports for final consumption overseas, which is thus considered to indicate the degree of engagement in the final assembly process.[3] The AIO data incorporates information on matching bilateral trade flows in its multi-country import matrices. To formulate the property of the AIO tables as mentioned above, the new equation for the VS index will be:

$$VS''/EX = \sum_{s} \underline{u}[A^{sr}(I - A^{rr})^{-1}\underline{EX^r}]/EX^r, \tag{4.7}$$

where r is the country in question, and s is a trade partner of r. A^{sr} is country r's import coefficient matrix from country s, while A^{rr} is country r's domestic input coefficient matrix. $\underline{EX}^r$ is country r's export vector to each destination country. To calculate VS_i and VS_f, export vector $\underline{EX}^r$ is constructed in two arrays, one of which consists of the products to be used as an intermediate input and the other as a final good in the subsequent stages.

3. VERTICAL SPECIALIZATION BEFORE AND AFTER THE CRISIS: CALCULATION RESULTS[4]

Figure 4.2 shows the regional averages of VS indices of the Asia-Pacific region from 1990 to 2008.[5] The entire span of the crossbar shows the total VS value: that is the degree of countries' participation in vertical production chains. The length of the bar towards the left from the centre (darkly-shaded) indicates VS_i, the degree of participation in the production of parts and components, while that extending to the right-hand side (lightly-shaded) shows VS_f, the degree of participation in the final assembly process.

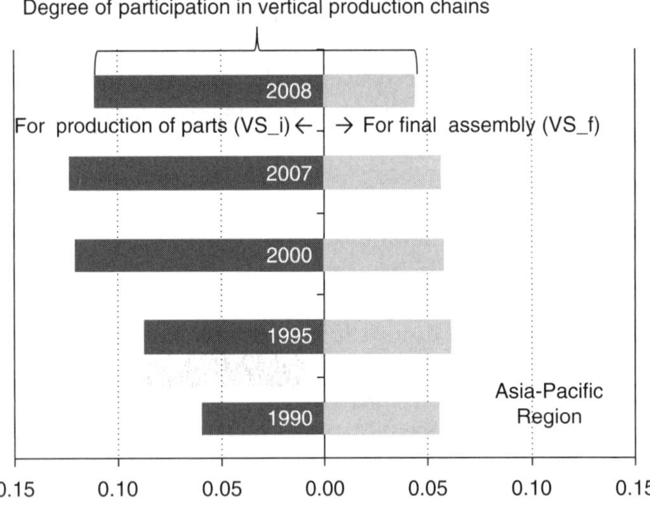

Note: The index value of 2007 is an estimate using 2007 trade statistics but based on the structure of the 2000 AIO table.

Source: The Asian International Input–Output Tables.

Figure 4.2 Vertical specialization: the whole region

The levels of VS_i and VS_f were almost equivalent in 1990. From that year onwards, however, the VS_i index grew much faster than VS_f. This implies that the vertical production networks in the Asia-Pacific region developed rapidly during the period, both in depth and scale, involving various industries from various countries supplying intermediate goods and services. The production chains of the region became increasingly complex, and highly efficient international division of labour was achieved through the sophisticated fragmentation and exchange of production processes among the countries concerned.

The total VS index peaked before the crisis and then declined significantly by 13.8 per cent. This is largely accounted for by the drop of the VS_f index, which decreased by 21.2 per cent compared to the 10.3 per cent decrease in the VS_i index.

The VS_i index is less likely to be affected by external shocks than VS_f for three possible reasons. Firstly, the time span of shock transmission differs. The collapse of the US final demand directly and immediately affects the demand for final goods of the region, while its effect on intermediate goods propagates with a lag, depending on the length of the production chains.

Secondly, there might be a contractual pre-commitment for orders of parts and materials. Manufacturers have to place orders well in advance to secure just-in-time delivery in accordance with their production plans. The transactions of intermediate goods thus tend to be downwardly inflexible to environmental changes compared to final goods, which usually assume point-of-purchase transactions.

Finally, there is a difference in demand elasticity. The VS_i index of an industry, by definition, will decline when the industry's intermediate exports decrease and/or the imports that are used in producing exports decrease. The magnitude of the decrease depends on the substitutability of goods between domestic and foreign products. If the imported intermediate inputs are easily substituted by domestic products all along the production chains, for example, in response to the depreciation of currencies, then the overall VS_i values are reduced immediately. This is, however, not the case for the production system of the Asia-Pacific region. The levels of production technology in the region differ significantly between the countries, compared to, say, the EU market where one country's product can be easily replaced by another's because of the homogeneity of their production technologies. Accordingly, the VS_i index, or the production chains of intermediate goods in the Asia-Pacific region, have been relatively 'resistant' to external shocks, at least in the short run.[6]

Figures 4.3a to 4.3c show the VS indices by country, from the group of countries with high VS values down to that with low VS values.

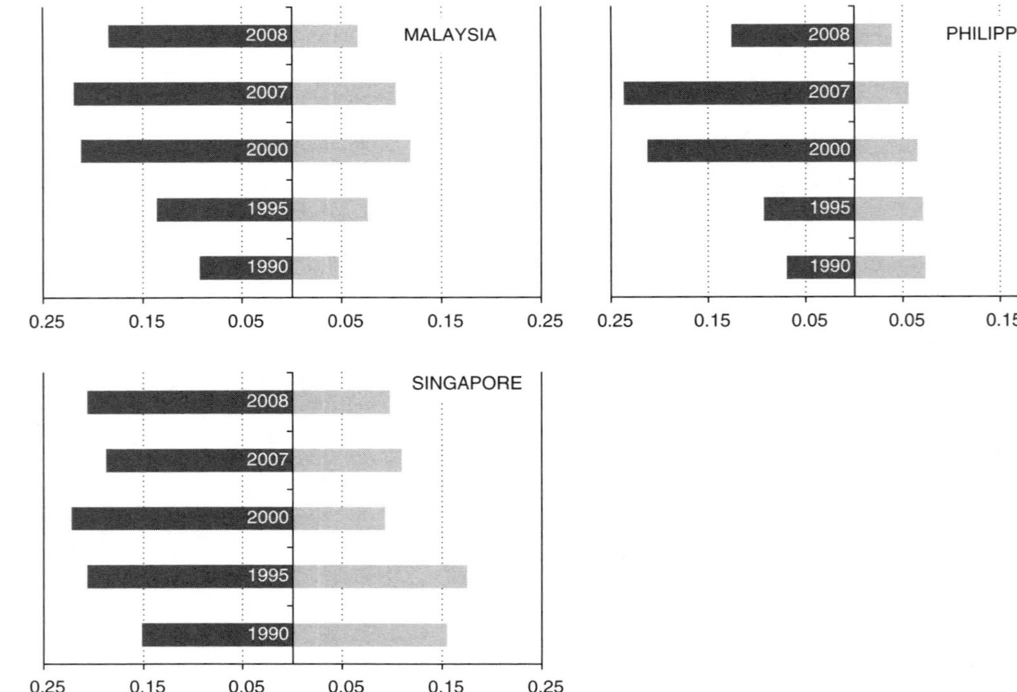

Source: The Asian International Input–Output Tables.

Figure 4.3a 'High VS' group countries

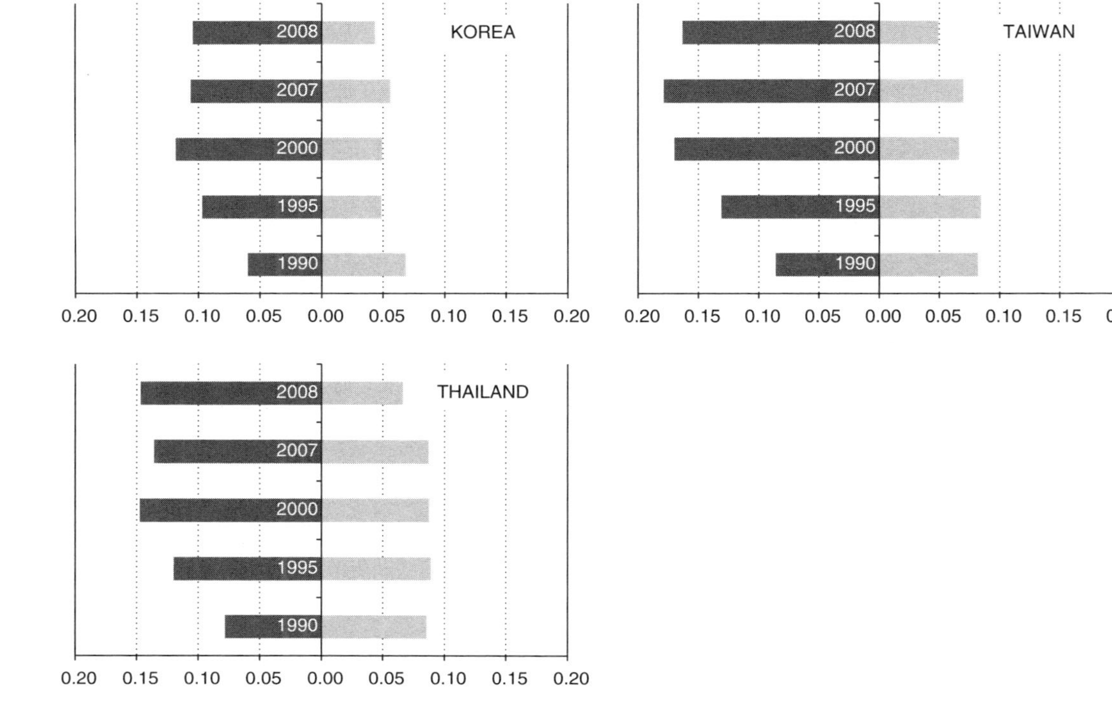

Source: The Asian International Input–Output Tables.

Figure 4.3b 'Middle VS' group countries

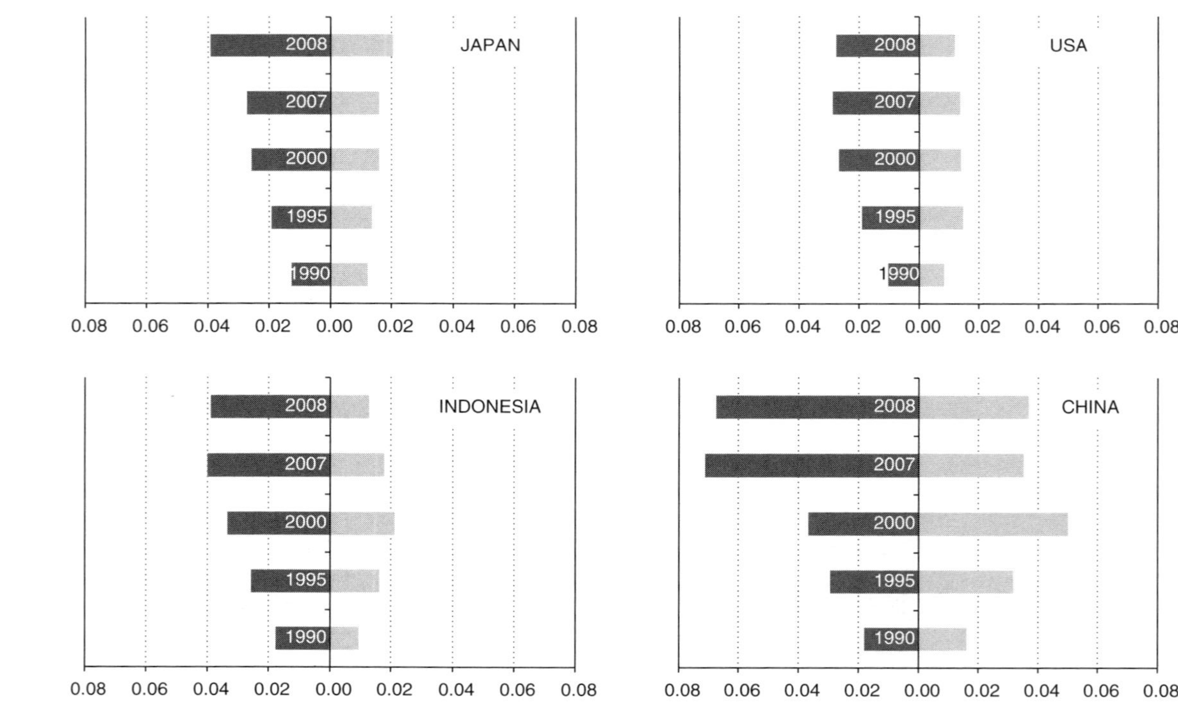

Source: The Asian International Input–Output Tables.

Figure 4.3c 'Low VS' group countries

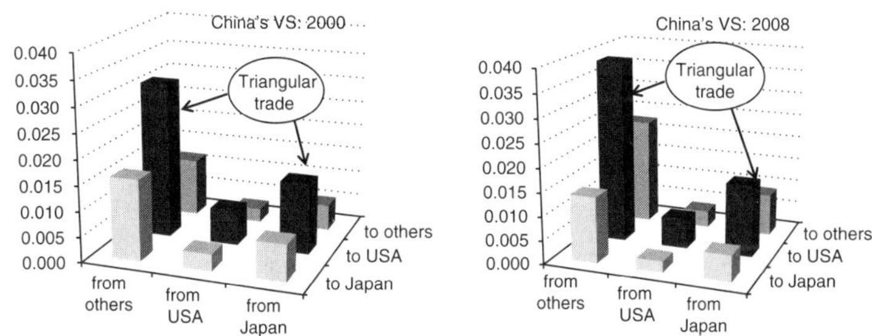

Note: 'Others' include all AIO countries except China, Japan and the USA.

Source: The Asian International Input–Output Tables.

Figure 4.4 Geographical decomposition of China's VS index

The level of the VS index seems to be negatively correlated with the size of the economy. In 2007 just before the crisis, the country with the highest VS value was Malaysia, followed by Singapore and the Philippines, while the lowest three were the USA, Japan and Indonesia. This is easily explained by the fact that small economies cannot rely on their own domestic markets and therefore become highly foreign-oriented, both for the sale of products and for the procurement of parts and materials, resulting in large values of VS indices.

Another finding is that values fluctuate more for small economies. This is again attributed to the foreign-orientation of these countries, making their economic trends more volatile and instantaneous in response to the change in the external environment.

In contrast, the VS indices of large economies show quite steady movements, yet among them, China exhibits an interesting shift in the VS structure. Until recently, the value of VS_i had always remained below that of VS_f. The share, however, reversed in 2007, where the VS_i value rose to more than double the VS_f value. This implies that China now engages more in the upstream segments of the vertical production process, such as the production of manufacturing parts and components, which may require more sophisticated production technology and logistics skills, as discussed in the previous section. China is considered to have 'stepped up' the technological ladder, shifting its position away from a mere assembler in the cross-national production networks.

This important finding is further investigated from a geographical perspective. Figure 4.4 shows the geographical decomposition of China's VS index in 2000 and 2008. Each bar indicates the degree of China's engagement in a particular segment of cross-national production chains, bridging

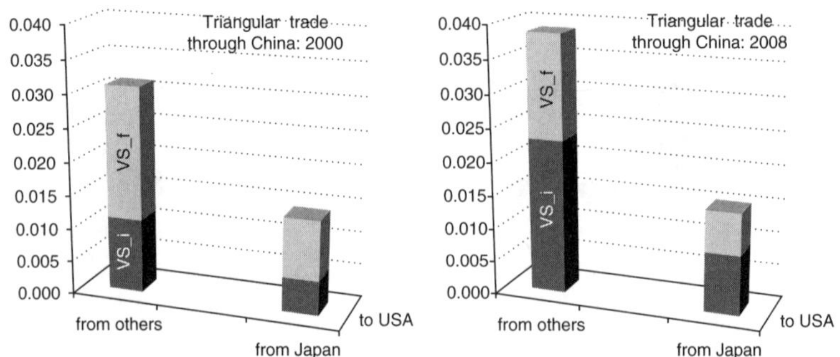

Note: 'Others' include all AIO countries except China, Japan and the USA.

Source: The Asian International Input–Output Tables.

Figure 4.5 Triangular trade through China

the input (import) of products from a country in a column and the output (export) of products to a country in a row.

Here, the side bars in the middle row stand out considerably and are of particular importance to our current study. They are the VS values of China's exports to the USA using intermediate parts and materials imported from Asian countries, which, of course, refer to the 'triangular trade through China', the fundamental motif of our research. It is shown that the structure developed steadily from 2000 to 2008, particularly with respect to the import contents of intermediate goods from other (non-Japan) Asian countries, which increased by 25 per cent, compared to the 8 per cent increase for the import contents of Japanese products. The prevalence of 'triangular trade through China' is thus verified from the viewpoint of vertical specialization as well.

So, are we just paraphrasing what has been already confirmed in the previous chapters of the book? . . . In fact, there is more to say.

Figure 4.5 picks up the bars for 'triangular trade' from Figure 4.4, but stratifies each bar between VS_i and VS_f. It is immediately clear that, from 2000 to 2008, the shares of VS_i increased remarkably, especially in terms of imports from other Asian countries. This is a striking observation. The 'triangular trade through China', which presumed China's role to be a mere assembler of final products, has undergone qualitative change in recent years in response to the promotion of China's technological profile. Although the 'triangular trade through China' remains prevalent in the Asia-Pacific region, its contents are no longer the same as we saw a decade ago.

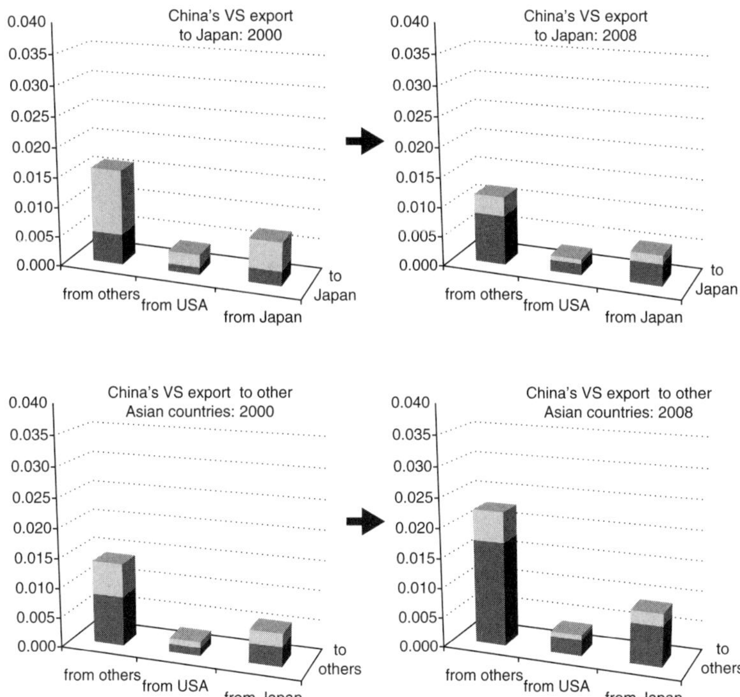

Note: 'Others' include all AIO countries except China, Japan and the USA.

Source: The Asian International Input–Output Tables.

Figure 4.6 Development of VS_i of China's exports

The shift in the role of China within vertical production networks is further confirmed by Figure 4.6. The diagrams pick up the rest of the rows from Figure 4.4: that for China's exports to Japan and the other for exports to the rest of Asia. Again, the increase in the share of VS_i is apparent in every bar. Also, particularly outstanding is the development of the production chain (Other Asia → China → Other Asia). China imports parts and materials from other Asian countries, and produces intermediate goods to be exported back to them for further processing. Indeed, we can observe a mirror image of this structural change from the viewpoint of other Asian countries. Figure 4.7 shows the VS index from the latter's perspective. From 2000 to 2008, a dramatic increase is apparent (8.6 times larger) in the VS value for the production chain (China → Other Asia → China), while other chains destined for the USA or Japan show significant

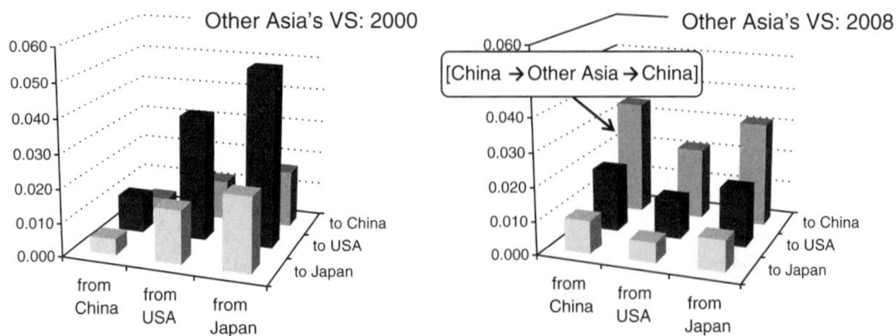

Note: 'Others' include all AIO countries except China, Japan and the USA.

Source: The Asian International Input–Output Tables.

Figure 4.7 Geographical decomposition of other Asian countries' VS index

declines. Together with the observation in Figure 4.6, this implies that the extensive and sophisticated production networks began to grow between China and other (non-Japan) Asian countries, whereby a product crosses national borders many times for a recursive value-adding process.

So, if China is to become the biggest customer for the final consumption goods of the region, after the relative decline of purchasing power of the United States, it is possible to envisage the formation of a highly self-sufficient market among these emerging Asian economies. There is no doubt that trade through China 'the Assembler' was the main leverage of regional trade growth for decades. However, the recent economic crisis had a significant impact on the production system of the Asia-Pacific region, and may continue to shake the foundations of its 'triangular trade' structure.

4. CONCLUSIONS

The last few decades have been marked by the rapid development of cross-national production networks in the Asia-Pacific region. Each country's production system is fragmented and transcends borders, amid continuous and extensive re-networking of production processes within the region in search of the efficient international division of labour.

The vertical specialization (VS) index measures the degree of a country's engagement in the cross-national production networks. The calculation results showed that the upstream production process of intermediate goods (as measured by the VS_i index) was relatively 'resistant' to the impact of the crisis, compared to the assembling process at the end of the production chains (as measured by the VS_f index), which was directly and immediately affected by the contraction of final demand.

The VS indices also revealed that the 'triangular trade through China' underwent qualitative change in recent years, as China promoted its position within the regional production networks from a mere assembler of final goods to a producer of parts and components. Also, extensive production chains of intermediate goods between China and other emerging economies are growing rapidly, which, in the near future, might result in breakdown of current 'triangular structure' and formation of a new production system in the Asia-Pacific region. Here, the geographical configuration of the production/trade of intermediate goods constitutes the core structure of the upcoming new system, since it determines the length of vertical production chains and the complexity of supply–demand networks. This subject is further investigated in the next chapter.

NOTES

1. There are other empirical approaches that calculate the degree of a country's participation in production networks, such as that using trade statistics (Ng and Yeats, 1999 and 2003), or using firm-level data (Feenstra and Hanson, 2004). Here, we choose the method based on I–O analysis since it is able to deal with the multiplier effect of production, an important aspect of vertical production networks.
2. The production network of hard disk drives (HDD) is a good example. A clear division of labour is observed among countries, with capital-intensive countries, such as Japan and Taiwan, producing parts and components, and labour-intensive countries, such as China, assembling components. Even within the production process of HDD parts, a sophisticated allocation of production engagement is prevalent in accordance with the country's technological level. See Hiratsuka (2006) for details.
3. Ng and Yeats (1999) provide the indices for a similar analytical purpose. Their indices, however, are based on the product categorization of trade statistics, which may be criticized for its arbitrariness and ad hoc formulation.
4. The VS indices shown in this section are for manufacturing sectors only.
5. The value of 2007 is an estimate using 2007 trade statistics but based on the structure of the 2000 AIO table.
6. Baldwin (2009) draws a different picture from the trade finance perspective. The shortage of trade finance at the time of the crisis will have a significant impact on the vertical specialization trade. Final goods producers cannot pay for the purchase of intermediate goods before selling their products. This is also the case for all the middle-stage producers, but, in the absence of short-term credit, the firms in the upper-end of production streams will be in the biggest trouble, since they receive their returns latest of all (Pitigala, 2009).

REFERENCES

Baldwin, R. (2006), 'Managing the noodle bowl: the fragility of East Asian regionalism', *CEPR Discussion Papers*, No. 5561.

Baldwin, R. (2009), 'Progress report: Vox's global crisis debate', available at www.voxeu.com.

Feenstra, R.C. (1998), 'Integration of trade and disintegration of production in the global economy', *Journal of Economic Perspectives*, **12**, 31–50.

Feenstra, R.C. and G.H. Hanson (2004), 'Ownership and control in outsourcing to China: estimating the property-rights theory of the firm', *NBER Working Papers*, No. 10198, National Bureau of Economic Research.

Hanson, G., R. Mataloni Jr. and M. Slaughter (2005), 'Vertical production networks in multinational firms', *Review of Economics and Statistics*, **87**(4), 664–78.

Hiratsuka, D. (2006), 'Catching up of manufacturing cum de facto economic integration in East Asia', in D. Hiratsuka (ed.), *East Asia's De Facto Economic Integration*, London: Palgrave Macmillan.

Hummels, D., J. Ishii and K. Yi (2001), 'The nature and growth of vertical specialization in world trade', *Journal of International Economics*, **54**, 75–96.

Krugman, P. (1995), 'Growing world trade: causes and consequences', *Brookings Paper on Economic Activity*, 1, 327–77.

Ng, F. and A.J. Yeats (1999), 'Production sharing in East Asia: who does what for whom, and why?', *Policy Research Working Paper*, No. 2197, World Bank.

Ng, F. and A.J. Yeats (2003), 'Major trade trends in East Asia: what are their implications for regional cooperation and growth?', *World Bank Policy Research Working Paper* No. 3084, World Bank.

Pitigala, N. (2009), 'Global economic crisis and vertical specialization in developing countries', *Prem Notes*, No. 133, World Bank.

APPENDIX 4A.1: VS INDICES BY INDUSTRIAL SECTOR AND BY COUNTRY: 2000 AND 2008

Table 4A.1 shows that 'Computers and electronic equipment' products have attained peak VS value in 2000, when cross-national production networks developed extensively in the Asia-Pacific region. The result is consistent with our intuition that products like 'Computers and electronics equipment' are most prone to outsourcing, since their production process is technically separable and the parts and components contain a relatively high degree of value-added at a manageable size and weight.

The table also shows that the index of 'Computers and electronic equipment' declined significantly after the crisis (except for China), reflecting industry's vulnerability to external shocks. This is, however, compensated for by increases in other industries' indices, such as 'Other electrical equipment' and 'Metal and metal products'. Consequently, the overall decrease of VS values was moderated to some extent.

Table 4A.1 VS indices by industrial sector and by country: 2000 and 2008

2000	CHINA	INDONESIA	JAPAN	KOREA	MALAYSIA	TAIWAN	PHILIPPINES	SINGAPORE	THAILAND	USA
Food, beverage and tobacco	0.0005	0.0006	0.0006	0.0018	0.0012	0.0010	0.0005	0.0018	0.0023	0.0002
Textile, leather, and the products thereof	0.0113	0.0042	0.0007	0.0064	0.0034	0.0038	0.0147	0.0032	0.0061	0.0006
Wooden furniture and other wooden products	0.0006	0.0002	0.0004	0.0004	0.0005	0.0009	0.0009	0.0003	0.0010	0.0001
Pulp, paper and printing	0.0025	0.0023	0.0005	0.0021	0.0029	0.0021	0.0019	0.0017	0.0022	0.0002
Chemical products	0.0174	0.0178	0.0034	0.0225	0.0183	0.0396	0.0140	0.0148	0.0217	0.0015
Petroleum and petro products	0.0027	0.0025	0.0020	0.0063	0.0112	0.0051	0.0085	0.0148	0.0022	0.0001
Rubber products	0.0005	0.0003	0.0006	0.0008	0.0012	0.0008	0.0015	0.0019	0.0005	0.0004
Non-metallic mineral products	0.0011	0.0001	0.0005	0.0018	0.0005	0.0037	0.0006	0.0022	0.0014	0.0003
Metals and metal products	0.0094	0.0052	0.0043	0.0147	0.0233	0.0211	0.0134	0.0162	0.0228	0.0025
Industrial machinery	0.0044	0.0144	0.0021	0.0064	0.0098	0.0135	0.0020	0.0312	0.0050	0.0020

Computers and electronic equipment	0.0264	0.0009	0.0192	0.0865	0.2259	0.1193	0.1869	0.1871	0.0995	0.0265
Other electrical equipment	0.0064	0.0032	0.0036	0.0132	0.0214	0.0179	0.0238	0.0295	0.0554	0.0034
Transport equipment	0.0008	0.0026	0.0028	0.0018	0.0025	0.0039	0.0017	0.0006	0.0053	0.0022
Other manufacturing products	0.0028	0.0004	0.0010	0.0029	0.0079	0.0034	0.0072	0.0090	0.0094	0.0008

2008	CHINA	INDONESIA	JAPAN	KOREA	MALAYSIA	TAIWAN	PHILIPPINES	SINGAPORE	THAILAND	USA
Food, beverage and tobacco	0.0001	0.0004	0.0003	0.0004	0.0030	0.0003	0.0013	0.0018	0.0012	0.0001
Textile, leather, and the products thereof	0.0019	0.0023	0.0020	0.0021	0.0011	0.0017	0.0015	0.0028	0.0012	0.0011
Wooden furniture and other wooden products	0.0001	0.0002	0.0004	0.0003	0.0009	0.0006	0.0003	0.0005	0.0009	0.0003
Pulp, paper and printing	0.0010	0.0011	0.0007	0.0012	0.0024	0.0025	0.0014	0.0017	0.0016	0.0003
Chemical products	0.0132	0.0112	0.0062	0.0203	0.0198	0.0363	0.0102	0.0190	0.0133	0.0024
Petroleum and petro products	0.0038	0.0072	0.0015	0.0021	0.0113	0.0051	0.0157	0.0626	0.0015	0.0002

Table 4A.1 (continued)

2008	CHINA	INDONESIA	JAPAN	KOREA	MALAYSIA	TAIWAN	PHILIPPINES	SINGAPORE	THAILAND	USA
Rubber products	0.0004	0.0005	0.0007	0.0004	0.0007	0.0006	0.0005	0.0010	0.0021	0.0006
Non-metallic mineral products	0.0005	0.0001	0.0009	0.0032	0.0010	0.0043	0.0006	0.0016	0.0004	0.0004
Metals and metal products	0.0127	0.0078	0.0115	0.0398	0.0291	0.0380	0.0156	0.0207	0.0264	0.0051
Industrial machinery	0.0025	0.0100	0.0059	0.0050	0.0125	0.0070	0.0062	0.0238	0.0190	0.0032
Computers and electronic equipment	0.0563	0.0032	0.0168	0.0531	0.1400	0.0942	0.0990	0.1005	0.0807	0.0170
Other electrical equipment	0.0090	0.0040	0.0066	0.0144	0.0232	0.0144	0.0081	0.0510	0.0586	0.0053
Transport equipment	0.0006	0.0031	0.0030	0.0016	0.0026	0.0013	0.0028	0.0095	0.0044	0.0014
Other manufacturing products	0.0022	0.0005	0.0033	0.0043	0.0026	0.0060	0.0021	0.0066	0.0018	0.0024

Source: The Asian International Input–Output Tables.

5. The impact of the financial crisis on Factory Asia

Kazunobu Hayakawa

1. INTRODUCTION

Due to the recent financial crisis, consumer demand has plummeted remarkably all over the world. Such a decrease gradually led to a stop in the running of 'Factory Asia'.[1] One of the key sources of recent Asian economic development was the expansion of exports in both consumption and intermediate products. Asia formed sophisticated international production networks in a period of dramatic activity, including the so-called 'Asian Miracle' period (the former half of the 1990s) and serious currency crisis in 1997–1998 (Kimura, 2006). It churned out millions of different consumption products with world-beating price–quality ratios by sourcing billions of different parts and components from plants spread across a dozen nations in Asia. Due to the recent decrease in global consumer demand, however, such products now seem to have nowhere to go.

The impacts of the changes in demand on Factory Asia have been explored by employing the well-known gravity equation. By applying gravity equations to bilateral trade data at the industrial level, some researchers have found more active trade in parts and components in country-pairs with one of the countries having a large GDP, either as an importer or an exporter (see, for example, Athukorala and Yamashita, 2006; Kimura et al., 2007). Also, Hayakawa (2007) examines what contributed to the trade growth of intermediate machinery goods in Asia in the 1990s. His empirical results suggest that the reduction in border barriers and the increase in production of intermediate goods are important factors for the rapid growth of trade in machinery parts in Asia. In short, the previous studies clarify the importance of economic conditions for importers and exporters.

Against this backdrop, the aim of this chapter is to investigate how the decrease in demand and other elements induced by the recent financial crisis affect the operation of Factory Asia. By employing the Asian International Input–Output Table (AIO table), compiled by the Institute of Developing Economies, we explore the impacts of such elements on intra-regional trade in intermediate goods, bearing in mind the input–output linkages between finished and intermediate goods. Specifically, unlike the above-mentioned previous studies, our empirical model incorporates not only the importer's demand but also that of the third country other than the importer and exporter. For example, it includes the US demand, despite the analyses of intra-Asian bilateral trade. Such inclusion of countries that are not related directly to those trading would be realistic, particularly in the context of intermediate goods trade in Asia, as discussed in the previous chapters of the book in relation to the 'triangular trade' structure. Consequently, our empirical analysis enables us to clarify more closely the driving forces of the intra-regional trade in intermediate goods in Asia.

The rest of the chapter is organized as follows. Section 2 takes an overview of Factory Asia by using several indicators. In section 3, we specify our empirical equation describing international transactions of intermediate goods, the regression results of which are reported in section 4, before section 5 concludes.

2. OVERVIEW OF FACTORY ASIA

This section takes an overview of Factory Asia by using several indicators. First of all, we examine the regional trade in and production of intermediate goods in Asia. Table 5.1 reports the average exports from one Asian country to another in an industrial sector[2] (as for more details of our variable construction, see Appendix 5A.1). The data are drawn from the AIO table. The AIO table includes nine Asian countries; China, Indonesia, Japan, Korea, Malaysia, the Philippines, Singapore, Taiwan and Thailand. The upper area shows their levels in four years (1990, 1995, 2000 and 2008), and the lower area their growth in each period.

From this table, we see immediately that the levels of the average bilateral intermediate goods exports experienced a steady increase during the period 1990–2008. However, when viewing their growth, we can find slower growth in the latter half of the 1990s, possibly due to the influence of the Asian Currency Crisis. Afterwards, although the slowdown in export growth stopped, it has not yet regained the pace of the former half of the 1990s. In summary, exports of regional intermediate goods in each Asian country have experienced a certain increase since 1990, but their growth in the latter half of the 1990s is not outstanding compared with that in the former half, namely the period known as the 'Asian Miracle'.

Second, we examine the production values of intermediate goods in an industrial sector, the country sector average of which is shown in Table 5.1, with the data again from the AIO table. The table shows that the production

Table 5.1 Changes in trade and production: million US$

	Trade	Production	US demand	Asian demand
Level: X				
1990	120	22 210	88 235	65 810
1995	268	36 409	112 558	108 512
2000	383	38 433	162 476	101 077
2008	1 012	67 447	224 054	187 262
Growth: $(\log X_T - \log X_t)/(T - t)$				
1990–1995	0.222	0.132	0.014	0.099
1995–2000	0.073	−0.008	0.065	−0.027
2000–2008	0.110	0.100	0.039	0.098

Notes: 'Trade' indicates the average exports from one Asian country to another in an industrial sector, while 'Production' refers to the average total production values of intermediate goods in an industrial sector in an Asian country. 'US demand' and 'Asian demand' are the average expenditures in the USA for the industrial sector and the average of the sum of nine Asian countries' expenditures for the same, respectively.

Source: The Asian International Input–Output Tables.

values follow the same pattern of changes as the exports, and although production has expanded since 1990, the growth in the first half of the 1990s is the swiftest during the entire 1990–2008 period. Particularly during the period 1995–2000, the average growth of their production values became negative. In sum, we can say that the expansion of Factory Asia decelerated significantly in the latter half of the 1990s and that its operation was on a slow road to recovery from its performance in the first half of the 1990s.

Third, as potential key elements for their exports and production, some demand side indicators are investigated. In Table 5.1, the average US expenditures per industrial sector and the average of the sum of nine Asian countries' expenditures for the same are reported, the data of which come from the AIO table. It is well recognized that US as well as intra-Asian demand is crucially important for the Asian economy. The table reports that intra-Asian demand has the same pattern of changes as exports and production, with the swiftest growth observed in the former half of the 1990s. Conversely, the change in US demand differs interestingly from other indicators, with peak growth experienced in the latter half of the 1990s, followed by a slight slowdown. The latter reflects the negative shocks, due not only to the collapse of the information and technology bubble in the early 2000s but also to the recent financial crisis.

Last, we explore an indicator more directly related to the financial environment. Figure 5.1 describes the changes of country credibility of selected

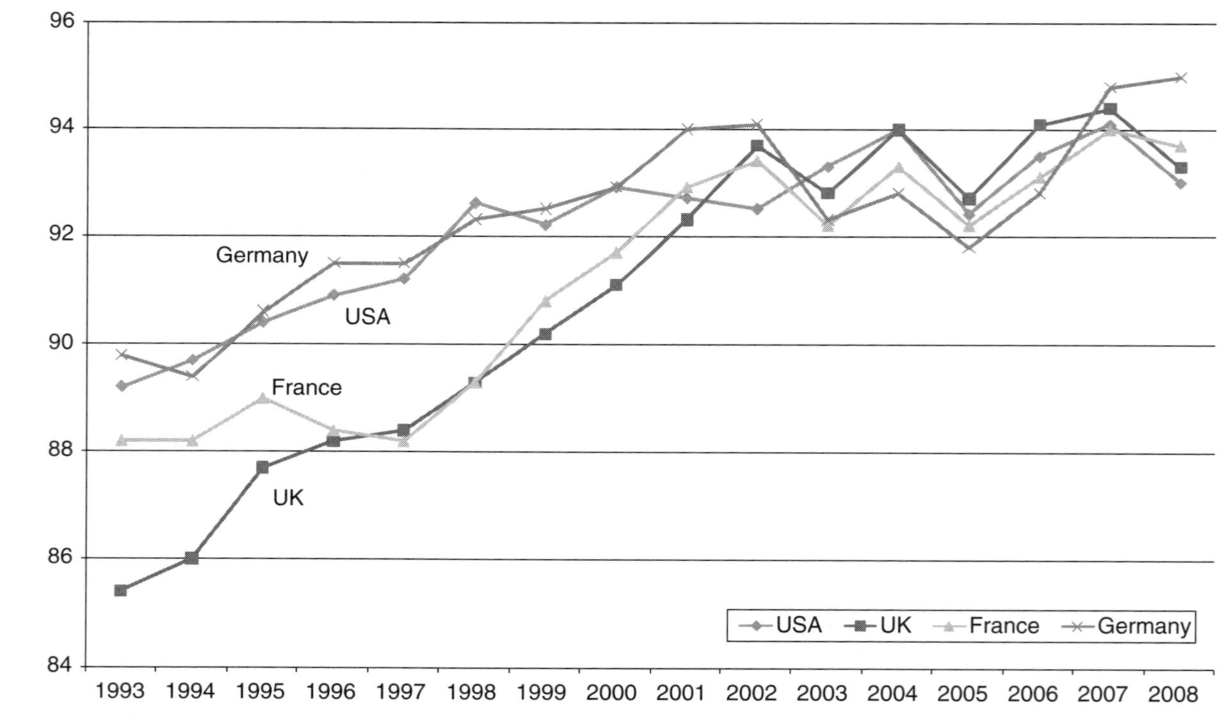

Source: *Institutional Investor*.

Figure 5.1 Trend of country credibility (%): developed countries

developed countries, the data of which are drawn from *Institutional Investor* (various issues). This index is constructed from the aggregate of bankers' evaluations on the risk of default, with higher index values indicating that the country has a smaller risk. These country credibility measurements correlate well with the changes in the international financial market. Here, we can find that their credibility index dropped from 2007 to 2008, except for Germany. On the other hand, from Figure 5.2, we can see a remarkable decline of this index in Asian developing countries in the latter half of the 1990s. Obviously, such decline reflects the influence of the Asian Currency Crisis in 1997–1998. Interestingly, however, unlike the Asian Currency Crisis, the recent financial crisis has not restricted the country credibility index in Asia. This might be attributed to the regional financial cooperation that developed in Asia in the 1990s after the Asian Currency Crisis.

3. EMPIRICAL METHODOLOGY

This section specifies the equation used to explore how the intra-Asian trade in intermediate goods can be determined. Our dataset has four dimensions: importer (s), exporter (r), industrial sector (i), and year (t). As in the dataset in section 2, it includes nine Asian countries as importers/exporters, nine industrial sectors, and four years (1990, 1995, 2000 and 2008). Our empirical equation is given by:

$$\begin{aligned}\ln Z^i_{rs} = {} & \beta_1 \ln (y^i_{US}/D_{s,US}) + \beta_2 \ln \textstyle\sum_{c \in A} (y^i_c/D_{sc}) + \beta_3 \ln D_{rs} + \beta_4 \ln Z^i_r \\ & + \beta_5 \ln w_r + \beta_6 \ln w_s + \beta_7 \ln G^i_s + \beta_8 \ln \mathit{Credibility}_r \\ & + \beta_9 \ln \mathit{Credibility}_s + u^i + u^t + u^i_{rs}.\end{aligned}$$

u^{it}_{rs} is an error term (for how this equation was obtained, see Appendix 5A.2). The dependent variable is a log of country r's total exports to country s in the intermediate products of industrial sector i. A time subscript is omitted for brevity and we have three kinds of independent variables: importer-specific, exporter-specific, and importer-exporter-specific.

3.1 Importer-specific Variables

The importer-specific variables are as follows: importer's wages (w_s), credibility ($\mathit{Credibility}_s$), access to finished goods markets, and sectoral price index (G^i_s).

First, lower wages in a country enable finished goods to be produced more cheaply and thus supplied in greater amounts all over the world.

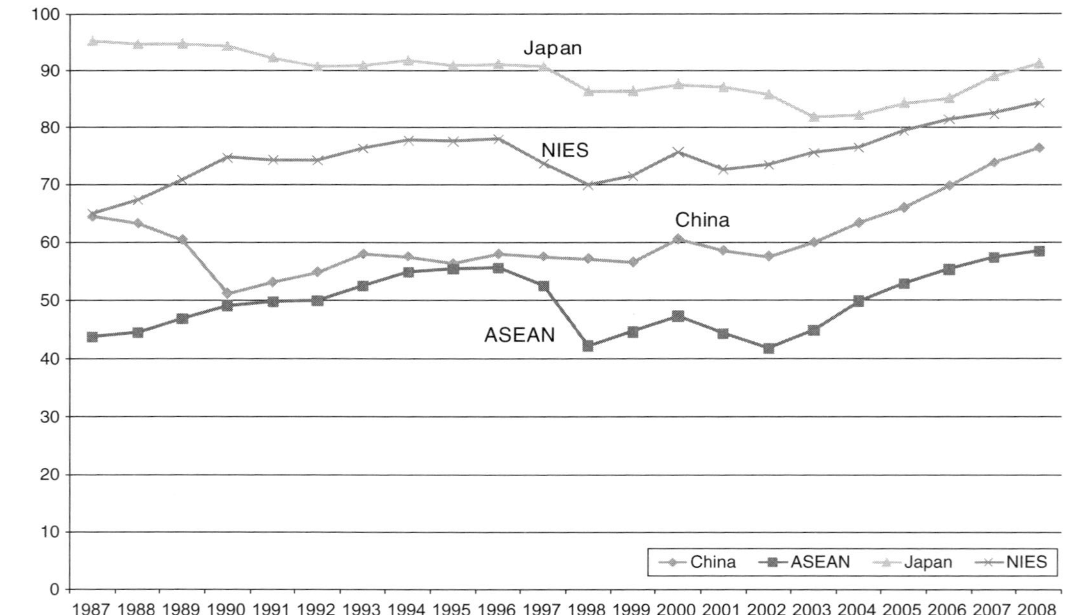

Notes: ASEAN indicates the average values among Thailand, Malaysia and Indonesia. NIES indicates those among Korea, Taiwan and Singapore.

Source: *Institutional Investor*.

Figure 5.2 Trend of country credibility (%): Asia

Consequently, in order to produce this larger volume of finished goods, countries with lower wages will import more intermediate goods. We use GDP per capita as their proxy, the data of which are from the International Financial Statistics (IFS) compiled by the International Monetary Fund. Since the data of some countries for 2008 are not yet available in the IFS, we also use the Asian Economic Statistics Database compiled by the Institute of Developing Economies.[3]

Second, a stable financial market is important, for example, in order to reduce exchange rate risks, meaning countries with stable financial markets import more intermediate goods as well as exporting more finished goods. To examine this, we introduce the importer's country credibility index as a proxy for the extent of stability in its financial markets. The data are drawn from the *Institutional Investor*, as in section 2.

Third, access to finished goods markets is key for the exports of finished goods, and thus for the imports of intermediate goods to produce such finished goods. In order to examine the role of market access in determining the import of intermediate goods, we introduce two distance-adjusted demand variables: the access to the US market (labelled US demand) and the access to Asian markets (Asian demand) respectively. The importer's access to the US market is captured by the US total expenditures on finished goods of an industrial sector, which are further adjusted by the geographical distance between the importer and the USA. Specifically, importer s's access to the US market in industrial sector i is $(y^i_{US}/D_{s,US})$, where y^i_{US} and $D_{s,US}$ are the US total expenditures on finished goods of industrial sector i and the geographical distance between country s and the USA, respectively. Similarly, its access to Asian markets is represented by the sum of each Asian country's expenditures adjusted by distance with the importer. Specifically, it is $\Sigma_{c \in A}(y^i_c/D_{sc})$, where A is a set of nine Asian countries. y^i_c and D_{sc} are country c's total expenditures on finished goods of industrial sector i and the geographical distance between countries s and c, respectively. Data of expenditure by country and by industrial sector are obtained from the AIO table. The CEPII website provides us with the data of geographical distance between countries.

Last, in order to control the effects of price index fluctuation in each industrial sector, we introduce a sector-specific price index. Our price index data are compiled by the Institute of Developing Economies and can be obtained from its website.[4] The import and export unit value indices are available by importer, exporter, industrial sector, and year and are formulated by a chain-linked index formula using each product's unit price data drawn from the UN Comtrade database. In order to incorporate as wide a range of products as possible, we use the square of (import unit-value index * export unit-value index), which is the Laspeyres index.[5]

3.2 Exporter-specific Variables

The exporter-specific variables are exporter's wages (w_r), credibility (*Credibility*$_r$), and the total production of intermediate goods (Z^i_r). First, as in the above case, GDP per capita is used as a proxy for wages. This time, however, GDP per capita is also considered in order to capture the workers' skill levels. In general, it is known that the production of intermediate goods requires workers to have higher skills than the production of finished goods. Consequently, the large GDP per capita may lead to the indication of their high skills, resulting in the significant exports of intermediate goods. Second, since a stable financial market, that is higher country credibility, also encourages the exports of intermediate goods, we introduce exporter's country credibility, the data of which are again from the *Institutional Investor*. Third, we explore the impacts of the increase in the number of intermediate goods firms. By assuming output per firm to remain largely similar among firms, the total production values of intermediate goods are used as a proxy for their number. Data of the total production by country and by industrial sector are obtained from the AIO table.

3.3 Importer–exporter-specific Variables and Other Variables

Other independent variables are as follows. The importer-exporter-specific variable is the geographical distance between trading partners (D_{rs}), the data of which come from the CEPII website. In order to control sectoral fixed effects and year fixed effects, we introduce the industrial sector dummy u^i and time dummy u^t.

To estimate this equation, we employ the ordinary least squares (OLS) method. However, it is worth pointing out one possible econometric issue. There could be a simultaneity problem between bilateral trade values (Z^i_{rs}) and total production value (Z^i_r). If we conduct an OLS estimation for our equation, a correlation between the production value and the error term could emerge. To address this problem, we move ln Z^i_r to the left-hand side; namely, the dependent variable is replaced with ln (Z^i_{rs}/Z^i_r).

4. EMPIRICAL RESULTS

This section reports our regression results. Column (I) in Table 5.2 shows the result of our baseline regression, the dependent variable of which is just ln Z^i_{rs}, not ln(Z^i_{rs}/Z^i_r). There are five points to be noted. First, coefficients for

Table 5.2 Regression results

Dependent	(I) Trade	(II) Ratio	(III) Trade	(IV) Ratio
US demand	1.216***	1.312***	1.219***	1.315***
	[0.169]	[0.189]	[0.169]	[0.189]
Asian demand	0.142**	0.162**	0.139**	0.160**
	[0.068]	[0.076]	[0.068]	[0.077]
Distance	−0.305***	−0.517***	−0.251**	−0.490***
	[0.045]	[0.053]	[0.102]	[0.121]
*1995			−0.004	0.034
			[0.132]	[0.155]
*2000			−0.074	−0.071
			[0.135]	[0.162]
*2008			−0.137	−0.070
			[0.130]	[0.157]
Production	0.444***		0.444***	
	[0.019]		[0.019]	
Ex wages	0.090**	0.202***	0.092**	0.204***
	[0.042]	[0.047]	[0.042]	[0.047]
Im wages	−0.093*	−0.102*	−0.090*	−0.100*
	[0.050]	[0.055]	[0.050]	[0.055]
Ex credibility	0.889***	−0.704***	0.880***	−0.712***
	[0.239]	[0.237]	[0.238]	[0.237]
Im credibility	2.154***	2.143***	2.147***	2.136***
	[0.221]	[0.245]	[0.221]	[0.246]
Price index	0.044	−0.074	0.036	−0.079
	[0.154]	[0.174]	[0.154]	[0.174]
Year dummy	YES	YES	YES	YES
Sector dummy	YES	YES	YES	YES
Obs.	2566	2566	2566	2566
R-sq	0.6048	0.3047	0.6050	0.3050

Notes:
***, ** and * show 1%, 5% and 10% significance, respectively.
Heteroscedasticity-consistent standard errors (White) are in brackets.
The dependent variables in the 'Trade' and 'Ratio' columns are $\ln Z^i_{rs}$ and $\ln(Z^i_{rs}/Z^i_r)$, respectively.

the US demand and Asian demand are estimated to be significantly positive. Interestingly, the coefficient for US demand is much larger than that for Asian demand. In this sense, we can say that the intra-Asian trade in intermediate goods is more sensitive to the final demand in the USA than to that in Asia itself. Second, importer's and exporter's country credibility shows expected signs. This result indicates that trading partners' financial market stability serves as a significant driving force for the regional trade in intermediate goods. Third, a production coefficient is estimated to be significantly positive, implying that the firms' active entry into the intermediate goods sector enhances their exports remarkably. Fourth, as usual, the coefficient for distance is inversely significant. Fifth, exporter's wages have a positive sign, while importer's wages show a negative sign. As mentioned in the previous section, this contrasting result between exporter and importer may indicate that both the quality and cost of labour are important factors for determining the level of production of intermediate and finished goods.

Table 5.2 reports three more results. Column (II) shows the result of the equation with ln (Z^i_{rs}/Z^i_r) as a dependent variable in order to address the previously mentioned problem of simultaneity. The results are qualitatively unchanged from those in column (I). In columns (III) and (IV), we introduce the interaction terms of geographical distance with the time dummy, to examine changes in the importance of geographical distance during our sample period. Consequently, we cannot detect any significant changes in its importance. In both columns, the results in other variables are qualitatively unchanged from before.[6]

Last, we decompose the growth of the intra-Asian intermediate goods trade by using the result in column (I) in Table 5.2. Specifically, taking the difference in our equation between times T and t, we obtain:

$$\frac{(\ln Z^i_{rs,T} - \ln Z^i_{rs,t})}{T-t} = \beta_1\left[\frac{\ln (y^i_{US,T}/D_{s,US}) - \ln (y^i_{US,t}/D_{s,US})}{T-t}\right]$$

$$+ \beta_2\left[\frac{\ln \sum_{c\in A}(y^i_{c,T}/D_{sc}) - \ln \sum_{c\in A}(y^i_{c,t}/D_{sc})}{T-t}\right] + \beta_4\left[\frac{\ln Z^i_{r,T} - \ln Z^i_{r,t}}{T-t}\right]$$

$$+ \beta_5\left[\frac{\ln w_{r,T} - \ln w_{r,t}}{T-t}\right] + \beta_6\left[\frac{\ln w_{s,T} - \ln w_{s,t}}{T-t}\right] + \beta_7\left[\frac{\ln G^i_{s,T} - \ln G^i_{s,t}}{T-t}\right]$$

$$+ \beta_8\left[\frac{\ln Credibility_{r,T} - \ln Credibility_{r,t}}{T-t}\right]$$

$$+ \beta_9\left[\frac{\ln Credibility_{s,T} - \ln Credibility_{s,t}}{T-t}\right] + \frac{u^T - u^t}{T-t} + \frac{u^{cT}_{rs} - u^{ct}_{rs}}{T-t}.$$

By substituting the estimated coefficients into a vector of β and the respective average values into variables, we simulate the average growth of intra-Asian trade in intermediate goods, for each period (1990–1995, 1995–2000, and 2000–2008). In Figure 5.3, the contribution of each independent variable is depicted by a stacked bar graph, and the transition of the average growth, the values of which are the same as those reported in Table 5.1, is by a line graph. 'Macro' indicates the contribution of changes in time dummy coefficients.

From Figure 5.3, we can find the following. During the 'Asian Miracle' period (1990–1995), the high growth of regional trade in intermediate goods was induced by their production expansion due to, for example, the development of global production networks. Subsequently, Asian trade in intermediate goods plummeted dramatically when the Asian Financial Crisis occurred (1995–2000). In the latter period, no elements within Asia functioned as the driving force. Instead, Asian trade was propped up by robust consumption in the USA. However, due to the serious financial crisis, US consumption has shrunk in the recent period (2000–2008) and it is Asia itself that has compensated for the impact of such contraction in US consumption. As in the period of the 'Asian Miracle', the expansion of production and consumption and the stability of the financial market in Asia have supported the intra-Asian trade in intermediate goods.

5. CONCLUSIONS

By employing the AIO table this chapter investigated how the decrease in demand and other impacts induced by the recent crisis affected the operation of Factory Asia. Our main finding is as follows. The recent financial crisis reduced the US final demand and thus slowed down the growth of intra-Asian trade in intermediate goods. However, the steady movement of production and consumption in Asian countries, backed up by their stable financial markets, has propped up its development. This finding implies that Factory Asia has begun to work and grow, at a certain level, without relying on other regional economies.

Thus, the expansion of intra-Asian demand and the facilitation of financial cooperation will further strengthen the regional production network and improve its resistance against shocks from the rest of the globe. Here, no one denies the crucial role of China in the formation of post-crisis Factory Asia. The next chapter will focus on this Asian giant, and complete our study by examining its influence on the neighbouring Asian countries in order to envisage the future of the region.

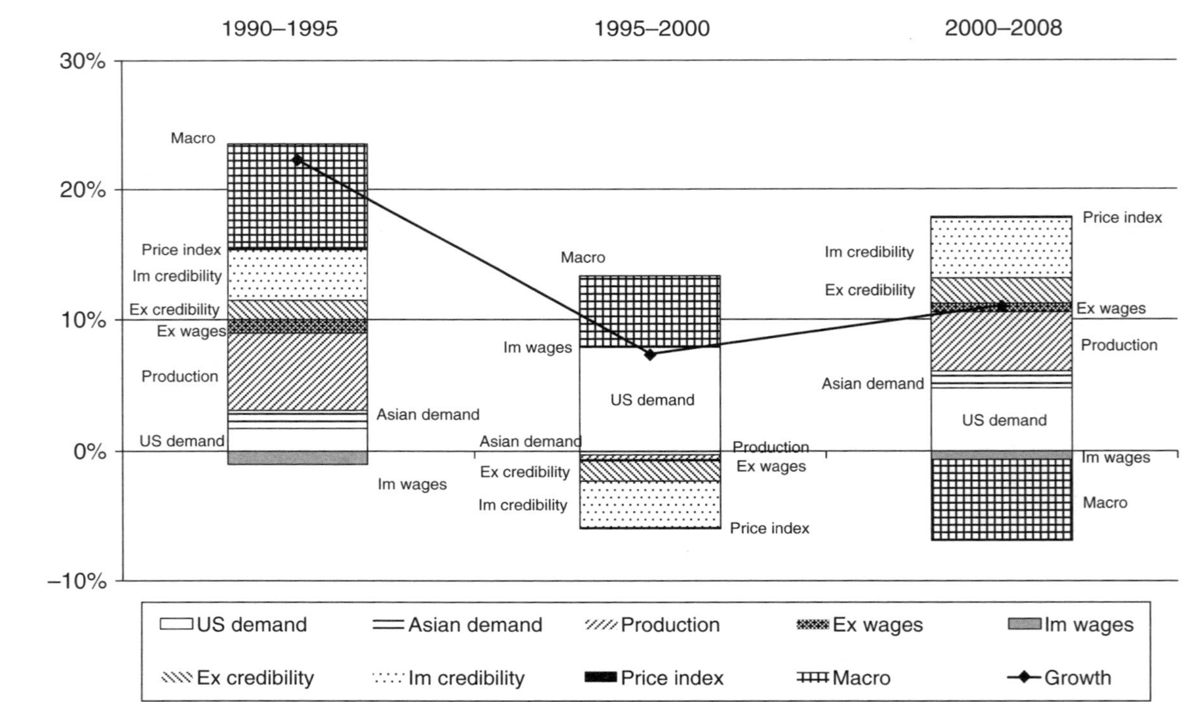

Source: Author's estimation based on the regression results in Table 5.2.

Figure 5.3 Decomposition of the growth of intra-Asia intermediate goods trade

NOTES

1. Baldwin (2006) states that 'Asian corporations set up Factory Asia'.
2. Our dataset includes nine industrial sectors (Timber and wooden products; Pulp, paper and printing; Chemical products; Petroleum and petro products; Rubber products; Non-metallic mineral products; Metal products; Machinery; Transport equipment).
3. http://www.ide.go.jp/Japanese/Publish/Periodicals/W_trend/tokei.html.
4. http://www.ide.go.jp/English/Data/Trade/index.html.
5. Since the price index data are unavailable in 2008, those in 2006 are used instead.
6. The negative results in Ex credibility would be due to its high correlation with Ex wages.

REFERENCES

Athukorala, P.C. and N. Yamashita (2006), 'Production fragmentation and trade integration: East Asia in a global context', *The North American Journal of Economics and Finance*, **17** (3), 233–56.

Baldwin, R. (2006), 'Managing the noodle bowl: the fragility of East Asian regionalism', *CEPR Discussion Papers*, No. 5561.

Harris, C. (1954), 'The market as a factor in the localization of industry in the United States', *Annals of the Association of American Geographers*, **64**, 315–48.

Hayakawa, K. (2007), 'Growth of intermediate goods trade in East Asia', *Pacific Economic Review*, **12** (4), 511–23.

Kimura, F. (2006), 'International production and distribution networks in East Asia: eighteen facts, mechanics, and policy implication', *Asian Economic Policy Review*, **1** (2), 326–44.

Kimura, F., Y. Takahashi and K. Hayakawa (2007), 'Fragmentation and parts and components trade: comparison between East Asia and Europe', *North American Journal of Economics and Finance*, **18** (1), 23–40.

APPENDIX 5A.1: VARIABLE CONSTRUCTION

This Appendix provides an explanation on how to construct our variables. Before that, some notations must be defined as follows:

a_{ij}^{rs}: inputs of country s in sector j from country r in sector i
f_i^{rs}: country s's total final demands on goods supplied by country r in sector i
A: a set of nine Asian countries
A^+: a set of nine Asian countries plus the USA
W: a set of all countries in the world
M: a set of nine industrial sectors
N: a set of all industrial sectors

Defining the mean values of X_i over i as $mean_i\{X_i\}$, we can express the mean values reported in Table 5.1 as follows:

$$Trade = \underset{r\in A, r\neq s, s\in A, j\in M}{mean}\left\{\sum\nolimits_{i\in N} a_{ij}^{rs}\right\},$$

$$PRODUCTION = \underset{r\in A, i\in M}{mean}\left\{\sum\nolimits_{s\in W}\sum\nolimits_{j\in N} a_{ij}^{rs}\right\},$$

$$US\ Demand = \underset{i\in M}{mean}\left\{\sum\nolimits_{r\in W} f_i^{r,US}\right\},$$

$$Asian\ Demand = \underset{i\in M}{mean}\left\{\sum\nolimits_{s\in A}\sum\nolimits_{r\in W} f_i^{rs}\right\}.$$

Similarly, variables for the regression equation are expressed as the following:

$$Z_{rs}^i = \sum\nolimits_{j\in N} a_{ij}^{rs},\ Z_r^i = \sum\nolimits_{s\in A^+}\sum\nolimits_{j\in N} a_{ij}^{rs},\ y_j^s = \sum\nolimits_{r\in W} f_j^{rs}.$$

APPENDIX 5A.2: THEORETICAL MODEL

In this Appendix, we formalize the simple theoretical model describing the international transactions of intermediate goods. This modelling aims to specify variables that affect their international transactions.

The representative consumer in each region is assumed to have a two-tier utility function, which becomes the standard in international trade and new economic geography literature. The upper tier is a Cobb–Douglas function of the utility derived from the consumption of downstream goods (finished goods). Specifically, we apply the following utility function of the consumer in region s:

$$U_s = \prod_{h=1}^{H} (C_s^h)^{\alpha_h}, \ \sum_{h=1}^{H} \alpha_h = 1,$$

where C_s^h is the aggregate consumption of a downstream good h in region s.

We formalize expenditure allocation in a downstream good i consisting of multiple varieties differentiated by country (Armington assumption) and omit the subscript representing the name of downstream goods for now. The consumer has the following preference specified as a constant elasticity of substitution (CES) function over the varieties:

$$C_s = \left(\sum_{r=1}^{R} X_{rs}^{\frac{\sigma-1}{\sigma}} \right)^{\frac{\sigma}{\sigma-1}},$$

where R and X_{rs} are the number of countries and the demand of country s for the downstream variety produced in country r, respectively. σ is the elasticity of substitution between downstream varieties and is assumed to be greater than unity. The utility maximization yields:

$$X_{rs} = \alpha \tau_{rs}^{-(\sigma-1)} p_r^{-\sigma} P_s^{\sigma-1} Y_s,$$

where p_r and P_s denote the price of the downstream variety produced in country r and the price index of downstream goods in country s, respectively, while Y_s is total expenditure in country s. Transactions in downstream goods between countries r and s are modelled as facing Samuelsonian iceberg costs, τ_{rs} (≥ 1). Consequently, the total production value of downstream goods in country s, which is denoted by E_s, is given by:

$$\begin{aligned} E_s &\equiv p_s X_s \\ &= p_s \sum_c \alpha \tau_{sc}^{-(\sigma-1)} p_s^{-\sigma} P_c^{\sigma-1} Y_c \\ &= \alpha p_s^{-(\sigma-1)} \sum_c \tau_{sc}^{-(\sigma-1)} P_c^{\sigma-1} Y_c \end{aligned}$$

The market structure in the downstream goods sector is assumed to be perfect competition. The downstream goods producer of each country combines a composite index aggregated across various intermediate inputs (intermediate goods) and primary factors, for example skilled and unskilled labour, using the Cobb–Douglas model. The composite enters the cost function for each producer through a CES aggregator. Specifically, we have the following cost function:

$$C(X_s) = w_s^{1-\mu} G_s^{\mu} X_s,\ G_s = \left[\sum_{r=1}^{R} \int_0^{M_r} t_{rs}^{-(\upsilon-1)} q_r(j)^{-(\upsilon-1)} dj \right]^{\frac{-1}{\upsilon-1}},$$

where w_s denotes the price index for primary factors employed by each producer to produce downstream output x_s, which is called simply wages. G_s is the price index for upstream products, and μ is a linkage parameter between downstream and upstream goods, The upstream products are differentiated by firm, unlike downstream goods, and their market structure is assumed to be monopolistic competition. Transactions in upstream products between countries r and s are modelled as facing Samuelsonian iceberg costs, $t_{rs}(\geq 1)$. M_r, $q_r(j)$, and υ are the number (mass) of upstream varieties produced in country r, the price of the j-th variety produced in country r, and the elasticity of substitution between upstream varieties, respectively. The elasticity is again assumed to be greater than unity.

In this setting, country s's demand for an upstream variety j produced in country r ($z_{rs}(j)$) can be derived as follows. First, applying Shephard's lemma to the above-defined cost function, we obtain:

$$Q_s = \mu w_s^{1-\mu} G_s^{\mu-1} X_s, \text{ where } Q_s = \left(\sum_r \int z_{rs}(j)^{\frac{\upsilon-1}{\upsilon}} dj \right)^{\frac{\upsilon}{\upsilon-1}}.$$

This is a country s's composite index of the consumption of upstream products. Applying the marginal cost-pricing rule to downstream products, we obtain:

$$p_s = w_s^{1-\mu} G_s^{\mu}.$$

Thus, the composite index can be simplified as:

$$Q_s = \mu G_s^{-1} E_s.$$

Second, since each upstream product needs to be chosen so as to minimize the cost of attaining Q_s, the following minimization problem is solved:

$$\min \sum_r \int t_{rs} q_r(j) z_{rs}(j) dj \text{ subject to } \left(\sum_r \int z_{rs}(j)^{\frac{\upsilon-1}{\upsilon}} dj \right)^{\frac{\upsilon}{\upsilon-1}} = Q_s.$$

Consequently, based on the assumption that all varieties produced in a particular country have the same technology and price, it is derived that:

$$z_{rs} = t_{rs}^{-(\upsilon-1)} q_r^{-\upsilon} G_s^{\upsilon-1} Q_s.$$

Last, substituting the simplified composite index into this, we obtain:

$$z_{rs} = \mu t_{rs}^{-(\upsilon-1)} q_r^{-\upsilon} G_s^{\upsilon-2} E_s.$$

Hence, country r's total exports to country s are given by:

$$\begin{aligned} Z_{rs} &\equiv M_r q_r z_{rs} \\ &= \mu M_r t_{rs}^{-(\upsilon-1)} q_r^{-(\upsilon-1)} G_s^{\upsilon-2} E_s \\ &= \mu M_r t_{rs}^{-(\upsilon-1)} q_r^{-(\upsilon-1)} G_s^{\upsilon-2} \left(\alpha p_s^{-(\sigma-1)} \sum_c \tau_{cs}^{-(\sigma-1)} P_c^{\sigma-1} Y_c \right) \\ &= \mu\alpha t_{rs}^{-(\upsilon-1)} (M_r q_r^{-(\upsilon-1)}) \left[G_s^{\upsilon-2} p_s^{-(\sigma-1)} \left(\sum_i \tau_{cs}^{-(\sigma-1)} P_c^{\sigma-1} Y_c \right) \right]. \end{aligned}$$

Taking its log, we can express our gravity-like equation as:

$$\begin{aligned} \ln Z_{rs} = {} & \ln(\mu\alpha) - (\upsilon - 1)\ln t_{rs} + \ln M_r - (\upsilon - 1)\ln q_r - (\sigma - 1)\ln p_s \\ & + (\upsilon - 2)\ln G_s + \ln\left(\sum_c \tau_{cs}^{-(\sigma-1)} P_c^{\sigma-1} Y_c \right). \end{aligned}$$

We will simply assume that upstream producers use only primary factors for the production (a marginal input requirement parameter is set as unity). Furthermore, its technology is assumed to follow the same specification as the component of primary factors in the downstream products. In other words, downstream products' prices are:

$$q_r = [\upsilon/(\upsilon - 1)]w_r.$$

Substituting these into the above gravity-like equation, we will obtain our equation to be estimated in this chapter:

$$\begin{aligned} \ln Z_{rs} = {} & \ln[\mu\alpha\upsilon/(\upsilon - 1)] - (\upsilon - 1)\ln t_{rs} + \ln M_r - (\upsilon - 1)\ln w_r \\ & - (\sigma - 1)(1 - \mu)\ln w_s + \{\upsilon - 2 - (\sigma + 1)\mu\}\ln G_s \\ & + \ln\left(\sum_c \tau_{cs}^{-(\sigma-1)} P_c^{\sigma-1} Y_c \right). \end{aligned}$$

This gravity-like equation tells us that exporter attributes, importer attributes and their joint attributes play a crucial role in determining trade in upstream products. First, upstream production scale and wages are the exporter attributes playing a crucial role in determining trade in upstream products. The more upstream firms there are in a country, or the lower the wages are in the country, the more upstream products the country exports. Second, in addition to the price index for upstream products and the wages, access to each country's final demand for downstream products becomes an important element for the importer. Such market access is a key variable in our model that distinguishes upstream and downstream processes. The better the access to global demand for downstream products produced by the country, the more upstream products the country imports. The usual gravity model lacks this term. Last, the important importer–exporter attribute is trade costs between them, as in the usual gravity model.

To make the equation estimable, we modify this equation as follows. First, as usual, trade costs between importer and exporter are assumed to be a function of the geographical distance between them (D_{rs}). Second, the third term is captured by introducing total production values of upstream products since in our model, firms are assumed to be homogeneous, so that $M_r = Z_r / q_r z$, where z and Z_r are their output per firm and total production, respectively. Third, for the last term, we use the simple measure of distance-weighted demand, that is Harris-type market potential measure (Harris, 1954). In order to avoid multi-colinearity of this variable with other explanatory variables such as wages, we use αY_c rather than Y_c. In other words, the last term is expressed as $\ln \Sigma(y_c / D_{sc})$, where y_c is a country c's total expenditure on downstream products of this industrial sector. Thus, our market potential measure is constructed by aggregating y_c / D_{sc} across all countries available in the input–output table, that is the US plus nine Asian countries. Furthermore, to evaluate US importance, we *assume* that $\ln \Sigma(y_c / D_{sc})$ can be approximated by:

$$\ln (y_{US} / D_{s,US}) + \ln \sum\nolimits_{c \in A} (y_c / D_{sc}),$$

where A is a set of nine Asian countries. This decomposition enables us to examine the impacts of changes in US demand and intra-regional demand separately.

Last, in order to explore the more direct impacts of the financial crisis, we introduce variables relating to the finance market, specifically, importer's country credibility ($Credibility_s$) and exporter's country credibility ($Credibility_r$), which are the same index as used in Figure 5.1. These country credibility measures will be well related to changes in the international financial market and a component of trade costs, t_{rs} and τ_{cs} Although the importer's credibility should be combined with market access measures because τ_{cs} should be so, we simply incorporate the credibility of both exporters and importers as separate independent variables. Consequently, adding an industrial sector dummy and time dummy and putting an appropriate industrial sector superscript, we can express our equation estimated as that presented in the text.

6. To what extent will the shock be alleviated? The evaluation of China's counter-crisis fiscal expansion

Nobuhiro Okamoto and Satoshi Inomata

1. INTRODUCTION

The year 2008 marked the 30th anniversary of the launch of the Reform and Open-door policy in the People's Republic of China. As is generally known, China has achieved a high level of economic growth since these internal changes occurred in 1978. Although there were occasional economic recessions caused by accidental factors such as the Tiananmen Square incident in 1989 or the Asian Currency Crisis in 1997, it is fair to say that China has realized rapid economic development in the last 30 years.

China's development model is based on an export-oriented strategy. China achieved its industrialization upon a high degree of export orientation, while shifting its focus from the export of primary products to that of labour-intensive processing industries, which enjoyed the comparative advantage of a massive labour force.

However, this strategy was bound to encounter obstacles when the international market started to shrink. For China, the impact of the financial crisis emerged as a result of a fall in exports due to the collapse of the global commodity market, despite the crisis itself originating in US financial markets. Since the Chinese economy is export-driven, the export reduction triggered an immediate economic slowdown; the growth rate fell as low as 6.1 per cent in the first quarter of 2009. An economic growth rate of under 8 per cent implied a significant loss of employment opportunities, thus causing social unrest and instability.

Recently, the Chinese government decided to launch a fiscal expenditure package with 4 trillion Chinese Yuan (approx. 520 billion US$), which records an unprecedented level of fiscal commitment in the history of Chinese economic policy. In evaluating the effect of China's recent fiscal measure, this chapter conducts the following analyses. First, we quantify the impact of the recent economic crisis on the Chinese economy. This is done by identifying the mechanism of spatial shock transmissions among regional economies within China, and also in relation to other Asian countries, by using the *Transnational Interregional Input–Output Table between China and Japan 2000* (IDE-JETRO, 2007). Subsequently, we evaluate the effect of the current fiscal measure in moderating or even reversing the downward spiral that severely haunted the Asian-Pacific economies.

2. ECONOMIC CRISIS IN CHINA: AN OVERVIEW

The timing of the global economic crisis was particularly unfortunate for China. After the overheating period of double-digit growth rates, the Chinese economy was already plunging into the deflationary phase of a business cycle in early 2008. Household consumption showed steady decline; stocks of cars were accumulating from March onwards, and the sale of large-size televisions was mediocre, disappointing manufacturers' expectation of a boom in consumption due to the Beijing Olympic Games.

This is considered to be the outcome of a series of government policies to cool down the overheating economy. For example, in order to control the massive outflow of exports, export tax rebates (reimbursement of export value-added taxes) were reduced in the second half of 2007. The appreciation of the Yuan against the US dollar was tacitly permitted, which also helped curb exports. The central bank (People's Bank of China) recurrently raised interest rates during the first half of 2008, to moderate the ever-increasing investment fever.

The government's projection for the soft landing of the economy, however, was abruptly disturbed by the onset of the crisis. The drastic change in the economic environment rendered government measures to tame the economy excessively deflationary, and resulted in serious downward pressure being inflicted on business activities in China (Onishi, 2009).

This is shown in Table 6.1. The growth rate of the pre-crisis 2007 was 11 per cent, yet the pace of growth fell as early as the first half of 2008, reflecting the effects of government measures to cool down the economy. Then, the Lehman shock occurred soon afterwards. The Chinese economy immediately felt the impact, and the growth rate dropped to 9 per cent in the third quarter of 2008. The downward trend accelerated and the

Table 6.1 GDP of China (annual and quarterly)

	2007	2008	2008 Q1 Jan–Mar	2008 Q2 Apr–Jun	2008 Q3 Jul–Sep	2008 Q4 Oct–Dec	2009 Q1 Jan–Mar	2009 Q2 Apr–Jun
							(100 million Yuan)	
GDP total	257 306	300 670	63 475	71 251	73 299	92 645	65 745	–
Primary	28 627	34 000	4 720	7 080	10 262	11 938	4 700	–
Secondary	124 799	146 183	31 658	37 672	34 644	42 209	31 968	–
Tertiary	103 880	120 487	27 097	26 499	28 393	38 498	29 077	–
Growth rate	11.4	9.0	10.6	10.1	9.0	6.8	6.1	7.9

Source: China Statistical Abstract 2009, National Bureau of Statistics Homepage.

fourth quarter registered 6.8 per cent, a further drop from the previous period. Indeed, the annual growth rate for 2008 was only 9 per cent, that is single-digit, which had never been experienced in China in the preceding six years.

The Chinese government emphasized efforts to keep economic growth at 8 per cent or higher. Yet, as announced by the National People's Congress (NPC) in 2009, pushing down the threshold of the 8 per cent bottom line seemed to be a realistic estimate. The reason why the Chinese government persisted in the 8 per cent growth rate was that it enabled it to maintain a level of employment to the extent that social unrest could be avoided. According to the Nikkei Shimbun (26 January 2009) the annual increase in the number of workers in China was estimated to be 8 400 000 persons, and, since jobs for 900 000 persons were expected to be created by a 1 per cent increase in economic growth, the 8 per cent growth was considered necessary to secure job opportunities for the increasing number of workers (see also Chapter 2). Therefore, an 8 per cent growth rate was a critical target for the Chinese government in order to pursue 'a harmonious society'.[1]

In general, there are three major channels for negative shock transmission of the financial crisis:

1. The direct damage to the financial sector of the country concerned;
2. The influence of the global credit crunch;
3. The contraction of export markets.

Table 6.2 Exports and imports of China (100 million US$)

		Export		Import	
2008	Jan–Aug	9378.3	22.3%	7862.3	30.1%
	Sep	1363.5	21.4%	1069.5	21.2%
	Oct	1282.3	19.0%	929.3	15.4%
	Nov	1149.8	−2.2%	748.1	−18.0%
	Dec	1111.6	−2.8%	721.8	−21.3%
2009	Jan	903.7	−17.5%	514.0	−43.1%
	Feb	648.5	−25.7%	600.3	−24.2%
	Mar	902.4	−17.2%	717.3	−25.2%
	Apr	919.2	−22.6%	788.2	−23.0%
	May	887.6	−26.4%	783.7	−25.2%

Note: The percentage ratios are the change from the figure for the same month the previous year.

Source: General Administration of Customs homepage.

As far as the financial sector of China is concerned, it is a question of how much Chinese money was trapped in sub-prime-related securities and hence damaged by the bad loans. According to Li (2009), the bad loans of China CITIC Bank amounted to only 0.05 per cent of its total assets, and this was the highest degree of 'contamination' among all Chinese banks. Also, the US real estate bonds that went bankrupt reached 1.7 per cent of the total assets of the Bank of China, yet this was the worst figure; all other banks suffered less than 1 per cent default of total assets. So, it is fair to say that the negative impact on the Chinese financial sector is considered quite limited.

On the other hand, the global credit crunch triggered a sharp decline in investment, and should have affected a number of firms in China. Moreover, the sudden drop of stock values cooled down Chinese consumers' confidence through a negative asset effect, which may have influenced their purchasing behaviour in daily life.

Looking at the export side, the United States is undoubtedly the biggest market for China. The contraction of the US markets caused by the financial crisis should have damaged China's business activities considerably, perhaps the largest impact among all the three channels considered above. As shown in Table 6.2, China's foreign trade kept expanding until September 2008, yet then began declining for the first time in the last seven and a half years. If we examine the percentage change from the figure for the same month the previous year, the magnitude of decline accelerated at the beginning of 2009; a 17 per cent decline was recorded in

January compared to the previous year, dropping further to 25 per cent in February.

Also, imports declined by approximately 20 per cent in the early stage of the crisis, and went on to plummet by 43 per cent in January 2009. Why was the change in import more sensitive to the shock than exports? Many manufacturers were forced to revise their production plans in response to the change in the business environment, including the global credit crunch in capital markets as mentioned above. If the import contents of their products are high, this should lead to a significant decrease in import demand. This is the case especially for foreign-affiliated firms located in coastal regions of China. Their products account for approximately 60 per cent of Chinese exports, with an extremely high percentage of import contents for parts and materials. In addition, the gloomy business prospects drove manufactures to run down their inventories instead of purchasing new parts and materials from abroad.

The fact that the export decline in China was coupled with a significant decrease in its imports (even on a larger scale) has important implications for our current study. Namely, this is directly relevant to the issue of an international, inter-regional shock transmission mechanism in the Asia-Pacific region, in which China plays a central role in the regional production networks. In what follows, we shall review related research on the spatial industrial structure of China as preliminaries to our empirical study.

3. LITERATURE REVIEW

The spatial industrial structure of China has been analysed in various research works such as Okamoto and Ihara (2005), Meng and Qu (2007), Hioki and Okamoto (2009) and Hioki et al. (2009). These studies use the China Interregional Input–Output Model for their analyses. The spatial linkages between Chinese and Japanese regions are investigated in only Yonemoto et al. (2008), yet this study is a policy simulation based on CGE models, which treats the linkages between the regions in China and Japan as a kind of 'black box'.

Zhang and Tao (2009) consider the impact of the export decline on the Chinese economy. The analysis of demand elasticity is introduced in this study; if the GDP of each country declines by 1 per cent, it results in a 9.52 per cent decrease of Chinese exports to the United States, a 5.28 per cent decrease to Japan, and a 2.75 per cent decrease to Europe. Namely, the decline of the US market has the biggest impact on Chinese exports. The study also demonstrates a simulation on the contribution of exports to economic growth using an input–output model. If the growth rate of domestic demand (consumption + investment) and the export value is the same as the year 2008, the total output in 2009 is estimated to grow at about 6 per cent (the estimated growth rate of GDP is almost the same). If it is to maintain an 8 per cent growth rate in 2009, exports must grow at 7.5 per cent, which, as the study concludes, is an unrealistic prospect.

As for regional differences within China, Kurata (2009) performs a simulation using a Multi-regional Input–Output Model for China 2000 (IDE-JETRO, 2003). This demonstrates the impact on the production and employment of each region when exports decrease by 10 per cent in each case. The result shows that a total output of 159 500 million Yuan is lost in the South Coast region, the largest decrease of all, followed by the Central Coast region losing 117 300 million Yuan. Employment suffers a similar loss; 4 130 000 jobs are lost on the South Coast and 2 200 000 jobs on the Central Coast. The study concludes that the impact of export decline is prevalent among inland regions although the initial impact attacks coastal regions.

In Zhang et al. (2009), a dynamic input–output model is constructed and the effect of 4 trillion Yuan of fiscal expenditure is analysed. In particular, the effects of individual projects, such as the subsidies on automobile purchases or the distribution of shopping vouchers, are investigated by using a CGE model. The simulation result shows that the subsidies on automobile purchases trigger a 0.2 per cent rise in GDP and create employment opportunities for 1 690 000 persons. As for the effect of shopping vouchers, their distribution to a value of 50 billion Yuan raises GDP by 0.22 per cent and creates 2 500 000 jobs.

4. DATA

The data used in this chapter is the *Transnational Interregional Input–Output Table between Japan and China* (IDE-JETRO, 2007) for the reference year of 2000. The table was constructed by combining three components: the 2000 Asian International Input–Output Table (AIO table), the inter-regional input–output table of China, and that of Japan. The basic idea of the construction scheme is that the information on inter-regional transactions within China and within Japan, taken from the two inter-regional tables, be 'plugged in' to the corresponding segments in the Asian International Input–Output Table.

The overall picture of the 2000 *Transnational Interregional Input–Output Table* is given in Table 6.3. Seen column-wise, each cell in the table shows the input composition of the industries of the respective country/region. A^{A00A00}, for example, shows the input compositions of the ASEAN5 industries *vis-à-vis* domestically produced goods and services. A^{C01A00},

Table 6.3 *Format of 2000* Transnational Interregional Input–Output Table *between China and Japan*

		Intermediate Demand (A)							
		ASEAN5	China-region 1	China-region n	China-region 7	Japan-region 1	Japan-region 8	East Asia	United States
	Code	(AA00)	(AC01)	(AC0n)	(AC07)	(AJ01)	(AJ08)	(AE00)	(AU00)
ASEAN5	(AA00)	A^{A00A00}	A^{A00C01}	A^{A00C0n}	A^{A00C07}	A^{A00J01}	A^{A00J08}	A^{A00E00}	A^{A00U00}
China-region 1	(AC01)	A^{C01A00}	A^{C01C01}	A^{C01C0n}	A^{C01C07}	A^{C01J01}	A^{C01J08}	A^{C01E00}	A^{C01U00}
China-region n	(AC0n)	A^{C0nA00}	A^{C0nC01}	A^{C0nC0n}	A^{C0nC07}	A^{C0nJ01}	A^{C0nJ08}	A^{C0nE00}	A^{C0nU00}
China-region 7	(AC07)	A^{C07A00}	A^{C07C01}	A^{C07C0n}	A^{C07C07}	A^{C07J01}	A^{C07J08}	A^{C07E00}	A^{C07U00}
Japan-region 1	(AJ01)	A^{J01A00}	A^{J01C01}	A^{J01C0n}	A^{J01C07}	A^{J01J01}	A^{J01J08}	A^{J01E00}	A^{J01U00}
Japan-region n	(AJ0n)	A^{J0nA00}	A^{J0nC01}	A^{J0nC0n}	A^{J0nC07}	A^{J0nJ01}	A^{J0nJ08}	A^{J0nE00}	A^{J0nU00}
Japan-region 8	(AJ08)	A^{J08A00}	A^{J08C01}	A^{J08C0n}	A^{J08C07}	A^{J08J01}	A^{J08J08}	A^{J08E00}	A^{J08U00}
East Asia	(AE00)	A^{E00A00}	A^{E00C01}	A^{E00C0n}	A^{E00C07}	A^{E00J01}	A^{E00J08}	A^{E00E00}	A^{E00U00}
United States	(AU00)	A^{U00A00}	A^{U00C01}	A^{U00C0n}	A^{U00C07}	A^{U00J01}	A^{U00J08}	A^{U00E00}	A^{U00U00}
International Freight and Insurance	(BF)	BA^{A00}	BA^{C01}	BA^{C0n}	BA^{C07}	BA^{J01}	BA^{J08}	BA^{E00}	BA^{U00}
Import from Rest of the World	(CW)	A^{WA00}	A^{WC01}	A^{WC0n}	A^{WC07}	A^{WJ01}	A^{WJ08}	A^{WE00}	A^{WU00}
Duties and Import Tax	(DT)	DA^{A00}	DA^{C01}	DA^{C0n}	DA^{C07}	DA^{J01}	DA^{J08}	DA^{E00}	DA^{U00}
Value Added	(VV)	V^{A00}	V^{C01}	V^{C0n}	V^{C07}	V^{J01}	V^{J08}	V^{E00}	V^{U00}
Total Input	(XX)	X^{A00}	X^{C01}	X^{C0n}	X^{C07}	X^{J01}	X^{J08}	X^{E00}	X^{U00}

Note: n = 2~6.

Source: IDE-JETRO (2007).

on the other hand, shows the input composition of ASEAN5 industries for imported goods and services from the China-region 1. Cells A^{C0nA00}, A^{C07A00}, A^{J01A00}, A^{J0nA00}, A^{J08A00}, A^{E00A00} and A^{U00A00} allow the same interpretation for imports from other countries/regions.

The basic scheme of the table is exactly the same as for the AIO tables, which can be referred to in the 'Explanatory notes' (see Chapter 8).

As shown in Table 6.4, the industrial classification covers 10 industrial sectors: 01 Agriculture, livestock, forestry and fisheries, 02 Mining and

Table 6.3 (continued)

Final Demand (F)											
ASEAN5 (FA00)	China-region 1 (FC01)	China-region n (FC0n)	China-region 7 (FC07)	Japan-region 1 (FJ01)	Japan-region n (FJ0n)	Japan-region 8 (FJ08)	East Asia (FE00)	United States (FU00)	Export to ROW (LW)	Discrepancies (QX)	Total Output (XX)
F^{A00A00}	F^{A00C01}	F^{A00C0n}	F^{A00C07}	F^{A00J01}	F^{A00J0n}	F^{A00J08}	F^{A00E00}	F^{A00U00}	L^{A00W}	Q^{A00}	X^{A00}
F^{C01A00}	F^{C01C01}	F^{C01C0n}	F^{C01C07}	F^{C01J01}	F^{C01J0n}	F^{C01J08}	F^{C01E00}	F^{C01U00}	L^{C01W}	Q^{C01}	X^{C01}
F^{C0nA00}	F^{C0nC01}	F^{C0nC0n}	F^{C0nC07}	F^{C0nJ01}	F^{C0nJ0n}	F^{C0nJ08}	F^{C0nE00}	F^{C0nU00}	L^{C0nW}	Q^{C0n}	X^{C0n}
F^{C07A00}	F^{C07C01}	F^{C07C0n}	F^{C07C07}	F^{C07J01}	F^{C07J0n}	F^{C07J08}	F^{C07E00}	F^{C07U00}	L^{C07W}	Q^{C07}	X^{C07}
F^{J01A00}	F^{J01C01}	F^{J01C0n}	F^{J01C07}	F^{J01J01}	F^{J01J0n}	F^{J01J08}	F^{J01E00}	F^{J01U00}	L^{J01W}	Q^{J01}	X^{J01}
F^{J0nA00}	F^{J0nC01}	F^{J0nC0n}	F^{J0nC07}	F^{J0nJ01}	F^{J0nJ0n}	F^{J0nJ08}	F^{J0nE00}	F^{J0nU00}	L^{J0nW}	Q^{J0n}	X^{J0n}
F^{J08A00}	F^{J08C01}	F^{J08C0n}	F^{J08C07}	F^{J08J01}	F^{J08J0n}	F^{J08J08}	F^{J08E00}	F^{J08U00}	L^{J08W}	Q^{J08}	X^{J08}
F^{E00A00}	F^{E00C01}	F^{E00C0n}	F^{E00C07}	F^{E00J01}	F^{E00J0n}	F^{E00J08}	F^{E00E00}	F^{E00U00}	L^{E00W}	Q^{E00}	X^{E00}
F^{U00A00}	F^{U00C01}	F^{U00C0n}	F^{U00C07}	F^{U00J01}	F^{U00J0n}	F^{U00J08}	F^{U00E00}	F^{U00U00}	L^{U00W}	Q^{U00}	X^{U00}
BF^{A00}	BF^{C01}	BF^{C0n}	BF^{C07}	BF^{J01}	BF^{J0n}	BF^{J08}	BF^{E00}	BF^{U00}			
F^{WA00}	F^{WC01}	F^{WC0n}	F^{WC07}	F^{WJ01}	F^{WJ0n}	F^{WJ08}	F^{WE00}	F^{WU00}			
DF^{A00}	DF^{C01}	DF^{C0n}	DF^{C07}	DF^{J01}	DF^{J0n}	DF^{J08}	DF^{E00}	DF^{U00}			

quarrying, 03 Household consumption products, 04 Basic industrial materials, 05 Processing and assembling, 06 Electricity, gas and water supply, 07 Construction, 08 Trade, 09 Transportation and 10 Services.

China is divided into the seven regions of Dongbei, Huabei, Huadong, Huanan, Huazhong, Xibei, and Xinan, whereas the eight regions in Japan are Hokkaido, Tohoku, Kanto, Chubu, Kinki, Chugoku, Shikoku, and Kyushu–Okinawa (Table 6.4 and Figure 6.1). For analytical brevity in this chapter, all the sub-regions of Japan are aggregated into a single region,

Table 6.4 Industrial sector and regional classification

Industrial sector classification

Code	Description	Code	Description
001	Agriculture, livestock, forestry and fishery	006	Electricity, gas and water supply
002	Mining and quarrying	007	Construction
003	Household consumption products	008	Trade
004	Basic industrial materials	009	Transportation
005	Processing and assembling	010	Services

Region classification

Code	Region	Description (countries or domestic provinces included)
AA00	ASEAN5	Indonesia, Malaysia, the Philippines, Singapore and Thailand
AC01	China's Dongbei	Liaoning(6), Jilin(7), Heilongjiang(8)
AC02	China's Huabei	Beijing(1), Tianjin(2), Hebei(3), Shandong(15)
AC03	China's Huadong	Shanghai(9), Jiangsu(10), Zhejiang(11)
AC04	China's Huanan	Fujian(13), Guangdong(19), Hainan(21)
AC05	China's Huazhong	Shanxi(4), Anhui(12), Jiangxi(14), Henan(16), Hubei(17), Hunan(18)
AC06	China's Xibei	Inner Mongolia(5), Shaanxi,(27), Gansu(28), Qinghai(29), Ningxia(30), Xinjiang(31)
AC07	China's Xinan	Guangxi(20), Chongqing(22), Sichuan(23), Guizhou(24), Yunnan(25), Tibet(26)
AE00	East Asia	Korea and Taiwan
AJ01	Japan's Hokkaido	Hokkaido(1)
AJ02	Japan's Tohoku	Aomori(2), Iwate(3), Miyagi(4), Akita(5), Yamagata(6), Fukushima(7)
AJ03	Japan's Kanto	Ibaraki(8), Tochigi(9), Gunma(10), Saitama(11), Chiba(12), Tokyo(13), Kanagawa(14), Niigata(15), Yamanashi(19), Nagano(20), Shizuoka(22)
AJ04	Japan's Chubu	Toyama(16), Ishikawa(17), Gifu(21), Aichi(23), Mie(24)
AJ05	Japan's Kinki	Fukui(18), Shiga(25), Kyoto(26), Osaka(27), Hyogo(28), Nara(29), Wakayama(30)

Table 6.4 (continued)

Code	Region	Description (countries or domestic provinces included)
AJ06	Japan's Chugoku	Tottori(31), Shimane(32), Okayama(33), Hiroshima(34), Yamaguchi(35)
AJ07	Japan's Shikoku	Tokushima(36), Kagawa(37), Ehime(38), Kochi(39)
AJ08	Japan's Kyushu & Okinawa	Fukuoka(40), Saga(41), Nagasaki(42), Kumamoto(43), Oita(44), Miyazaki(45), Kagoshima(46), Okinawa(47)
AU00	USA	The United States

Source: IDE-JETRO (2007).

'Japan'. There are also three other regions to be considered: 'ASEAN5 (the Philippines, Thailand, Malaysia, Singapore, Indonesia)', 'South Korea – Taiwan', and 'the USA'.

The input–output model used here is a simple impact analysis model, yet the unique feature of the *Transnational Interregional Input–Output Table* described above enables us to view the 'intra-regional' and 'inter-regional' effects individually, so as to probe the detailed, region-to-region linkage structure from a geographical perspective.

5. EMPIRICAL RESULTS

5.1 The Inter-regional Production Structure between China and other Asian Regions

Before starting the simulation analysis, let us first trace the history of regional development in China in order to facilitate understanding of the spatial linkage structure between China and other Asian regions. In 1979, China established the Special Economic Zone (SEZ) at Shenzhen, Zhuhai, Shantou and Xiamen in Huanan, the purpose of which was to support foreign-affiliated firms to set up factories in the areas by providing them with an improved investment environment. In 1984, 14 other cities in coastal areas were opened to foreign companies, and Hainan in Huanan region also became an SEZ in 1988. In 1987, Zhao Ziyang, the former president, proposed the so-called 'Coastal Area Development Strategy', which involved inviting foreign companies into coastal areas. The policy aimed to exploit their technology and trading know-how, and to combine

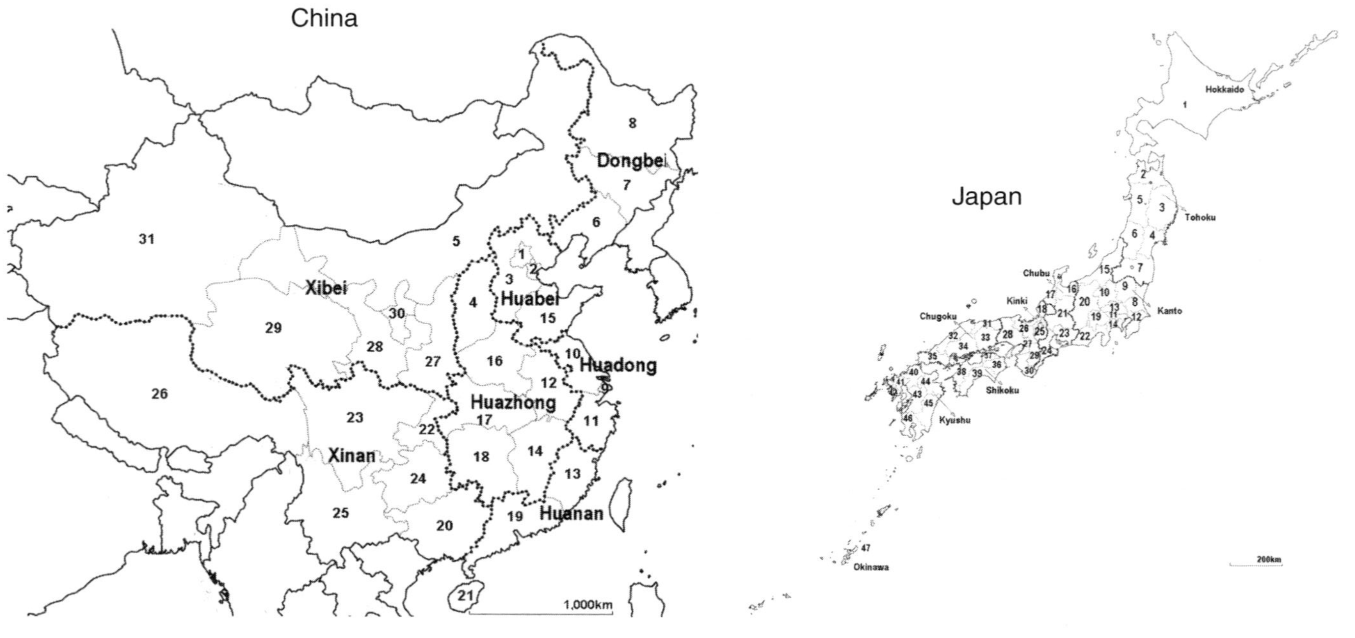

Source: IDE-JETRO (2007).

Figure 6.1 The regional definition of China and Japan

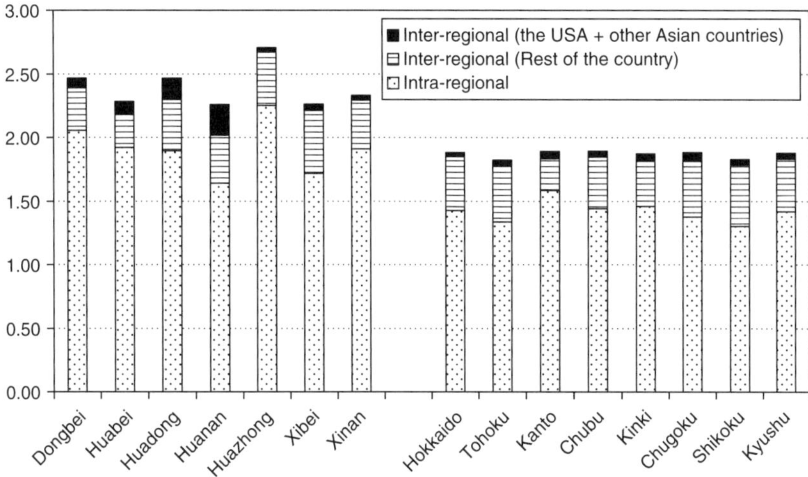

Source: Calculated by the authors.

Figure 6.2 Multiplier effect of each region

them with the massive labour force in China. Consequently, various kinds of basic materials and intermediate goods flowed into the country, whereupon the products were assembled and processed by Chinese workers to produce the final goods, mostly directed to foreign markets. This production system was further strengthened in the early 1990s, and rapid economic growth followed thereafter under this export-driven development strategy.

The high degree of dependence on foreign capital and overseas commodity markets formed a very special production structure in China. More than 90 per cent of foreign firms are concentrated in coastal regions, especially in Huanan and Huadong, and they utilize the cheap and massive labour force in China to produce labour-intensive products. These labour-intensive products such as apparel and electronic appliance are then exported to the markets of developed countries like the USA, the EU and Japan, as analysed in Chapter 1.

Figure 6.2 compares the magnitudes of 'intra-regional' and 'inter-regional' multipliers, among the seven regions of China and eight regions of Japan respectively. A multiplier measures the degree of influence of each region over the economy. If its magnitude is large, it means that a shock occurring in that region, regardless of whether positive or negative, has a significant impact on its own and/or the rest of the economy. A multiplier is calculated as a column sum of the elements in the Leontief inverse matrix

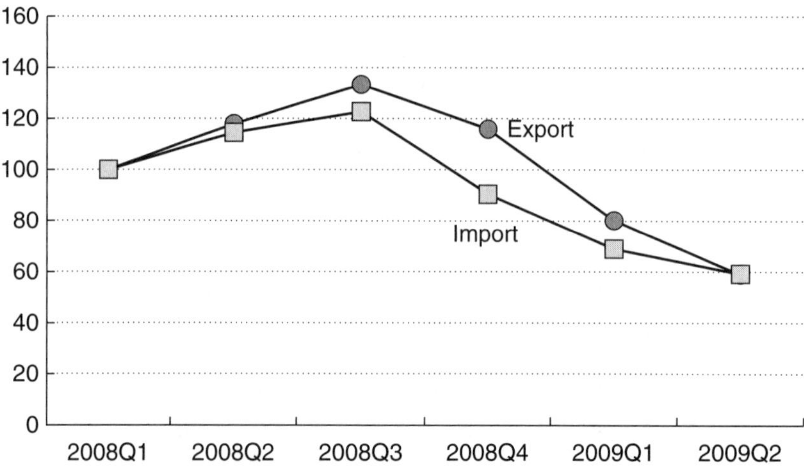

Note: 2009Q2 indicates only 2 months from April to May due to limited data.

Source: General Administration of Customs homepage.

Figure 6.3 Trend of China's exports and imports

constructed from the *Transnational Interregional Input–Output Table* and further divided into intra-regional and inter-regional multipliers, depending on which parts of the Leontief inverse are observed. Referring back to Table 6.3, for example, if we examine the segment of the Leontief inverse that corresponds to A^{C01C01}, this gives us the intra-regional multiplier of China-region 1. If we look at the rest of the column, we are referring to the inter-regional multipliers of China-region 1 with respect to other regions.

It is observed in Figure 6.2 that the multipliers of Chinese regions are generally higher compared to those of Japanese regions. Chinese regions have much more influence over the Asia-Pacific economy and are hence deserving of the title 'growth engine'.

The variation of the magnitudes of multipliers is also prominent for Chinese regions, while all Japan's multipliers remain within the range [1.83–1.89]. Huazhong has the largest multiplier, while Huanan has the smallest. A comparison of these two reveals an interesting implication. As stated above, Huanan is a hub where foreign-affiliated firms are concentrated, and has developed strong and extensive production networks beyond the national border. This is clearly indicated by the magnitude of its inter-regional multiplier with respect to the USA and other Asian countries (the black segment), as well as that for Huadong, which is another foreign-oriented coastal region. Huazhong, in contrast, has the largest total multiplier of all, but a very small international component. This implies that the shock that occurs in Huazhong induces the biggest impact, yet the majority will be transmitted to domestic regions of China (especially itself). On the other hand, a significant portion of the shock in Huanan will reverberate among neighbouring foreign countries. Together with Huadong, these coastal regions are considered to be China's 'shock outlets' to foreign nations.

5.2 Impact of the Financial Crisis

As discussed in section 2, the impact of the financial crisis on China was mainly channelled through the contraction of foreign trade. Figure 6.3 shows that both exports and imports expanded favourably between the first and third quarters of 2008. In the fourth quarter, however, the index values dropped by 18 and 32 points, respectively, from the preceding period, whereas in the second quarter of 2009 the index values are 40 points lower for both exports and imports compared to the initial period (the first quarter of 2008).[2]

In Figure 6.4, the total outputs induced by the production of China's export are compared between the pre- and post-crisis periods. This is not the data of official estimates, but rather the simulation result using our input–output table data (for the calculation method of 'induced output', see the 'Explanatory notes' in Chapter 8). The impacts on the Huadong and Huanan production show virtually overlapping movement; both regions recorded output exceeding 300 billion US$ in the third quarter of 2008, yet declined to 140 billion US$ after the financial crisis. This was followed by the production decline of Huabei, decreasing from 170 to 75 billion US$, while the impacts on Huazhong and Dongbei were also significant.

It is worth pointing out that the export decline in China had noticeable impacts on Japan and Korea–Taiwan, as well as on the USA and ASEAN5 to some degree. In fact, the magnitude of impact on Japan or Korea+Taiwan is even greater than that on Xinan or Xibei. Figure 6.5 shows the structure of inter-regional linkages from China to these four foreign regions. It takes a proportion of the magnitude of inter-regional multiplier effects from each region in China in order to illustrate the relative degree of influence of Chinese regions on the neighbouring Asian countries and the USA. It is apparent from Figure 6.5 that Huanan has the largest influence on all four regions, followed by Huadong and Huabei.

Figure 6.6 gives the structure of inter-regional linkages from the other perspective. It is a composition of the size of multipliers of each Chinese region according to its impact destinations. Particularly interesting is the relationship between the level of multiplier and inter-regional distance.

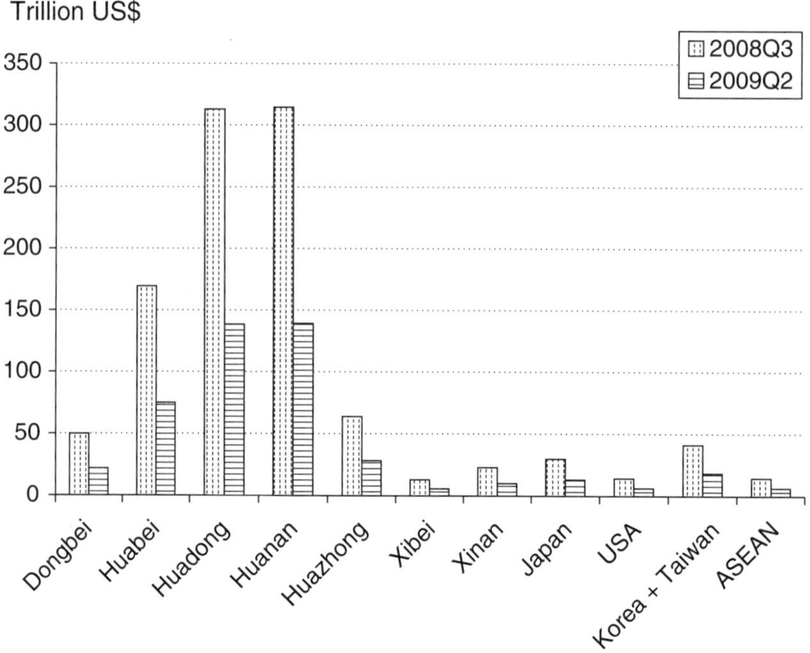

Source: Calculated by the authors.

Figure 6.4 The output decrease caused by China's export decline

For the first four Chinese regions, that is Dongbei, Huabei, Huadong and Huanan, the share of influence on ASEAN5 is increasing in that order. The result matches the descending order of distance from each region to the ASEAN5 countries. Referring to the map in Figure 6.1 helps to confirm this. In the same way, the share of Japan is decreasing from northern Donbei towards southern Huanan, with the exception of Huabei. The reason why the value of Huabei is lower than that of Huadong is that 'shipping distance' rather than geographical distance counts here. As seen in the map, the Korean peninsula lies between Huabei and Japan, making the shipping route between the two regions longer than that between Huandong and Japan. As far as the other three inland regions of China (Xibei, Xinan and Huazhong) are concerned, here again the geographical distance is irrelevant since economic linkages with foreign countries depend on the location of shipping ports of adjacent regions, meaning that the relationship between linkage and distance is less obvious than that for coastal regions.[3]

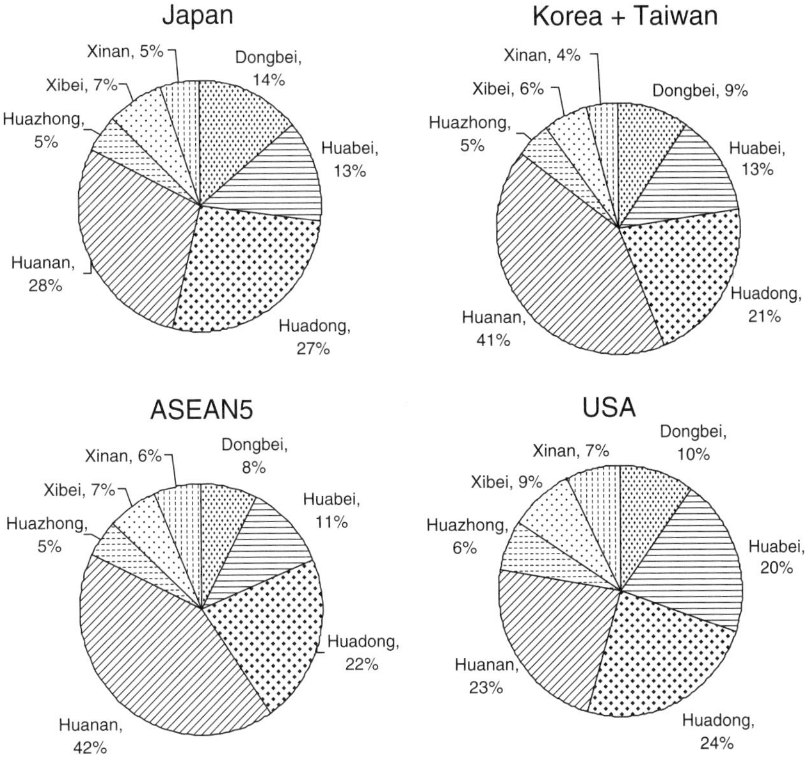

Source: Calculated by the authors.

Figure 6.5 Influence from Chinese regions

The preceding analyses enable us to identify the shock transmission mechanism through regional production networks around China. The decline in China's exports had a considerable negative impact on coastal regions such as Huanan and Huadong, both of which are extremely dependent on foreign markets. These regions have a large influence on the production of neighbouring Asian countries and the USA, meaning that a significant part of the shock was transmitted to these outer regions. Interestingly, the degree of influence is closely related to the shipping distance between the countries concerned, and hence Korea, Taiwan and ASEAN countries are considered more sensitive and vulnerable to the deterioration of coastal economies in China.

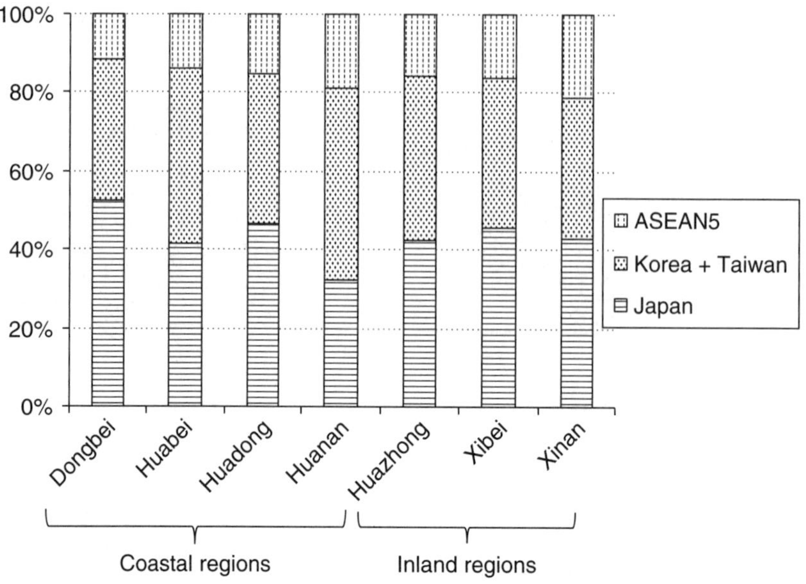

Source: Calculated by the authors.

Figure 6.6 Economic linkages with Asian countries

5.3 Evaluation of Counter-crisis Fiscal Expansion

On the evening of 9 November 2008, the Chinese government announced a counter-crisis fiscal measure of 4 trillion Yuan (about 520 billion US$). This was a fiscal commitment of an unprecedented scale, surpassing the previous financial injection of 3 trillion Yuan in 1998 to offset the Asian Currency Crisis.

The contents of the fiscal package included the supply of cheap residences, development of countryside infrastructure, and the construction of roads, railroads, airports, and so on. Corporate and individual taxes were to be reduced by a total of 500 billion Yuan, while other special taxes were also to be cut by 120 billion Yuan, especially in the form of export tax rebates for enterprises as well as the value-added tax reform. From 20 January 2009, the acquisition tax rate of small cars was also halved, from 10 per cent to 5 per cent.

The People's Bank of China decided to cut interest rates three times in just six weeks after mid-September, while the loan ceiling was also lifted. This induced 5 trillion Yuan or more of new credit creation.

Particular attention should be paid to the policy of so-called 'Household

Table 6.5 Counter-crisis policies

Stimulation of domestic demand	Total of 4 trillion Yuan fiscal expenditure Tax reduction of 0.5 trillion Yuan for households and enterprises 40 billion Yuan of subsidies to the countryside Over 5 trillion Yuan of new bank loans
Industrial policy	Improved access to finance for small- and medium-sized firms Promotion of R&D Support for energy-saving and pollution control projects
Stabilization of society	4.2 billion Yuan for employment policy 293 billion Yuan for social security Prevention of subversive activities

Source: *Nikkei Shimbun*, 9 March 2009.

Appliances to the Countryside (Jia Dian Xia Xiang)'. In this policy, the government provided 13 per cent subsidies for the purchase of home electrical appliances (colour/liquid crystal display televisions, refrigerators, washing machines, cellular phones) to households in farm villages. This is equivalent to a '40 billion Yuan subsidy to a farm village' (Table 6.5). The policy was experimentally implemented in Shangdong, Henan and Sichuan at the end of 2007, and then extended to 14 provinces by the end of 2008, and finally nationwide by February 2009. According to an estimate by the Department of Commerce, 3 500 000 people were expected to be using this scheme one year after the implementation, which should raise the sale of household appliances by about 40 per cent, adding extra consumption demand of 920 billion Yuan by 2012.

Along these lines, the policy of 'Automobiles to the Countryside (Qi Che Xia Xiang)' was introduced from March 2009 onwards, to facilitate the purchase of a compact car in the countryside (switching from the popular three-wheelers), as an additional measure to stimulate household consumption. On top of this, 'Consumption vouchers' for shopping and travelling were distributed in provinces such as Zhejiang and Jiangsu (though the scheme was not introduced nationwide due to possible management difficulties).[4]

Next we evaluate whether these counter-crisis policies can be effective measures to alleviate the negative shocks of the financial crisis.

One of the government's major motivations behind this large-scale fiscal commitment is to correct the persistent regional disparity in China. After the launch of Reform and the Open-door policy, the policy focus was

Table 6.6 Allocation of 4 trillion Yuan fiscal expenditure

Allocation to:	%
Priority projects on roads, railways, airways, water supply and improvement of city electric networks	37.5
Reconstruction of the Sichuan region	25.0
Construction of low rent/price housings	10.0
Construction of countryside infrastructure	9.3
Investment for R&D to adjust the industrial structure	9.3
Investment for energy saving, environmental protection and to restore ecosystem	5.3
Investment for health, education, culture and social work	3.8

Note: Investment is to be carried out in both 2009 and 2010.

Source: *21st Century Business Herald* (21 Shiji Jingji Baodao), 22 May 2009.

switched to the development of coastal regions. With historical and geographical advantages, coastal regions enjoyed rapid economic development compared with inland regions. During the periods of the seventh and eighth five year plans (1985–1995), the government expected that inland regions could support the development of coastal regions by supplying a cheap labour force, energy and primary products. During the ninth five year plan, the government manifested the 'Cooperated Development' among the regions, yet regional disparity grew ever higher through the 1990s.

With this in mind, the 'Western Regions Development' was proposed in 1999, and the 'Promotion of the North-east Region' was undertaken in 2003 to alleviate regional imbalances. These programmes focused on the development of social infrastructure, especially the transportation system.

The operation of the schemes seemed to go well in the first few years, yet, before its completion, a devastating earthquake attacked south-west Sichuan province; hence the ongoing fiscal expenditure was designed to take this irregular situation into account. As seen in Table 6.6, the amount of 4 trillion Yuan fiscal injection was mainly allocated to infrastructure construction, which occupies approximately 80 per cent of total expenditure. This includes 1 trillion Yuan (25 per cent of the total) for reconstruction of Sichuan province from the devastating earthquake damage.

In order to calculate the effect of China's counter-crisis measure, some assumptions were made in our simulation. The composition of fiscal injection is designed on the basis of the information given in Table 6.6. In particular, 25 per cent of the expenditure is considered to go to Xinan region, for the reconstruction of Sichuan province. As far as the timing of fiscal

Table 6.7 Comparison of crisis impacts and policy impacts

(Million US$)	Crisis impacts	Policy impacts	Net effects
Dongbei	−27 808	102 378	74 570
Huabei	−94 309	202 131	107 822
Huadong	−174 268	206 354	32 086
Huanan	−175 170	116 925	−58 245
Huazhong	−35 622	276 871	241 250
Xibei	−7 231	66 123	58 892
Xinan	−12 746	394 174	381 428
Japan	−16 613	17 512	900
USA	−7 927	9 691	1 764
Korea + Taiwan	−22 995	17 616	−5 379
ASEAN5	−8 039	6 959	−1 080
Total	−551 692	1 416 734	834 008

injections is concerned, it is assumed that 40 per cent of the expenditure is to be carried out in 2009 and 60 per cent in 2010, in accordance with the information given in the *21st Century Business Herald*, which states that fiscal commitment will be completed in two years' time.[5]

We compare the magnitudes of output lost due to the crisis and the output gained due to counter-crisis measures, with the results shown in Table 6.7 and Figure 6.7. As for the magnitude of output loss (crisis impacts), coastal areas such as Huadong and Huanan suffered most, due to their export-dependent structure as explained in the previous section. As for the output gain (policy impacts), the impact was felt most in the Xinan region, which is unsurprising due to the reconstruction programme in Sichuan province. This is followed by Huazhong, which may have benefited from Xinan's expansion thanks to its geographical proximity.

Particularly alarming is the fact that the net effect on Huanan is negative. This is partly attributed to the magnitude of the crisis impact which struck all along the coastal regions, but the weakness of policy impact on Huanan is equally astonishing. It is so ironic that the export-oriented strategy, intended to promote coastal regions, is now causing a serious structural problem for Huanan. The region was strategically shaped into a highly foreign-dependent constitution with poor economic linkages with inner China. Consequently, Huanan suffered a lot from the worldwide depression but is unable to pick up the benefit of the massive government commitment in the development of inland regions.

The impacts on foreign countries are also noticeable. For Japan and the USA, the output gains cancel out the output losses, though this is not the case for Korea+Taiwan and ASEAN5. The backdrop to this observation

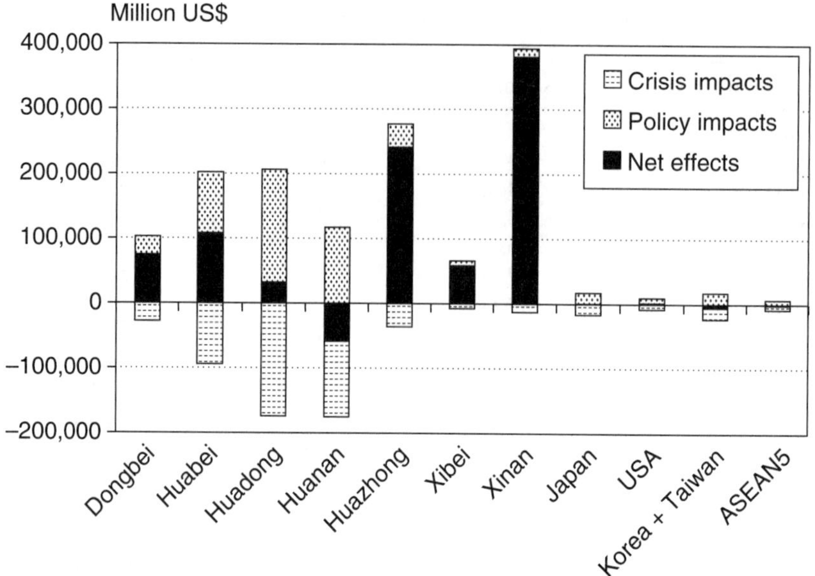

Notes: Crisis impact is the sum of declining amount from 2008Q3. Policy Impact is the total result of two years' expenditure.

Source: Calculated by the authors.

Figure 6.7 Comparison of crisis impacts and policy impacts

is found in Table 6.8, whereby the same analysis is implemented for these foreign regions with respect to major industries. It is shown that 'Basic industrial materials' and 'Processing and assembling' in Japan and the USA receive a positive net effect of China's fiscal expenditure, because China is critically dependent on intermediate materials from Japan and the USA for its infrastructure construction. In contrast, the type of intermediate goods supplied by Korea, Taiwan or ASEAN countries are considered to be used in China to produce export goods, meaning that the development of inland regions has a very limited impact on these countries.

6. CONCLUSIONS

In the last decade, China became a principal engine of growth for the Asian region, as indicated by the outstanding magnitude of its production multiplier, and undoubtedly towed the regional economic growth. The

Table 6.8 The effect of China's fiscal measure on major industries in foreign countries

Region	Industry	Crisis impacts	Policy impacts	Net effects
Japan (Kanto region)	Household consumption products	−260	192	−68
	Basic industrial materials	−2074	2219	145
	Processing and assembling	−2631	2946	315
USA	Household consumption products	−440	332	−108
	Basic industrial materials	−2366	2735	369
	Processing and assembling	−2218	3160	942
Korea+Taiwan	Household consumption products	−3070	1586	−1485
	Basic industrial materials	−9375	7939	−1436
	Processing and assembling	−5514	4297	−1217
ASEAN5	Household consumption products	−725	516	−209
	Basic industrial materials	−1871	1753	−118
	Processing and assembling	−2962	2260	−702

Source: Compiled by the authors.

opposite picture, however, is equally valid. When business slows down in China, it has a considerable negative impact on the rest of the Asian region. As seen in the empirical analysis, the production of export-driven districts such as Huadong and Huanan significantly declined in the second quarter of 2009, to almost half the level of the third quarter of 2008. This triggered further declines in output, not only in neighbouring Huazhong and Huabei, but also in other Asian economies such as Japan, South Korea, Taiwan and ASEAN countries.

The recent fiscal measures adopted by the Chinese government, however, are expected to turn the situation around. According to our simulation, it is revealed that the policy mainly functions to stimulate the economies of inland regions such as Xinan and Huazhong, although the coastal areas Huabei and Huadong may also benefit through inter-regional economic linkages. Moreover, the impact of fiscal expansion transcends international borders and reaches other Asian countries through extensive trade channels. For instance, the construction of infrastructure in China's inland areas induces an increase in the output of basic materials in Japan and in the United States. Although the stimuli may not be sufficient for the whole Asian region to completely restore its economic position, China's current fiscal measures are undoubtedly helping to create better prospects for the region to overcome the global economic crisis.

NOTES

1. The Hu Jintao government, which started in 2002, aimed at realizing 'a harmonious society' (He Xie She Hui).
2. The figures presented in this section include seasonal factors.
3. This is in line with the basic premise of the Gravity model. See Chapter 5 for more details.
4. Most of the information is based on articles from the *Nikkei Shimbun*, November 2008–March 2009.
5. Zhang et al. (2009) assume that the fiscal expenditure will be conducted over a four-year time span.

REFERENCES

Hioki, S. and N. Okamoto (2009), 'How have China's intra- and inter-regional input–output linkages changed during reform?', in Nazrul Islam (ed.), *Resurgent China: Issues for the Future*, Basingstoke: Palgrave Macmillan.

Hioki, S., G.J.D. Hewings and N. Okamoto (2009), 'Identifying the structural changes of China's spatial production linkages using a qualitative input–output analysis', *The Journal of Econometric Study of Northeast Asia*, **6**(2), 25–48.

Institute of Developing Economies-JETRO (2003), *Multiregional Input–output Model for China 2000*, Statistical Data Series No. 86, Chiba: Institute of Developing Economies-JETRO.

Institute of Developing Economies-JETRO (2007), *Transnational Interregional Input–Output Table between China and Japan 2000*, AIO Series No. 68, Chiba: Institute of Developing Economies-JETRO.

Kurata, D. (2009), 'The structure of multi-regional economic interdependence in China' (Chugoku chiiki keizai – tachiikikan keizaisogo izonkozo), *Research Fellow Reports*, Mimeo (in Japanese).

Li, R. (2009), 'The effect of subprime lending crisis on Chinese financial market' (Cidai xinfengbao dui woguo jinrong xingshi de yingxiang fenxi), in Wang Changsheng (ed.), *Annual Report on China and the World Economic Development (Zhongguo yu shijie jingji fazhang baogao)*, Social Sciences Academic Press (in Chinese).

Meng, B. and C. Qu (2007), 'Application of the input–output decomposition technique to China's regional economies', *IDE Discussion Papers* No.102.

Okamoto, N. and T. Ihara (2005), *Spatial Structure and Regional Development in China? Interregional Input–Output Approach*, Basingstoke: Palgrave Macmillan.

Onishi, Y. (2009), 'Turning point of China economy and international financial crisis' (Tenki no chugoku keizai to kokusai kinyu kiki), *International Affairs (Kokusai Mondai)*, No. 581 (in Japanese).

J.I. Round (2001), 'Feedback effects in interregional input–output models: what have we learned?', in Michael L. Lahr and Erik Dietzenbacher (eds), *Input–Output Analysis: Frontiers and Extensions*, London: Palgrave Macmillan.

Yonemoto, K., R. Shibasaki and T. Watanabe (2008), 'Analyzing the effects of trade and development policies by transnational interregional input–output table between China and Japan' (Nitchu chiikikan azia kokusai sangyorenkan-hyo wo mochiita boueki kaihatsu seisaku no chiiki betu eikyo bunseki), *Technical Note of NILIM (Kokudo gijutsu seisaku sogo kenkyusyo shiryo)*, No. 451 (YSK-N-150) (in Japanese).

Zhang, Y. and L. Tao (2009), 'Estimation analysis on contribution of export to 2009 China economy' (Chukou dui woguo 2009 nian jingji gongxian de cesuan fenxi), *Economic Perspectives (Jingjixue Dongtai)*, Institute of Economics Chinese Academy of Social Sciences, No.3.

Zhang, Y., K. Zhao, X. Li and P. Zhang (2009), 'The impacts of the current investment and consumption stimulation policy to the economic growth' (Jinyibu kuoda neixu zhengce dui 'bao zengchang' de gongxian fenxi), *Reform (Gaige)*, *Chongqing Reform Magazine*, No. 5.

APPENDIX 6A.1: THE EFFECT OF THE 'HOUSEHOLD APPLIANCES TO THE COUNTRYSIDE' POLICY

The simulation result is shown in Figure 6A.1. Here, it is assumed that the demand of 50 billion Yuan for home electric appliances has been generated. It is obvious and self-evident that the regions in China are affected most significantly, yet the impacts on foreign countries, especially Japan and Korea+Taiwan, are also noticeable. The positive impact, however, is very small in magnitude, and accounts for less than 1 per cent of the entire effect of the total 4 trillion Yuan injection.

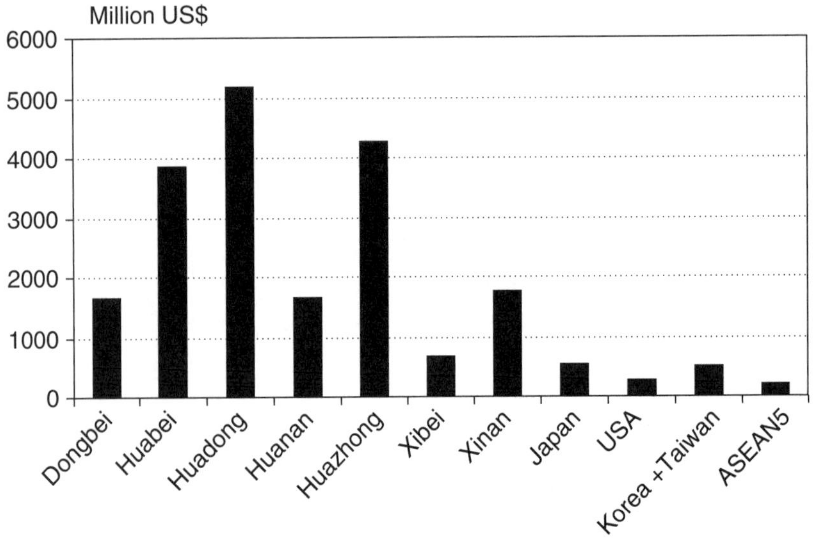

Source: Calculated by authors.

Figure 6A.1 Impact of 'Household appliances to the countryside'

7. An input–output analysis of post-crisis rebalancing in the Asia-Pacific economy[1]

Peter A. Petri

1. INTRODUCTION

Reducing international imbalances and achieving sustainable demand growth in surplus and deficit economies have emerged as key policy priorities in the wake of the 2008–2009 economic crisis. Global current account imbalances shrank in 2009 – due in part to increased US household savings and depressed investment – but are beginning to grow again in the recovery. Rebalancing is the main objective, for example, of the G-20 surveillance process launched in 2009.

Rebalancing raises policy challenges among and within countries. First, it requires changes in the composition of demand, with expenditures shifting from net exports to domestic absorption in surplus economies such as China, and from domestic absorption to net exports in deficit economies, including especially the United States. Such parallel shifts would reduce the scale of net international capital flows. Second, rebalancing requires adjustments in supply, with resources shifting from tradable goods sectors to non-tradable goods sectors in surplus economies and vice versa in deficit economies. Large adjustments of this kind could force changes in Asia's growth strategy from industrialization to, say, fostering services.

Relatively little work has been done so far on the implications of these adjustments. The Asian Development Bank (2009) traces the history of imbalances and explores the general case for rebalancing. The Pacific Economic Cooperation Council's Taskforce on the Global Economic Crisis examines the implications of rebalancing for the Asia-Pacific, and proposes a policy framework for coordinated initiatives (Petri, 2009). Prasad (2009) and a McKinsey Global Institute study (Woetzel et al., 2009) provide insight into the determinants of expenditures that need to change, and specifically on increasing consumption in China. Most work so far has addressed the demand side of rebalancing.

This study addresses the supply side, or the sectoral production shifts likely to be associated with rebalancing. Its unexpected finding is that the production implications of eliminating excessive international imbalances would be modest in both surplus and deficit countries and are unlikely to cause serious dislocations in either the United States or emerging Asia. A little known characteristic of production is responsible for these findings: different types of final demand ultimately result in similar production patterns due to 'structural overlap' in their induced input requirements. This does not mean that rebalancing will be easy to accomplish; spending reallocations are politically difficult. But it does mean that the production shifts involved in rebalancing will require incremental rather than revolutionary adjustments in output; they do not call for wholesale changes in the structure of production or investment.

The chapter is structured as follows. Section 2 reviews the economics of rebalancing. Section 3 develops a quantitative scenario for rebalancing expenditures. Although rebalancing involves economies around the world, the study addresses rebalancing in the Asia-Pacific, partly because this region includes the key protagonists in the drama – China, other Asian surplus economies, and the United States – and partly because an excellent data source, the Asian International Input–Output (AIO) table, permits tracing the implications of expenditure changes in the region. Section 4 develops a methodological approach for examining supply-side effects using the AIO dataset. Section 5 then applies the framework to examine the production implications of expenditure rebalancing, with emphasis on the role of structural overlaps in production. Section 6 presents conclusions.

2. THE ECONOMICS OF REBALANCING

The case for rebalancing rests, first, on building sustainable foundations for demand. As the crisis demonstrated, a decade of demand growth based on the exceptional appreciation of asset prices in the United States could not be sustained indefinitely. Another build-up of imbalances – driven, say, by continuing large-scale US government borrowing – would be likewise unsustainable and could risk renewed financial instability. Second, Asia's substantial net exports to the United States and Europe are unlikely to contribute 'their share' to Asia's future growth. These markets are expanding more slowly than Asia's, and it will be difficult to achieve further export penetration in them. Third, continued pressure to expand exports in these markets could intensify pressures for protectionism in the context of a weak global economy.

Rebalancing does not have to be handled entirely by policy. Even without interventions markets will resist unsustainable expenditures by anticipating and penalizing the build-up of imbalances. For example, *ex ante* expectations of imbalances may result in the depreciation of the US dollar and/or increase in dollar interest rates. These reactions would slow US spending by making it more expensive to borrow and by raising the cost of traded goods. Similar mechanisms could lead to opposite adjustments in surplus economies.[2] But under substantial uncertainty, market-driven adjustments could lead to costly volatility in exchange rates and asset prices.

Nevertheless, the pressure on market adjustments can be mitigated by policy. A recent Pacific Economic Cooperation Council study (Petri, 2009) suggests, for example, that China could increase government spending and income flows to households, and improve household safety nets, while the United States could adopt tighter regulation of consumer finance and restrain government spending. But such policies have long lead times and have to be deployed well in advance of the potential imbalances that they are designed to contain. The outlook for sustained growth – reasonable global growth with moderate US deficits – is uncertain. Two contrasting views are shown in Figure 7.1. The IMF (2009) forecasts that US deficits will remain under 3 per cent of GDP (a level widely considered sustainable) even as world growth approaches pre-crisis levels, but only if the United States adopts ambitious government targets for fiscal consolidation. Cline (2009) assumes unchanged US fiscal policy and projects that US current account deficits will grow to 5 per cent of US GDP by 2011 and to 16 per cent by 2030. That prospect argues for preemptive policy. This chapter does not address the debate about what policies need to be implemented; its contribution is to characterize the structural dislocations that might follow from them.

Rebalancing raises issues similar to those addressed in the 'transfer problem' debate, by Keynes (1919, 1929) and Ohlin (1929) and more recently by Krugman (1999) after the 1997–98 Asian financial crisis.[3] In those cases, as today, large changes were required in international payments. The literature is concerned with possible differences in the composition of expenditures between the transferor and transferee. If the expenditure bundles are the same, then the transfer will not affect relative prices. If they differ, then the transfer will generate additional pressures – secondary burdens – due to the adjustment of supply–demand balances and factor prices.

In its simplest form, the transfer problem is a disturbance in global markets for goods and services that are initially in equilibrium:

$$S(p) = D(p, y) \quad (7.1)$$

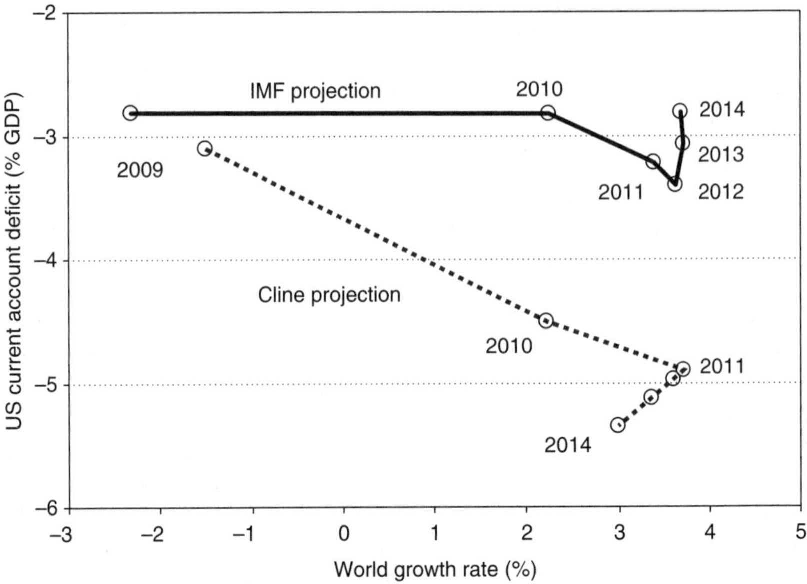

Sources: IMF, *WEO*, October 2009 and Cline (2009).

Figure 7.1 Not all paths lead to sustained growth

where

D = demand vector for goods (countries × goods)
S = supply vector for goods (countries × goods)
p = price vector (countries × goods)
y = real expenditures vector (countries)

We will introduce an expenditure disturbance dy into this equilibrium, which reduces national imbalances to 'sustainable' levels while leaving total expenditures, and by implication total GDP, unchanged in each country. This constraint implies that no further prices pressures would result from general under- or over-employment in any country. (It leaves open the possibility of positive or negative excess demands for specific factors, as examined below.) For simplicity, dy is treated as exogenously determined, although in practice price and production responses would feed back into expenditure effects. The finding that these responses turn out to be modest provides justification for omitting second-order effects.

A disturbance in y generates excess demands in product markets which induce price changes dp to restore equilibrium. Differentiating and solving yields:

$$dp = -(S_p - D_p)^{-1} D_y \, dy \tag{7.2}$$

where

D_p = derivatives of D with respect to prices
D_y = derivatives of D with respect to expenditure
S_p = derivatives of S with respect to prices
S_y = derivatives of S with respect to income

If demand is homogeneous in prices, there will be one fewer product market to clear than there are goods and only $n - 1$ prices will be determined, with the nth serving as the numeraire.

Below, we use the international input–output system to empirically analyse the impact matrix D_y that translates real expenditure changes into changes in detailed production sectors, as well as the particular market pressures $D_y \, dy$ that would result from a specific rebalancing scenario. We also calculate impacts on factors of production. We express effects as percentages of supply and demand in order to help the reader gauge the price adjustments that might result, although we do not actually estimate price changes.

3. SCENARIOS OF ASIA-PACIFIC EXPENDITURE SHIFTS

Recent global imbalances arose in the wake of the Asian financial crisis of 1997–98 and the 2000 US Internet bubble. The currency attacks of 1997–98 fuelled improvements in Asian current accounts and led to large-scale accumulation of foreign currency reserves. Whether as insurance or simply to drive export growth, Asia generated large capital flows to the United States and other countries. Meanwhile, the collapse of the US 'dot com' bubble and 9/11 led to highly accommodative US macroeconomic policies. The results included a sudden increase in asset prices and, as is now well understood, varied excesses in US financial markets.

The US current account deficit peaked at 7 per cent of GDP in 2006. At that time, US net savings began to rise and the dollar began to depreciate against the euro and other currencies – the Chinese RMB was also allowed to rise slowly – and the US current account deficit began to decline. But it exceeded 5 per cent of GDP on the eve of the crisis, a level most economists still considered unsustainable. In 2009, the deficit fell below 3 per cent of GDP, due to a drop in US investment and increased household savings. But in the meantime, the US government embarked on massive stimulus spending that pushed its budget deficit above 10 per cent of GDP. It remains to be seen how quickly this deficit will be reduced;

Table 7.1 Pre-crisis expenditures were not sustainable (2007 in US $billion)

	C	I	G	X	M	GDP	X − M	CA
AIO countries								
China	1216	1450	472	1342	1035	3445	308	372
Indonesia	275	108	36	127	110	436	17	11
Japan	2469	1057	786	772	699	4384	73	211
Korea	571	309	154	440	424	1049	16	6
Malaysia	85	41	23	206	168	187	38	29
Taiwan	227	83	47	283	254	385	29	33
Philippines	100	22	14	62	61	137	1	7
Singapore	64	35	16	384	332	168	53	39
Thailand	132	66	31	180	161	247	19	14
United States	9826	2289	2676	1656	2370	14078	−714	−727
Others								
European Union	8998	3359	3227	6147	6006	15724	141	−103
Middle East	589	347	203	811	556	1394	255	254
Rest of world	7283	3646	2126	4740	4588	13207	151	98
World	31835	12810	9810	17149	16763	54841	386	244

Source: CEIC, IMF World Economic Outlook database.

in the meantime, many observers predict that additional net international capital inflows will be required to fund the budget deficits as the recovery accelerates.

There is no precise 'sustainable' rate for US deficits. As the issuer of the world's dominant reserve currency, the United States can be expected to run a deficit to satisfy the rising demand for global liquidity. It is widely argued (c.f. Bergsten, 2009) that a 3 per cent deficit could be sustained for some time without risking currency instability or inflation. This rate is roughly the expected long-term growth rate of the US economy and implies that the US external debt to GDP ratio would not grow beyond 100 per cent. There is nothing compelling about this level of indebtedness; it may be higher than desirable, on one hand, and also lower than what might be required to meet global liquidity needs, on the other.

In any case, rebalancing is not about imbalances in the immediate aftermath of the crisis – which appear sustainable – but about those that would recur after economy activity returns to 'normal', say, to patterns similar to those of 2007. Table 7.1 therefore provides an overview of global imbalances as they stood in 2007, along with data on underlying expenditures on consumption (C), government (G), investment (I), exports (X) and imports (M). The table also shows the current account deficit (CA), which equals net exports plus net factor payments from abroad. (Note that the table shows a surplus for the world as a whole, reflecting statistical inconsistencies.)

As Table 7.1 shows, global current account imbalances were dominated by surpluses in China, Japan and the Middle East (totalling $837 billion, or 9 per cent of GDP) and the deficit in the United States ($727 billion, or 5 per cent of GDP). What would it have taken to reduce such imbalances to sustainable levels? We next develop a scenario based on three assumptions: (i) a target for sustainable current account balances for the United States; (ii) rules for allocating the change in the US deficit internationally to changes in the surpluses of other economies; and (iii) rules for allocating the current account changes within each economy to specific expenditure categories.

1. *Target for imbalances.* We assume that the excessive US deficit should be no higher than 3 per cent of GDP ($422 billion). This means that the deficit has to be reduced by $304 billion from the 2007 actual current account deficit of $727 billion.
2. *International allocations.* We allocate the US deficit reduction to surplus countries based on the share of each country or region in the sum of surpluses. (Although the world as a whole also has a surplus, presumably due to statistical inconsistencies, this total is assumed to stay unchanged, and adjustments are allocated to surplus countries only.) The scenario assigns China and Japan 35 per cent and 20 per cent of the rebalancing effort, respectively, based on their shares of 2007 surpluses, translating into expenditure increases of $106 billion and $60 billion, respectively. The other seven Asian countries of the AIO system are allocated an additional 12 per cent. The European Union had an overall deficit in 2007, but this masked large internal imbalances. In this scenario, the European Union is excluded from the global exercise, assuming that its rebalancing efforts occur within Europe.
3. *Expenditure allocations.* Within each country or region, we allocate changes in total national absorption to specific expenditure categories based on common prescriptions for how countries might best adjust expenditures (say, as summarized in Petri, 2010). In China, for example, discussion has focused on raising the share of consumption in GDP, which is unusually low. In the United States, we assume that absorption comes primarily from consumption and government expenditures. And in South-east Asia, where investment has not returned to pre-1997 levels, we assign a large share of rebalancing to

Table 7.2 Assumptions for rebalancing global expenditures (% of US excess deficit allocated to expenditure categories)

Rationale of change	Economies affected	C	I	G
Rebalancing objective	Shift expenditures from deficit economy to surplus economies	$304 billion		
Deficit economy	United States	−60%	−20%	−20%
Surplus economies with adequate investment	China, Japan, Korea, Taiwan, Singapore	+60%	+20%	+20%
Surplus economies with low investment	Indonesia, Malaysia, Philippines, Thailand	+20%	+60%	+20%

Table 7.3 Scenario changes to 2007 expenditures (US $billion)

	C	I	G	X	M	GDP	X − M
AIO countries							
China	63.1	21.0	21.0	−52.6	52.6	–	−105.2
Indonesia	0.6	0.6	1.8	−1.5	1.5	–	−3.0
Japan	35.9	12.0	12.0	−29.9	29.9	–	−59.9
Korea	0.9	0.3	0.3	−0.8	0.8	–	−1.5
Malaysia	1.6	1.6	4.9	−4.1	4.1	–	−8.2
Taiwan	5.7	1.9	1.9	−4.7	4.7	–	−9.4
Philippines	0.4	0.4	1.3	−1.1	1.1	–	−2.1
Singapore	6.7	2.2	2.2	−5.6	5.6	–	−11.2
Thailand	0.8	0.8	2.4	−2.0	2.0	–	−4.0
United States	−182.4	−60.8	−60.8	152.0	−152.0	–	304.0
Others							
European Union	–	–	–	–	–	–	–
Middle East	37.3	21.9	12.8	−36.0	36.0	–	−72.0
Rest of World	15.5	7.8	4.5	−13.9	13.9	–	−27.8
World	−13.8	9.8	4.4	–	–	–	–

investment. With respect to trade, we assume that half of the rebalancing required would involve export changes and half import changes. (This is equivalent to assuming equal elasticities of demand in exports and imports.)

These assumptions, summarized in Table 7.2, result in *dy*, a country- and expenditure-specific pattern of shifts consistent with global rebalancing. The resulting changes to expenditures are shown in Table 7.3.

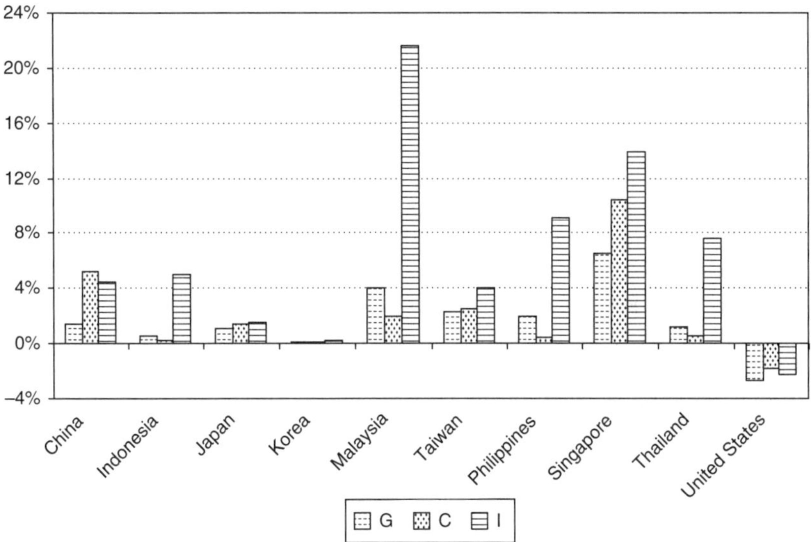

Figure 7.2 Expenditure changes sufficient for rebalancing (% of 2007 levels)

The striking result of this exercise is that it suggests quantitatively modest changes in most countries (Figure 7.2). In China, for example, the scenario increases consumption by only 5 per cent over its 2007 level – a change that would normally take place in less than one year given China's rapid growth path.[4] The proportional changes are smaller in Japan, the second largest surplus country. They are absolutely large only in Malaysia and Singapore because these economies have large surpluses relative to GDP, and because the scenario envisions a focus on investment, which is a relatively small expenditure category. In the United States, the scenario calls for 2 per cent reductions in US consumption expenditures and government spending. These results are consistent with other general equilibrium studies that also find modest overall effects (Kawai and Zhai, 2009). International imbalances that may have serious destabilizing impacts on financial markets are not large relative to major expenditure categories in large economies.

4. METHODOLOGY FOR IMPACT ANALYSIS

The expenditure shifts envisioned by the rebalancing scenario would lead to latent disequilibrium in product and factor markets. To study these, we examine induced production effects that operate through multiple layers of intermediate inputs. The methodology is based on the Asian International Input–Output (AIO) table, a comprehensive dataset for 10 major Asia-Pacific economies including the United States (IDE, 2006). Developed by Japan's IDE-JETRO institute, the AIO combines trade statistics with national input–output systems to construct detailed linkages throughout the fragmented production system of the Asia-Pacific (Athukorala, 2005). The AIO is currently available for 2000. It will be important to update the present findings, but for reasons discussed below, they are likely to become stronger with more recent information.

The AIO identifies transactions among 76 sectors in 10 economies, represented in a 760 × 760 matrix. In addition, the system traces sector-specific demand by each of seven types of final users, and sector-specific value-added generated by four types of factors of production. Most transactions are within economies (on or near the diagonal blocks of the international table) but the system also incorporates detailed international transactions (say, sales of the Malaysian electronics industry to the Korean machinery industry). The AIO is structured around the identity:

$$x^r = Z^{rs}\underline{u} + F^{rs}\underline{u} \tag{7.3}$$

where

x^r = output of goods produced in country r (each x^r is a 76-industry vector)

Z^{rs} = sales of goods produced in r to producers in s (each Z^{rs} is a 76×76 matrix)

F^{rs} = sales of goods produced in r to final users in s (each F^{rs} is a 76×7 matrix).

$\underline{u}$ = aggregator (column of ones)

Based on the transactions data, coefficients can be derived for inputs into production and into categories of final demand:

$$a_{ij}^{rs} = x_{ij}^{rs}/x_j^s \text{ and } b_{ik}^{rs} = f_{ik}^{rs}/y_k^s \tag{7.3}$$

where

a_{ij}^{rs} = input of i produced in r per unit of output j produced in s

b_{ik}^{rs} = purchase of i produced in r per unit of expenditure k in s

y_k^s = *expenditure* k in country s

By assembling these coefficients into region-wide matrixes, we can rewrite equation (7.3) as:

$$x = Ax + By \tag{7.4}$$

where
$A = \{a_{ij}^{rs}\}$, $B = \{b_{ik}^{rs}\}$, $x = \{x_i^r\}$ and $y = \{y_i^s\}$.
and solve for output levels:

$$x = (I - A)^{-1}By \tag{7.5}$$

Imports and exports are transactions that take place between different countries of the system, that is, *off* the diagonal blocks of the input–output system that capture intra-economy transactions. Trade flows among countries are given by:

$$t^{rs} = A^{rs}x^s + B^{rs}y^s \textit{ for } r \neq s \tag{7.6}$$

where
t^{rs} = vector of exports from country r to country s
Bilateral trade flow vectors summed across partners generate total import and export vectors m^s and e^s.

Factor demand[5] consequences can be derived using value-added coefficients:

$$u_{kj}^r = w_{kj}^r / x_j^r \tag{7.7}$$

where
u_{kj}^r = input of value-added k per unit of output of j produced in r
w_{kj}^r = value-added k generated in the production of j in r
which, when post-multiplied by output changes, yield value-added impacts:

$$v = U\,x \tag{7.8}$$

where
$U = \{u_{kj}^r\}$, block diagonal matrix of $k \cdot j$ value-added blocks for countries
$v = \{v_k^r\}$, stacked vector of value-added vectors of countries

Equations (7.5), (7.6) and (7.8) represent a tool kit for analysing the consequences of expenditure changes (see Table 7.4). Each contains a reduced form 'impact matrix' with rows for affected markets and columns for categories of final demand. Differences among the columns of these matrixes will determine the extent to which expenditure shifts affect specific markets.

Table 7.4 Summary of impact computations

Variable affected	Eqn.	Impact matrix	Consequence analysed
Industries	7.5	$(I - A)^{-1}B$	Effects on goods demands
Imports	7.6	$A^* \Lambda^r Q_x + \Lambda^r B^*$	Effects on net trade
Exports	7.6	$A^* Q_x + B^*$	
Value-added	7.8	UQ_x	Effects on factor demands

Note: Λ^r = is an aggregrator matrix consisting of zeroes, except for an identity matrix corresponding to the sectors of country *r*.

5. STRUCTURAL IMPLICATIONS OF REBALANCING

Using the scenario of section 3 and impact equations summarized in Table 7.4, we calculated the direct and indirect production implications of rebalancing for 76 industries and 4 value-added sectors in the 10 AIO economies. We present only a summary of the results; details are available on request.

5.1 Sectoral Consequences

Since global demand is fixed under the rebalancing scenario, the distribution of percentage changes in demand in the 760 sectors (76 sectors in 10 economies) is clustered around zero (see Figure 7.3). What is surprising is just how tight the cluster is; two-thirds of all sectors change by less than 1 per cent. Only 12 sectors (2 per cent) show an absolute change larger than 5 per cent. Most sectors in most countries – even those in countries facing relatively large expenditure shifts, such as Malaysia and Singapore – appear to be unaffected by rebalancing. The explanation for the stability of the output mix must be sought in the similarity of the production requirements of the different kinds of demand affected by rebalancing. We will return to analysing these similarities in a later section.

One general pattern that emerges from the results is that the industries that expand (shrink) in countries where household expenditures rise (fall) are those that produce goods such as beverages and tobacco, with few applications outside consumer demand. The industries that expand (shrink) in countries where investment expenditures rise (fall) are those, such as construction, with few markets except for investment. Most industries apparently do not fall into these extremes. As Table 7.5 shows, positive changes appear in consumption-related sectors in China, in investment-related

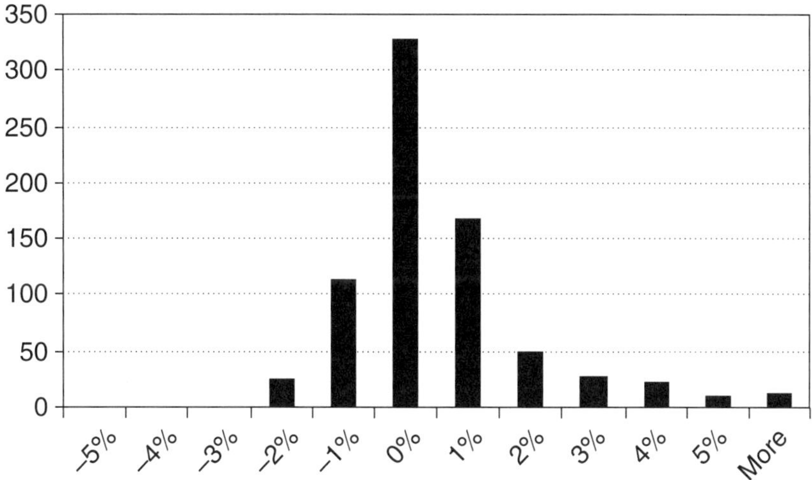

Source: Computations explained in the text.

Figure 7.3 Production effects of rebalancing (number of sectors by size of change)

sectors in Malaysia, and in export-related sectors in the United States. Conversely, negative changes appear in export-related sectors in China and Malaysia, and in sectors such as administration, health and education, which serve consumers and government in the United States.

A second general pattern that emerges is that tradable sectors expand in deficit countries and decline in surplus countries. This relationship is also far from direct, since a sector's reaction is also affected by the kinds of demand it serves. We defined a tradability index for each sector based on the ratio of the region's exports and imports to total regional demand. Plotting this index against output changes (Figure 7.4) shows that the more tradable a sector is, the more likely it is to shrink in China, and to expand in the United States as a result of rebalancing. But the changes are a few percentage points or less; in other words, even in highly tradable sectors the impacts are muted.

A third finding is that rebalancing generally favours labour in economies that shift from net exports to consumption (surplus economies with adequate initial investment, such as China and Japan), and capital in economies that shift from consumption and government expenditures to investment or net exports (deficit economies, and surplus economies with inadequate initial investment). It is worth noting that the income effects generated by these production effects would reinforce the objectives of

Table 7.5 Largest increases and decreases in demand by sector (% changes)

	China		Malaysia		United States	
Largest increases	Building construction	3.6	Building construction	16.5	Leather products	5.1
	Other construction	3.6	Other construction	9.4	Motor cycles	4.6
					Hotels	4.2
	Tobacco	3.5	Cement products	9.2	Iron ore	4.2
	Beverages	2.9	Public administration	4.0	Other transport eqp.	4.1
	Milled grain products	2.9	Non-metallic mining	3.9		
Largest decreases	Other electronics	−3.6	Metalworking machinery	−1.9	Public administration	−2.7
	Semiconductors	−3.5	Specialized machinery	−1.8	Other construction	−2.3
	Knitting	−3.1				
	Made-up textiles	−3.0	Synthetic resins	−1.8	Education and research	−2.0
			Boilers, engines	−1.7		
	Timber	−2.9	Other electronics	−1.7	Building construction	−1.8
					Health services	−1.8

Source: Computations explained in the text.

rebalancing by increasing household incomes in surplus countries and by reducing household incomes in deficit countries.

Factor demands are affected because consumption and government expenditures typically have larger service components and are more labour-intensive than investment or export expenditures. But because factor effects are based on small changes in output mix, the production implications are ultimately small. For China, for example, the results show the compensation of employees rising by only 0.4 per cent of the base level. For the US, the effect works in reverse, but employee compensation would fall by only 0.1 per cent of its base level. Table 7.6 summarizes factor requirement differences across expenditure types; more than other measures of impact, these intensity measures vary across economies.[6]

5.2 Structural Overlap

Why are most production effects so muted? The answer to this question lies in the similarities of the production effects of different expenditures.

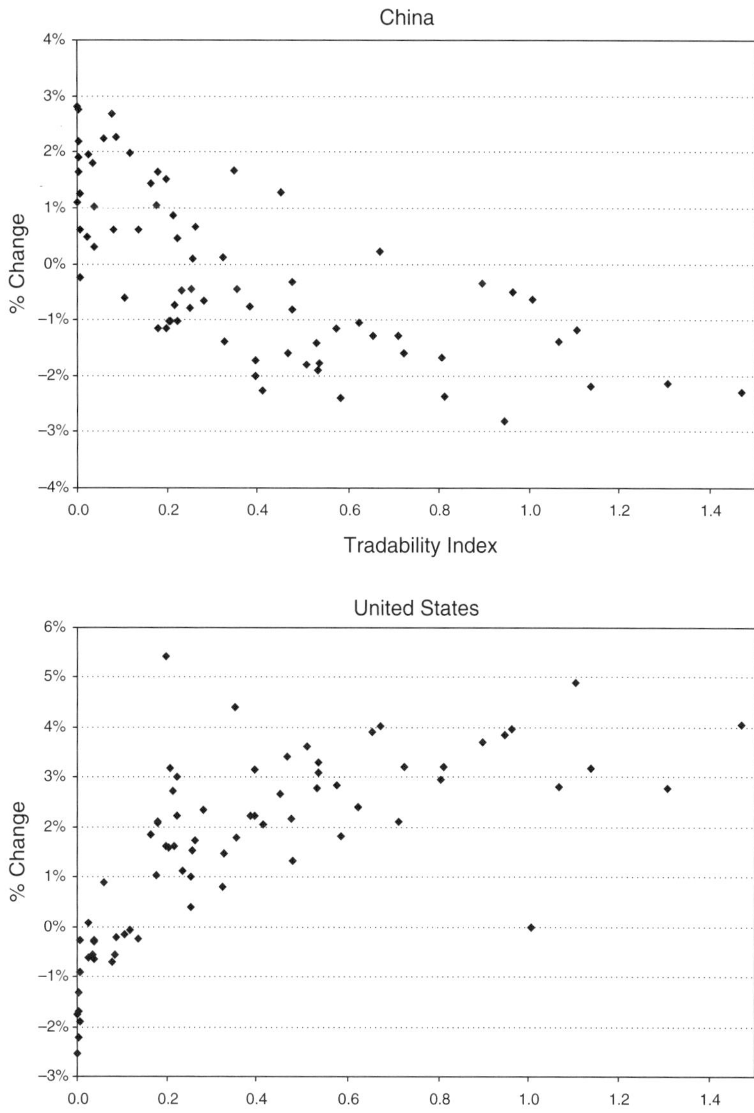

Note: Tradability index = (regional exports + imports)/regional demand.

Figure 7.4 Production changes due to rebalancing and tradability

Table 7.6 Factor demand effects of rebalancing

	Compensation	Surplus	Depreciation	Tax-subsidy
China	0.4%	−0.4%	−0.1%	−0.3%
Indonesia	0.2%	−0.3%	−0.1%	−0.1%
Japan	0.0%	0.0%	0.0%	−0.1%
Korea	0.1%	0.0%	0.0%	0.0%
Malaysia	1.1%	−0.6%	0.0%	0.0%
Taiwan	0.2%	0.0%	−0.2%	0.0%
Philippines	0.0%	0.0%	0.0%	0.0%
Singapore	0.9%	−0.1%	−0.3%	1.0%
Thailand	0.3%	−0.1%	−0.1%	−0.2%
United States	−0.1%	0.1%	0.0%	−0.1%

Source: Computations explained in the text.

To quantify the similarities among expenditure categories, we develop an 'overlap index' to measure the share of production that is common to different types of demand. The overlap is defined simply as the share of the total induced production that stays in place – in the same detailed production sector – if $1 of expenditure is shifted from one expenditure category to another:

$$p^r_{jk} = \sum_l \min\,(v^r_{lj}, v^r_{lk}) \tag{7.9}$$

where

p^r_{jk} = overlap of value-added induced by demand categories j and k in country r

v^r_{lj} = value-added induced in sector l by $1 demand in category j in country r

The maximum overlap is 1 (when $v^r_{lj} = v^r_{lk}$). The actual overlap will be determined by similarities in the composition of direct demand (final demand), and by similarities in the composition of indirect demand – the 'deeper' inputs required to produce various final goods and services. Even if consumption and investment involve a different final product, both may generate similar induced input requirements – for example, for inputs such as energy, primary materials, financial services, and other business services. Sectors that produce such deeper inputs would remain unaffected as demand shifts from consumption to investment or vice versa.

Overlap indexes are reported for pairs of expenditures in China and the United States for each economy in Table 7.7. For example, the total overlap index for shifting expenditures from Chinese exports to Chinese

Table 7.7 Structural overlap indexes for expenditure shifts

A. China

From: \ To:		C	G	I	X	M
C	Total		0.46	0.47	0.57	0.52
	Direct		0.09	0.10	0.29	0.22
	Indirect		0.67	0.67	0.78	0.73
G	Total	0.44		0.39	0.39	0.38
	Direct	0.08		0.00	0.00	0.00
	Indirect	0.70		0.77	0.74	0.73
I	Total	0.52	0.45		0.61	0.65
	Direct	0.15	0.00		0.16	0.21
	Indirect	0.58	0.64		0.74	0.77
X	Total	0.63	0.44	0.61		0.77
	Direct	0.40	0.00	0.14		0.55
	Indirect	0.71	0.65	0.77		0.87
M	Total	0.56	0.43	0.64	0.76	
	Direct	0.28	0.00	0.18	0.51	
	Indirect	0.69	0.66	0.84	0.91	

B. United States

From: \ To:		C	G	I	X	M
C	Total		0.34	0.52	0.59	0.47
	Direct		0.11	0.27	0.34	0.16
	Indirect		0.73	0.82	0.91	0.86
G	Total	0.32		0.30	0.31	0.31
	Direct	0.10		0.07	0.07	0.07
	Indirect	0.84		0.82	0.88	0.88
I	Total	0.57	0.35		0.69	0.61
	Direct	0.35	0.11		0.44	0.31
	Indirect	0.71	0.61		0.90	0.92
X	Total	0.60	0.34	0.63		0.76
	Direct	0.41	0.10	0.40		0.56
	Indirect	0.72	0.61	0.83		0.93
M	Total	0.49	0.34	0.58	0.78	
	Direct	0.22	0.11	0.31	0.62	
	Indirect	0.66	0.58	0.81	0.90	

Source: Computations based on the AIO, explained in text.

consumption is 63 per cent, indicating that nearly two-thirds of the value-added induced by exports would remain in place if expenditures on exports were replaced by expenditures on consumption. In the United States, the shift from consumption to exports would leave 59 per cent of the related value-added unaffected. Coefficients in other countries are similar.[7]

Table 7.7 further reports overlap indexes for two aspects of total production, production for final demand directly, and production induced indirectly, via the layers of input requirements tracked by the input–output system. This decomposition clearly shows that overlap indexes are large due to similarities in indirect production. For example, the direct requirements of Chinese exports and consumption have only a 40 per cent overlap, while the indirect inputs generated by them have a 70 per cent overlap. This difference is even greater for other pairs of demands; for example the direct overlap between Chinese consumption and government expenditures is only 9 per cent, but the indirect overlap is 67 per cent. In this case the total overlap works out to a significant 46 per cent. A general rule of thumb is that about half of value-added generated by a unit of final demand is direct and half is indirect.

These results suggest that the structure of the production system is quite 'modular': final sectors represent a narrow production stage that combines relatively similar baskets of inputs from upstream general inputs. This process may well have strengthened over time, with value-added shifting from direct into indirect production. Modularization is likely to reflect increased specialization, driven by economies of scale and international trade. Economies of scale reduce the cost of inputs that are common to multiple downstream uses. International trade, in turn, concentrates domestic production into a relatively small subset of inputs – those in which the economy has comparative advantage – while other, more exotic inputs are imported. Both processes increase demand for common, general inputs. As these processes unfold, production becomes more flexible, permitting final expenditures to shift with limited impact on upstream production.

To be sure, the method used here to calculate overlap indexes is sensitive to the level of sectoral aggregation in the underlying data; the calculated coefficients would be smaller if the analysis distinguished among more than 76 industries. But such additional disaggregation is not necessarily meaningful. A highly detailed classification would separate activities with substantially similar production efforts, for example based on similar technologies, skills and institutions. More refined overlap analysis might account for substitution in production by calculating partial overlaps, with sectors producing different but similar products (which can therefore shift from one output to another) treated as partially overlapping from the viewpoint of expenditure shifts.

Table 7.8 Non-tradable production by type of expenditure (% of value-added)

	C	G	I	X	M
China	0.36	0.69	0.44	0.17	0.17
Indonesia	0.32	0.80	0.53	0.11	0.18
Japan	0.57	0.86	0.53	0.22	0.25
Korea	0.62	0.90	0.61	0.22	0.29
Malaysia	0.57	0.89	0.56	0.19	0.19
Taiwan	0.63	0.93	0.52	0.26	0.31
Philippines	0.44	0.95	0.72	0.23	0.26
Singapore	0.65	0.91	0.68	0.31	0.37
Thailand	0.28	0.86	0.36	0.17	0.15
United States	0.65	0.90	0.56	0.30	0.23

Source: Computations explained in the text.

A related finding is that production relies heavily on non-traded goods and services, even in open economies. We used the tradability index introduced above and classified 15 of the 76 sectors as non-tradable (T) using a 5 per cent cut-off for the trade to demand ratio. Although few in number, the non-tradable sectors include some of the largest in a typical economy, consisting of sectors such as construction, education, real estate, utilities, finance and other business services. (Of course some trade takes place in these sectors but typically accounts for only a few percent of total trade.) The share of these non-tradable sectors in value-added generated by different types of expenditures is reported in Table 7.8. Notably even exports and imports incorporate significant non-tradable inputs.

Theoretical models typically draw sharp distinctions between tradable and non-tradable production and on spending in different expenditure categories. But reality is blurred: traded goods have significant non-traded components, and different kinds of final demand share similar input requirements. Thus production shifts have more muted implications than one might infer from theory. Indeed, the changes presented here are likely to be *overstated*, since the potential sectoral and factor imbalances that are derived from an input–output model (a model that does not explicitly account for price changes) would be dampened by price adjustments. For example, if consumption increases in China raised the prices of services, then consumers would likely turn to other consumption goods – say, to household electronics, which are likely to be in excess supply due to reductions in exports – with falling relative prices.

6. CONCLUSIONS

Economists broadly agree that the world economy needs to rebalance expenditures to forestall the reemergence of international imbalances. Implementing this strategy will require demand changes that affect the distribution of income and expenditures, and supply changes that facilitate reallocations of resources. This study addressed the latter.

Using a simple rebalancing scenario for 10 Asia-Pacific economies, we find that the expenditure changes required to achieve sustainable current account deficits are modest relative to the large domestic expenditures of Asia-Pacific economies. The proportional changes would be greatest in smaller South-east Asian economies, where investment levels are envisioned returning to levels similar to those before the 1997–98 crisis. The changes would be much smaller in the largest protagonists of the rebalancing drama – China, Japan and the United States.

The Asian International Input–Output table provides a framework for examining the ripple effects of these shifts through 76 sectors in 10 Asia-Pacific countries. It turns out that differences among expenditure categories become less significant the deeper one looks into the production structure: even quite different final goods and services are produced from relatively similar ('modular') inputs. Across a wide range of end products, production appears to rely intensively on inputs of non-traded goods and services, and on products in which the home economy specializes (with other inputs more often imported). Thus expenditure shifts tend to affect mainly on a 'top' layer of production and have strongly overlapping overall production effects.

To be sure, the impact of rebalancing is affected by the *kind* of domestic absorption that is targeted. If rebalancing targets investment, for example, then it will induce tradable-goods production, perhaps even more so than the net exports that it replaces. The induced production effects of investment may help to explain, for example, why Chinese industry experienced a very rapid recovery in 2009 despite the sluggish performance of exports. If instead rebalancing targets government spending, then it will generate demand for non-traded goods and employment. Had government-oriented absorption been more actively targeted by the Chinese stimulus programmes (to some extent of course it was), for example, it might have made larger contributions to employment and consumption spending, but smaller contributions to the recovery of firms hurt by export cutbacks.

The results are notable for what they fail to show. However important $300 billion is to particular exporters and importers in China and the United States, this order of expenditure is not large compared to consumption, investment or government expenditures in the Asia-Pacific region. Moreover, overlap effects limit the impacts of shifts in expenditures in most industries and countries. The politics of rebalancing may be daunting, but its production implications appear to be manageable. Policy makers should be comforted knowing that the expenditure adjustments required are achievable without serious dislocations in industrial structure or patterns of economic growth.

NOTES

1. The author is grateful to Manjola Tase for excellent research assistance. The chapter addresses issues raised in preliminary form in the report of the PECC Taskforce on the Global Economic Crisis (Petrin, 2010).
2. If the foreign exchange rate is fixed, as in China, the mechanisms would have to work through other channels, including a rise in the general price level. These effects would likely take longer and would also introduce additional distortions.
3. Krugman noted that 'despite the evident centrality of the transfer problem to what actually happened to Asia, this issue has been remarkably absent from formal models.' (Krugman, 1999, p. 463).
4. The change calculated here is an increment in the trend line. If reached over three years, for example, it would mean that Chinese consumption would have to grow 1.7 per cent more rapidly than GDP, or, say, by 11.7 per cent rather than 10 per cent.
5. Under AIO conventions, value-added is defined as 'domestic' rather than 'national' and thus measures value-added generated in country r regardless of the producer's nationality.
6. These variations may reflect in part measurement differences, since input–output tables measure factor demand in terms of employee compensation rather than labour income. Some 'operating surplus' is in fact labour income, especially in lower-income economies.
7. Even small countries have large overlap coefficients, suggesting that their *domestic* production requirements are similar. They may of course have very different imported input requirements (which are typically greater in smaller economies than in large ones) that do not affect the structure of domestic production.

REFERENCES

Asian Development Bank (2009), *Asian Development Outlook*, various issues.

Athukorala, P. (2005), 'Product fragmentation and trade patterns in East Asia', *Asian Economic Papers*, **4** (3), 1–27.

Bergsten, F.C. (2009), 'The dollar and the deficits', *Foreign Affairs*, November.

Cline, W.R. (2009), 'Long-term fiscal imbalances, US external liabilities, and future living standards', in F. Bergsten (ed.), *The Long-Term International Economic Position of the United States*, Special Report 20, Washington: Peterson Institute for International Economics.

Corsetti, G., M. Philippe and P. Paolo Presenti (2008), 'Varieties and the transfer problem: the extensive margin of current account adjustment', *EUI Working Paper* RSCAS 2008/01, Florence: European University Institute.

De Gregorio, J., G. Alberto and W. Holger (1994), 'International evidence on tradables and nontradables inflation', *European Economic Review*, 38, June, 1225–44.

Dornbusch, R. (1983), 'Real interest rates, home goods and optimal external borrowing', *Journal of Political Economy*, **91**, February, 141–53.

Institute of Developing Economies (2006), *Asian International Input–Output Table 2000*, (2 volumes), Tokyo: Institute of Developing Economies-Japan External Trade Organization.

International Monetary Fund (2009), *World Economic Outlook*, various issues.

Johnson, H.G. (1975), 'The classical transfer problem: an alternative formulation', *Economica*, **42** (165) (1929), February, 20–31.

Kawai, M. and F. Zhai (2009), 'China–Japan–United States integration and global economic crisis: a dynamic general equilibrium analysis', presented at People's Republic of China (PRC), Japan, and the United States: Deeper Integration Workshop, 28 May, Tokyo.

Keynes, J.M. (1919), *The Economic Consequences of the Peace*, London: Macmillan.

Keynes, J.M. (1929), 'The German transfer problem'; "The Reparation Problem: A Discussion". II. A Rejoinder'; 'Views on The Transfer Problem. III. A Reply', *Economic Journal*, **39**, March, pp. 1–7; June, pp. 172–8; September, pp. 404–8.

Krauss, M.B. (1975), 'Income redistribution and the transfer problem', *Economica*, **42** (168), November, 438–42.

Krugman, P. (1999), 'Balance sheets, the transfer problem and financial crises', *International Tax and Public Finance*, **6** (4), November.

Masson, P., K. Jeroen and J. Horne (1994), 'Net foreign assets and international adjustment: the United States, Japan and Germany', *Journal of International Money and Finance*, **13**, 27–40.

McDougall, I.A. (1965), 'Non-traded goods and the transfer problem', *The Review of Economic Studies*, **32** (1) January, 67–84.

Mori, T. and H. Sasaki (2007), 'Interdependence of production and income in Asia-Pacific economies: an international input–output approach', *Working Paper* No. 07-E-26, Tokyo: Bank of Japan.

Ohlin, B. (1929), 'The reparation problem: a discussion. I. Transfer Difficulties, Real and Imagined'; 'Mr. Keynes' views on the Transfer Problem. II. A Rejoinder', *Economic Journal*, **39**, pp. 172–82; 400–404.

Petri, P.A. (ed.) (2010), *Inclusive, Balanced, Sustained Growth in the Asia Pacific*, Report of the PECC Taskforce on the Global Economic Crisis, Singapore: Institute of Southeast Asian Studies.

Prasad, E.S. (2009), 'Rebalancing growth in Asia', *NBER Working Paper* 15169, Cambridge: National Bureau of Economic Research.

Pula, G. and T.A. Peltonen (2009), 'Has emerging Asia decoupled? An analysis of production and trade linkages using the Asian International Input–Output Table', *Working Paper* No. 993, Frankfurt: European Central Bank.

Samuelson, P.A. (1954), 'The transfer problem and transport costs: the terms of trade when impediments are absent', *Economic Journal*, **62**, 278–304.

Woetzel, J., J. Devan, R. Dobbs, A. Eichner, S. Negri and M. Rowland (2009), 'If you've got it, spend it: unleashing the Chinese customer', August, Seoul: McKinsey Global Institute.

8. Explanatory notes

Satoshi Inomata

I. A QUICK GUIDE TO THE INTERNATIONAL INPUT–OUTPUT ANALYSES

1. What is an Input–Output Table?

An input–output (I–O) table is a map of an economy, which compactly depicts all the flows of goods and services for a given period of time (usually one year), using recorded transaction values between industries. Its image is just like a piece of textile, woven from woof and warp. The woof (horizontal thread) is called a 'row', and the warp (vertical thread) is called a 'column'. In the I–O framework the rows represent the supply sectors of goods and services while the columns are demand sectors, and their intersection gives the value of transactions made between these two industries.

Table 8.1 shows a schematic image of an I–O table, of a hypothetical economy with only three industrial sectors: 'Machinery' manufacturing industry, 'Steel' manufacturing industry, and 'Transport' service industry. For example, looking at the intersection between the 'Steel' in the rows and the 'Machinery' in the columns, the value of '1600' indicates that the 'Machinery' industry purchased steel products from the 'Steel' industry in a quantity of 1600 units. We may consider the case where a car manufacturer uses steel to produce car bodies. Subsequently, if we look at the intersection between 'Transport (row)' and 'Machinery (column)', the value is '400', which shows that the 'Machinery' sector purchased transport services in a quantity of 400; say, the car manufacturer pays for the delivery of steel to its own factories.

Accordingly, goods and services are processed through the progressive commitment of various industries, in which the product of one industry is used as an intermediate input of others. This segment of the table, called the Intermediate transactions matrix, presents the entire nexus of transactions between industries, and forms the core apparatus of input–output analyses, as shown later.

Table 8.1 Input–output table (three industrial sectors)

		Intermediate transactions			Final demand				
		Machinery	Steel	Transport	Con-sumption	Investment	Export	Import	Total Output
Intermediate transactions	Machinery	800	1800	200	600	400	300	−100	4000
	Steel	1600	600	500	0	350	200	−250	3000
	Transport	400	300	900	350	50	0	0	2000
Value-added	Wages	800	200	250					
	Profits	250	50	100					
	Depreciation	100	30	40					
	Taxes	50	20	10					
	Total Input	4000	3000	2000					

Apart from Intermediate transactions, an I–O table integrates certain other segments, which closely correspond to the specification of national accounts.

Final demand

After the sequential processing through supply-use production chains between industries, the final/finished products are consumed by households or the government, used for investment purposes, or exported overseas. The terminal sectors that absorb these final/finished products are called Final demand sectors, which generally include 'private (households + non-profit organizations) consumption expenditure', 'government consumption expenditure', 'fixed capital formation', 'net increase in inventory', and 'net exports'.

Value-added

In addition to payments for intermediate goods and services, productive activities involve various costs such as wages and taxes. The payment to the production factors that are not reproduced by industries are recorded in Value-added items, generally comprising 'employee income (wages)' paid for labour, 'operating surplus (profit)' paid into capital, 'capital depreciation', which is an imputed yearly payment to machines, 'indirect taxes' upon the production of goods and services, and 'subsidies (deduction items)'.

Control totals (total input/total output)

The column end of the I–O table shows the value of total supply (= total input: value of intermediate input + Value-added) of each industry, and at the row end lies the value of total demand (= total output: value of Intermediate demand + value of Final demand) for each product. Since total supply equals total demand in a static framework, the column and row totals for a given industry should match exactly. These total values are used as 'footholds' to balance the figures between rows and columns in the process of constructing the I–O table, and are hence also dubbed 'Control totals'.[1]

2. Extension to International Input–Output Tables

Table 8.2 presents an image of the bilateral international I–O table between China and the USA. Indeed, an international I–O table is nothing but a patchwork of the pieces taken from each national I–O table, and can be read in exactly the same manner as for a national table; the rows and columns are supply and demand sectors respectively, and there are segments that correspond to Intermediate transactions (A), Final demands

Table 8.2 A schematic image of the China–US International Input–Output Table

		Intermediate demand CHINA			Intermediate demand USA			Final demand CHINA		Final demand USA		Export by country of destination			
		Mach-inery	Steel	Trans-port	Mach-inery	Steel	Trans-port	Con-sumption	Invest-ment	Con-sumption	Invest-ment	Export to Japan	Export to EU	Export to . . .	Export to RoW
CHINA	Machinery														
	Steel		A^{CC}			A^{CU}		F^{CC}		F^{CU}		L^{CJ}	L^{CO}	$L^{C..}$	L^{CW}
	Transport														
USA	Machinery														
	Steel		A^{UC}			A^{UU}		F^{UC}		F^{UU}		L^{UJ}	L^{UO}	$L^{U..}$	L^{UW}
	Transport														
REST OF THE WORLD	Machinery														
	Steel		A^{WC}			A^{WU}		F^{WC}		F^{WU}					
	Transport														
Value-added	Wages														
	Profits														
	Depreciation		V^{C}			V^{U}									
	Taxes														

(F) and Value-added (V). In addition, there is also a set of export columns for selected countries of destination (L).

The superscripts appended to each symbol show the direction of flows of goods and services for a particular transaction. They are the national code of the country of origin (to the left) and the country of destination (to the right). In this example, 'C' is for China and 'U' is for the USA. So, the segment 'CC' indicates domestic transactions within China, and 'UU' represents those within the USA. The off-diagonal segments are what we call 'import matrices'. The segment 'CU', for example, corresponds to the import matrix of the USA for goods and services produced in China. Therefore, the intersection 'C-Steel × U-Machinery' includes the transaction of an American car manufacturer purchasing steel products from China. The table also has the import matrices for Final demand transactions. If Chinese consumers buy American cars, it is recorded at 'U-Machinery × C-Consumption'.

What we saw above is a bilateral international I–O table linking two national tables; in this case, the Chinese table and the US table. The idea is easily extended to multilateral outlay covering more than three countries.

Table 8.3 presents the format of the Asian International Input–Output Table, linking the national tables of 10 countries in the Asia-Pacific region: Indonesia, Malaysia, the Philippines, Singapore, Thailand, China, Taiwan, Korea, Japan and the USA. The lightly-shaded parts correspond to the pieces taken from the Chinese table, and the darkly-shaded parts to those from the US table. Note that each cell herein represents the transactions among 76 industrial sectors; namely, each of them is a matrix of 76 × 76 dimensions.[2]

The way to read the table is the same as for bilateral tables. Viewing it column-wise, we have, for both Intermediate and Final demands: (1) domestic transactions; (2) import matrices by the 9 countries of origin; (3) the values of international freight and insurance incurred on these import transactions; (4) import matrices from other countries; and (5) the values of import duties and import commodity taxes levied on imported goods. Note that BA/BF and DA/DF are presented separately, so that the record of transactions among the 10 member countries are all valued at producers' price, while import matrices from Hong Kong, the EU and the Rest of the World are valued at CIF. At the bottom of the table lie Valued-added and Control totals (total supply), as in the case of a national table.[3]

3. Impact Analysis of the Global Economic Crisis

The last few decades have been marked by the rapid development of cross-national production networks. An economic shock that occurs in

Table 8.3 The Asian International Input–Output Table

	Intermediate demand (A)									
	Indonesia	**Malaysia**	**Philippines**	**Singapore**	**Thailand**	**China**	**Taiwan**	**Korea**	**Japan**	**USA**
Indonesia	A^{II}	A^{IM}	A^{IP}	A^{IS}	A^{IT}	A^{IC}	A^{IN}	A^{IK}	A^{IJ}	A^{IU}
Malaysia	A^{MI}	A^{MM}	A^{MP}	A^{MS}	A^{MT}	A^{MC}	A^{MN}	A^{MK}	A^{MJ}	A^{MU}
Philippines	A^{PI}	A^{PM}	A^{PP}	A^{PS}	A^{PT}	A^{PC}	A^{PN}	A^{PK}	A^{PJ}	A^{PU}
Singapore	A^{SI}	A^{SM}	A^{SP}	A^{SS}	A^{ST}	A^{SC}	A^{SN}	A^{SK}	A^{SJ}	A^{SU}
Thailand	A^{TI}	A^{TM}	A^{TP}	A^{TS}	A^{TT}	A^{TC}	A^{TN}	A^{TK}	A^{TJ}	A^{TU}
China	A^{CI}	A^{CM}	A^{CP}	A^{CS}	A^{CT}	A^{CC}	A^{CN}	A^{CK}	A^{CJ}	A^{CU}
Taiwan	A^{NI}	A^{NM}	A^{NP}	A^{NS}	A^{NT}	A^{NC}	A^{NN}	A^{NK}	A^{NJ}	A^{NU}
Korea	A^{KI}	A^{KM}	A^{KP}	A^{KS}	A^{KT}	A^{KC}	A^{KN}	A^{KK}	A^{KJ}	A^{KU}
Japan	A^{JI}	A^{JM}	A^{JP}	A^{JS}	A^{JT}	A^{JC}	A^{JN}	A^{JK}	A^{JJ}	A^{JU}
USA	A^{UI}	A^{UM}	A^{UP}	A^{US}	A^{UT}	A^{UC}	A^{UN}	A^{UK}	A^{UJ}	A^{UU}
Freight and Insurance	BA^{I}	BA^{M}	BA^{P}	BA^{S}	BA^{T}	BA^{C}	BA^{N}	BA^{K}	BA^{J}	BA^{U}
Import from Hong Kong	A^{HI}	A^{HM}	A^{HP}	A^{HS}	A^{HT}	A^{HC}	A^{HN}	A^{HK}	A^{HJ}	A^{HU}
Import from EU	A^{OI}	A^{OM}	A^{OP}	A^{OS}	A^{OT}	A^{OC}	A^{ON}	A^{OK}	A^{OJ}	A^{OU}
Import from the ROW	A^{WI}	A^{WM}	A^{WP}	A^{WS}	A^{WT}	A^{WC}	A^{WN}	A^{WK}	A^{WJ}	A^{WU}
Import duty and Sales tax	DA^{I}	DA^{M}	DA^{P}	DA^{S}	DA^{T}	DA^{C}	DA^{N}	DA^{K}	DA^{J}	DA^{U}
Value-added	V^{I}	V^{M}	V^{P}	V^{S}	V^{T}	V^{C}	V^{N}	V^{K}	V^{J}	V^{U}
Total inputs	X^{I}	X^{M}	X^{P}	X^{S}	X^{T}	X^{C}	X^{N}	X^{K}	X^{J}	X^{U}

Notes:
In a column-wise direction, each cell in the table shows the input compositions of the industries of the respective country. $\mathbf{A}^{II}$, for example, shows the input compositions of Indonesian industries *vis-à-vis* domestically produced goods and services, i.e. domestic transactions of Indonesia. $\mathbf{A}^{MI}$, in contrast, shows the input composition of Indonesian industries for imported goods and services from Malaysia. Cells $\mathbf{A}^{PI}$, $\mathbf{A}^{SI}$, $\mathbf{A}^{TI}$, $\mathbf{A}^{CI}$, $\mathbf{A}^{NI}$, $\mathbf{A}^{KI}$, $\mathbf{A}^{JI}$, $\mathbf{A}^{UI}$, $\mathbf{A}^{HI}$, $\mathbf{A}^{OI}$, $\mathbf{A}^{WI}$ allow the same interpretation for imports from other countries. **BA** and **DA** give international freight & insurance and taxes on these import transactions.

one country will be quickly and widely transmitted to the rest of the world through extensive cross-border supply chains. The decline in US demand for Japanese cars, for example, causes a decrease of Japanese car exports, and hence of car production in Japan. The output decline of Japanese cars reduces its import demand for tyres made in Korea, which further reduces

Table 8.3 (continued)

Final demand (F)										Export (L)					
Indonesia	Malaysia	Philippines	Singapore	Thailand	China	Taiwan	Korea	Japan	USA	Export to Hong Kong	Export to EU	Export to ROW	Statistical Discrepancy	Total Outputs	
F^{II}	F^{IM}	F^{IP}	F^{IS}	F^{IT}	F^{IC}	F^{IN}	F^{IK}	F^{IJ}	F^{IU}	L^{IH}	L^{IO}	L^{IW}	Q^{I}	X^{I}	Valued at producer's price
F^{MI}	F^{MM}	F^{MP}	F^{MS}	F^{MT}	F^{MC}	F^{MN}	F^{MK}	F^{MJ}	F^{MU}	L^{MH}	L^{MO}	L^{MW}	Q^{M}	X^{M}	
F^{PI}	F^{PM}	F^{PP}	F^{PS}	F^{PT}	F^{PC}	F^{PN}	F^{PK}	F^{PJ}	F^{PU}	L^{PH}	L^{PO}	L^{PW}	Q^{P}	X^{P}	
F^{SI}	F^{SM}	F^{SP}	F^{SS}	F^{ST}	F^{SC}	F^{SN}	F^{SK}	F^{SJ}	F^{SU}	L^{SH}	L^{SO}	L^{SW}	Q^{S}	X^{S}	
F^{TI}	F^{TM}	F^{TP}	F^{TS}	F^{TT}	F^{TC}	F^{TN}	F^{TK}	F^{TJ}	F^{TU}	L^{TH}	L^{TO}	L^{TW}	Q^{T}	X^{T}	
F^{CI}	F^{CM}	F^{CP}	F^{CS}	F^{CT}	F^{CC}	F^{CN}	F^{CK}	F^{CJ}	F^{CU}	L^{CH}	L^{CO}	L^{CW}	Q^{C}	X^{C}	
F^{NI}	F^{NM}	F^{NP}	F^{NS}	F^{NT}	F^{NC}	F^{NN}	F^{NK}	F^{NJ}	F^{NU}	L^{NH}	L^{NO}	L^{NW}	Q^{N}	X^{N}	
F^{KI}	F^{KM}	F^{KP}	F^{KS}	F^{KT}	F^{KC}	F^{KN}	F^{KK}	F^{KJ}	F^{KU}	L^{KH}	L^{KO}	L^{KW}	Q^{K}	X^{K}	
F^{JI}	F^{JM}	F^{JP}	F^{JS}	F^{JT}	F^{JC}	F^{JN}	F^{JK}	F^{JJ}	F^{JU}	L^{JH}	L^{JO}	L^{JW}	Q^{J}	X^{J}	
F^{UI}	F^{UM}	F^{UP}	F^{US}	F^{UT}	F^{UC}	F^{UN}	F^{UK}	F^{UJ}	F^{UU}	L^{UH}	L^{UO}	L^{UW}	Q^{U}	X^{U}	
BF^{I}	BF^{M}	BF^{P}	BF^{S}	BF^{T}	BF^{C}	BF^{N}	BF^{K}	BF^{J}	BF^{U}	←International freight and insurance on the trade between member countries (A**, F**).					
F^{HI}	F^{HM}	F^{HP}	F^{HS}	F^{HT}	F^{HC}	F^{HN}	F^{HK}	F^{HJ}	F^{HU}						
F^{OI}	F^{OM}	F^{OP}	F^{OS}	F^{OT}	F^{OC}	F^{ON}	F^{OK}	F^{OJ}	F^{OU}	Valued at C.I.F					
F^{WI}	F^{WM}	F^{WP}	F^{WS}	F^{WT}	F^{WC}	F^{WN}	F^{WK}	F^{WJ}	F^{WU}						
DF^{I}	DF^{M}	DF^{P}	DF^{S}	DF^{T}	DF^{C}	DF^{N}	DF^{K}	DF^{J}	DF^{U}	←Import duties and import commodity taxes levied on all trade.					

The parts made out of the Chinese I–O table

The parts made out of the US I–O table

Turning to the 11th column from the left side of the table, this shows the compositions of goods and services having gone to the final demand sectors of Indonesia. $\mathbf{F}^{II}$ and $\mathbf{F}^{MI}$ for example, map the inflow into Indonesian final demand sectors, of goods and services domestically produced and those imported from Malaysia, respectively. The rest of the column is read in the same manner as for the 1st column of the table.
$\mathbf{L}^{*H}$, $\mathbf{L}^{*O}$, $\mathbf{L}^{*W}$ are exports (vectors) to Hong Kong, EU and the Rest of the World, respectively. **V**s and **X**s are value-added and total input/output, as seen in the conventional national I–O table.

Korea's import demand for rubber from Malaysia, and so on. What has happened over the last few years or so is a clear reflection of this intertwined global production system. In what follows, we simulate the shock propagation mechanism across countries, using the international I–O model of two industries and two countries (Table 8.4).

Table 8.4 Mechanics of shock propagation: China–USA

(a) Intermediate transactions matrix

	China Ind.1	China Ind.2	USA Ind.1	USA Ind.2
China Ind.1	1200	400	400	20
China Ind.2	600	600	200	40
USA Ind.1	90	80	1600	400
USA Ind.2	90	20	800	600
Total Output	3000	2000	4000	2000

(b) Derivation of input coefficients

	China Ind.1	China Ind.2	USA Ind.1	USA Ind.2
China Ind.1	1200 ÷3000	400 ÷2000	400 ÷4000	20 ÷2000
China Ind.2	600 ÷3000	600 ÷2000	200 ÷4000	40 ÷2000
USA Ind.1	90 ÷3000	80 ÷2000	1600 ÷4000	400 ÷2000
USA Ind.2	90 ÷3000	20 ÷2000	800 ÷4000	600 ÷2000
Total Output	3000	2000	4000	2000

(c) Input coefficient matrix

	China Ind.1	China Ind.2	USA Ind.1	USA Ind.2
China Ind.1	0.40	0.20	0.10	0.01
China Ind.2	0.20	0.30	0.05	0.02
USA Ind.1	0.03	0.04	0.40	0.20
USA Ind.2	0.03	0.01	0.20	0.30

Table 8.4 (continued)

(d) Initial shock

	China Ind.1	China Ind.2	−100M$ ↓ USA Ind.1	USA Ind.2
China Ind.1	**0.40**	**0.20**	**0.10 ×(−100M$)**	**0.01**
China Ind.2	**0.20**	**0.30**	**0.05 ×(−100M$)**	**0.02**
USA Ind.1	**0.03**	**0.04**	**0.40 ×(−100M$)**	**0.20**
USA Ind.2	**0.03**	**0.01**	**0.20 ×(−100M$)**	**0.30**

(e) First-round (direct) impacts

	China Ind.1	China Ind.2	USA Ind.1	USA Ind.2	
China Ind.1	**0.40**	**0.20**	**0.10 ×(−100M$) =−10M$**	**0.01**	**→ to China's industry 1**
China Ind.2	**0.20**	**0.30**	**0.05 ×(−100M$) =−5M$**	**0.02**	**→ to China's industry 2**
USA Ind.1	**0.03**	**0.04**	**0.40 ×(−100M$) =−40M$**	**0.20**	**→ to US industry 1**
USA Ind.2	**0.03**	**0.01**	**0.20 ×(−100M$) =−20M$**	**0.30**	**→ to US industry 2**

Table 8.4 (continued)

(f) Feedback of the first-round impacts

	−10M$ ↓	−5M$ ↓	−40M$ ↓	−20M$ ↓	Feedback of 1st-round impacts
	China Ind.1	**China Ind.2**	**USA Ind.1**	**USA Ind.2**	
China Ind.1	**0.40 ×(−10M$)**	**0.20 ×(−5M$)**	**0.10 ×(−40M$)**	**0.01 ×(−20M$)**	
China Ind.2	**0.20 ×(−10M$)**	**0.30 ×(−5M$)**	**0.05 ×(−40M$)**	**0.02 ×(−20M$)**	
USA Ind.1	**0.03 ×(−10M$)**	**0.04 ×(−5M$)**	**0.40 ×(−40M$)**	**0.20 ×(−20M$)**	
USA Ind.2	**0.03 ×(−10M$)**	**0.01 ×(−5M$)**	**0.20 ×(−40M$)**	**0.30 ×(−20M$)**	

(g) Second-round impacts

	China Ind.1	**China Ind.2**	**USA Ind.1**	**USA Ind.2**	
China Ind.1	**0.40 ×(−10M$) =−4M$**	**0.20 ×(−5M$) =−1M$**	**0.10 ×(−40M$) =−4M$**	**0.01 ×(−20M$) =−0.2M$**	**Total of −9.2M$ to China's industry 1**
China Ind.2	**0.20 ×(−10M$) =−2M$**	**0.30 ×(−5M$) =−1.5M$**	**0.05 ×(−40M$) =−2M$**	**0.02 ×(−20M$) =−0.4M$**	**Total of −5.9M$ to China's industry 2**
USA Ind.1	**0.03 ×(−10M$) =−0.3M$**	**0.04 ×(−5M$) =−0.2M$**	**0.40 ×(−40M$) =−16M$**	**0.20 ×(−20M$) =−4M$**	**Total of −20.5M$ to US industry 1**
USA Ind.2	**0.03 ×(−10M$) =−0.3M$**	**0.01 ×(−5M$) =−0.05M$**	**0.20 ×(−40M$) =−8M$**	**0.30 ×(−20M$) =−6M$**	**Total of −14.35M$ to US industry 2**

Table 8.4 (continued)

(h) n*th-round impacts*

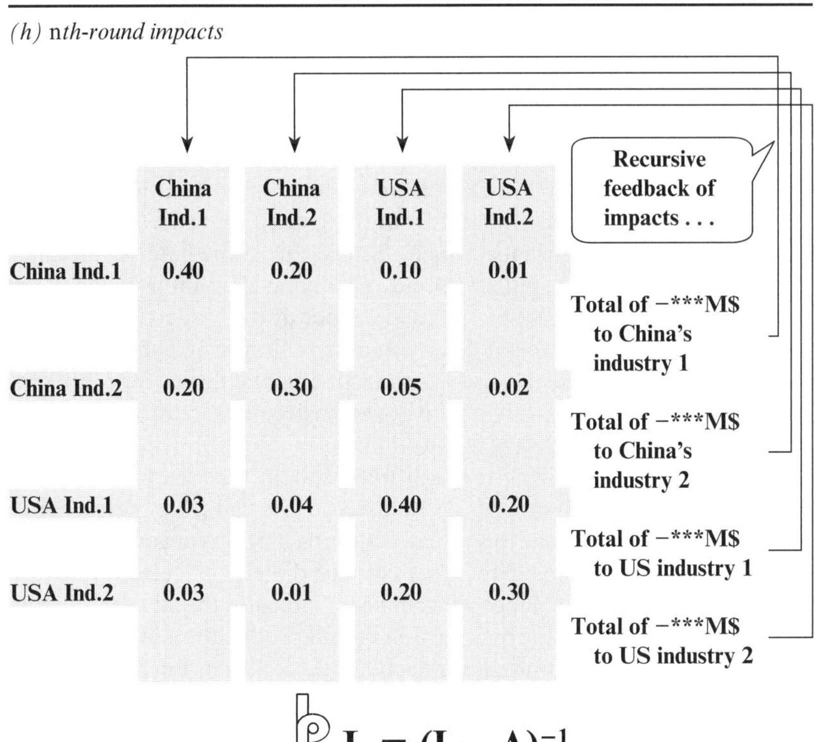

	China Ind.1	China Ind.2	USA Ind.1	USA Ind.2
China Ind.1	0.40	0.20	0.10	0.01
China Ind.2	0.20	0.30	0.05	0.02
USA Ind.1	0.03	0.04	0.40	0.20
USA Ind.2	0.03	0.01	0.20	0.30

$$\mathbf{L} = (\mathbf{I} - \mathbf{A})^{-1}$$

(i) Leontief inverse matrix

	China Ind.1	China Ind.2	USA Ind.1	USA Ind.2
China Ind.1	1.88	0.56	0.41	0.16
China Ind.2	0.55	1.60	0.27	0.13
USA Ind.1	0.18	0.17	1.89	0.55
USA Ind.2	0.14	0.09	0.56	1.59

×

Decrease in Final Demand
0
0
−100M$
0

Before we start the simulation exercise, we have to prepare what is known as the Input coefficient matrix. An 'input coefficient' is defined as 'the amount of goods/services which is directly required to produce one unit of output', and can be derived from the Intermediate transaction matrix of an I–O table. For example, in the case of Industry 1 in China, we know from the table that, in order to produce the industry's total output, which is 3000, this industry has to use 1200 units of its own product, 600 units of the product of Industry 2, and has to import 90 units each of the product of Industries 1 and 2 from the United States. So, in order to derive the input coefficients, which specify the immediate requirement for producing just one unit of output, we divide each input value in the column (1200, 600, 90, 90) by the total output of the industry (3000). The result of the operation for all four columns is shown in Table 8.4c. This matrix of input coefficients serves as the fundamental device for every kind of input–output analysis since it gives the basic structure of the technical requirement of each industry in question.

Now, suppose, following the sub-prime shock, that the US consumption demand declined and the production of US Industry 1 thus fell by 100 million US$. We want to simulate the impact of this negative shock on each industry. The immediate impact can be directly calculated from the Input coefficient matrix. Since the coefficient indicates the amount of intermediate use per unit of output, the first-round propagation of the negative shock can be given by multiplying each input coefficient by the amount of decreased production, as shown in Tables 8.4d and 8.4e.

The story, however, does not end here. The first-round impacts propagate further and trigger secondary repercussion. This is calculated by feeding back the first-round impacts on the corresponding input coefficients on an industry-by-industry basis, which simulates the second-round propagation of the initial shock (Tables 8.4f and 8.4g).

This operation will continue until the marginal decline of outputs subsides (Table 8.4h). In order to calculate the total impact of the negative shock, from the first to the *n*th-round, we derive the 'Leontief inverse matrix' from the Input coefficient matrix by mathematical transformation $(I - A)^{-1}$, where A is a matrix form of the Input coefficient matrix and I is an identity matrix. While the input coefficient represents just the immediate requirement for goods and services, the Leontief inverse coefficient indicates both direct and indirect requirements, and is hence able to capture the entire impact of the negative shock delivered through every possible channel of the production networks. Mathematically, our simulation exercise of the US demand shock can be represented as a matrix multiplication of the Leontief inverse and the vector of US Final demand components, with the entry of −100M$ for the element of 'USA Ind. 1' (Table 8.4i).

The formal presentation of the 'output loss induced by a negative shock' is given as follows:[4] The Input coefficient matrix of the production system with two industries (1, 2) / two countries (r, s) is defined as

$$A = \begin{bmatrix} a_{11}^{rr} & a_{12}^{rr} & a_{11}^{rs} & a_{12}^{rs} \\ a_{21}^{rr} & a_{22}^{rr} & a_{21}^{rs} & a_{22}^{rs} \\ a_{11}^{sr} & a_{12}^{sr} & a_{11}^{ss} & a_{12}^{ss} \\ a_{21}^{sr} & a_{22}^{sr} & a_{21}^{ss} & a_{22}^{ss} \end{bmatrix}.$$

The Leontief inverse matrix is then derived as

$$L = \begin{bmatrix} l_{11}^{rr} & l_{12}^{rr} & l_{11}^{rs} & l_{12}^{rs} \\ l_{21}^{rr} & l_{22}^{rr} & l_{21}^{rs} & l_{22}^{rs} \\ l_{11}^{sr} & l_{12}^{sr} & l_{11}^{ss} & l_{12}^{ss} \\ l_{21}^{sr} & l_{22}^{sr} & l_{21}^{ss} & l_{22}^{ss} \end{bmatrix} = (I - A)^{-1}$$

where I is an identity matrix of the same dimension (4 × 4).

The 'output loss induced by a negative shock (i.e. the decrease in Final demand)' is calculated as

$$\Delta X = L \cdot \Delta F$$

where ΔF is a column vector of the length (4 × 1) with negative entries in the elements corresponding to the industries from which the shock originates, and ΔX is a column vector of the same size that shows the consequent decrease in the output of each industry. For example, in the case that the shock occurred in Industry 1 of Country s in a quantity of $-$q, ΔF and the consequent ΔX are given as

$$\Delta F = \begin{bmatrix} \Delta f_1^r \\ \Delta f_2^r \\ \Delta f_1^s \\ \Delta f_2^s \end{bmatrix} = \begin{bmatrix} 0 \\ 0 \\ -\mathrm{q} \\ 0 \end{bmatrix}, \Delta X = \begin{bmatrix} \Delta x_1^r \\ \Delta x_2^r \\ \Delta x_1^s \\ \Delta x_2^s \end{bmatrix} = L \cdot \Delta F = \begin{bmatrix} l_{11}^{rs} * (-\mathrm{q}) \\ l_{21}^{rs} * (-\mathrm{q}) \\ l_{11}^{ss} * (-\mathrm{q}) \\ l_{21}^{ss} * (-\mathrm{q}) \end{bmatrix}.$$

II. UPDATING PROCEDURE FOR THE 2008 ASIAN INTERNATIONAL I–O TABLE

Although the international I–O table is such a powerful tool for studying the cross-national impact of external shocks, its compilation is highly resource-intensive and therefore the trade-off between the speed of release

Table 8.5 Industrial classification (26 sectors)

Code	Description
001	Paddy
002	Other agricultural products
003	Livestock and poultry
004	Forestry
005	Fishery
006	Crude petroleum and natural gas
007	Other mining
008	Food, beverage and tobacco
009	Textile, leather, and the products thereof
010	Wooden furniture and other wooden products
011	Pulp, paper and printing
012	Chemical products
013	Petroleum and petro products
014	Rubber products
015	Non-metallic mineral products
016	Metals and metal products
017	Industrial machinery
018	Computers and electronic equipment
019	Other electrical equipment
020	Transport equipment
021	Other manufacturing products
022	Electricity, gas, and water supply
023	Construction
024	Trade and transport
025	Other services
026	Public administration

and the accuracy of the data is inevitable. Usually, a lag of five to seven years has to be assumed between the reference year and the time of release. However, due to the urgent nature of the current studies, the *Asian International Input–Output Table for 2008* was newly constructed in order to meet the analytical needs of present concerns.

This section illustrates the updating procedure of the 2008 AIO table.

Input Data: at 26 Sector Classification (see Table 8.5)

- 2000 national I–O tables of the competitive import type, constructed from the 2000 AIO table;
- Export and import matrix of 2008, constructed from the foreign trade database = the 'World Trade Atlas';

- 2000 TTM ratios and Import duties & import commodity taxes ratio;
- GDP growth rate between 2000 and 2008;
- 2008 total value of each final demand item based on national account statistics.

Updating Procedure

1. Control totals
   Control totals are blown up from 2000 values by using the GDP growth rate between 2000 and 2008.
2. Exports and imports
   - Export vector (FOB) and import vector (CIF: subtraction) are constructed from the foreign trade database for the year 2008.
   - The export vector is converted into the producer's price by using the 2000 TTM ratios.
   - Import duties and the import commodity taxes vector (subtraction) is constructed, using the 2000 import duties and import commodity taxes ratios.
3. Value-added
   The total value-added is calculated based upon the national account identity VA = Domestic final demand + Exports − Imports. The value is then made into a row vector by using the distribution ratio from the 2000 AIO table.
4. Balancing
   Using all the components prepared above, intermediate and final demand transactions are estimated though an RAS procedure based on the 2000 input and final demand structure.
   R vector (column) = CT – Exports + Imports
   S vector (row: intermediate demand) = CT – Value-added
   S vector (row: final demand) = CT − total final demand values from 2008 national accounts
5. Linking
   Using all the updated national I–O tables and the 2008 trade matrix, the 2008 Asian International Input–Output Table is compiled by manual balancing and adjustment.

The procedure is illustrated in Figure 8.1.

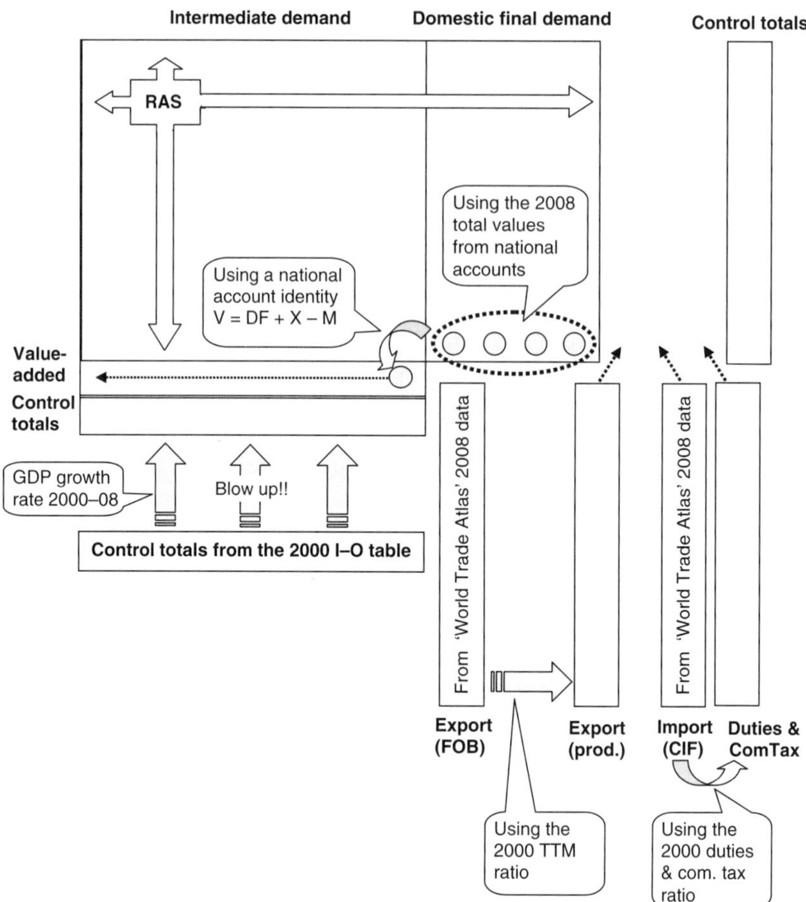

Figure 8.1 A schematic image of the updating procedure

Table 8.6 Availability of IDE input–output tables

	Reference year					
	1970	1975	1985	1990	1995	2000
Asian International I–O Table			✓	✓	✓	✓
Transnational Interregional I–O Table between China and Japan						✓
Multi-regional I–O Model for China						✓
ASEAN International I–O Table		✓				
Korea–Japan International I–O Table	✓	✓	✓	✓		
Philippines–Japan International I–O Table	✓		✓	✓		
Thailand–Japan International I–O Table		✓	✓	✓		
Indonesia–Japan International I–O Table		✓	✓	✓		
China–Japan International I–O Table			✓	✓		
Singapore–Japan International I–O Table			✓	✓		
Malaysia–Japan International I–O Table			✓	✓		
Taiwan–Japan International I–O Table			✓	✓		
Philippines I–O Table				✓		
China I–O Table			✓	✓		
Singapore I–O Table			✓	✓		
Malaysia I–O Table			✓	✓		
Taiwan I–O Table			✓	✓		

The following two tables will be released in September 2011:

1. Asian International Input–Output Table for 2005
   - Industrial sector classification: 76 sectors
   - Country coverage: Indonesia, Malaysia, the Philippines, Singapore, Thailand, China, Taiwan, Korea, Japan and the USA.
2. BRICs International Input–Output Table for 2005
   - Industrial sector classification: 26 sectors
   - Country coverage: Brazil, Russia, India, China, Japan, EU25[5] and the USA.

All data may be purchased from IDE website: http://www.ide.go.jp/English/Publish/Books/Sds/material.html.

NOTES

1. In this light, an I–O table can provide double information from a single matrix: if we look at the table in a column-wise direction, we observe the cost structure of each industry. If we read it row-wise, we see the distribution structure of each product according to its destination.
2. For analytical purposes, the data used in the current studies are aggregated to 26 industrial sectors. See Table 8.5 for the sector classification.
3. For the list of national and international I–O tables constructed by IDE-JETRO see Table 8.6.
4. The basic assumptions of I–O models are:

   (1) A one-to-one correspondence between commodities and industries: this implies the absence of an alternative choice of techniques for production, and the absence of by-products and/or secondary products arising out of the productive process.
   (2) Constant returns to scale: if the output level is doubled, the input requirement is also doubled (for materials, service inputs, production factors and so on). If the output is tripled, inputs are also tripled. Neither increasing nor decreasing returns to scale exist, and there is a fixed proportionality between inputs and outputs.
   (3) No externalities: there is no physical interference in the economic activity of one industry over others, so that the sum of the products of individual economic activities equals the level of the products expected when these activities are carried out collectively; in other words, economic activities are additive.

   Premises (2) and (3) guarantee the linearity of the input–output data, upon which all the theoretical models of input–output analysis are constructed.
5. Austria, Belgium, Cyprus, Czech Republic, Denmark, Estonia, Finland, France, Germany, Greece, Hungary, Ireland, Italy, Latvia, Lithuania, Luxembourg, Malta, the Netherlands, Poland, Portugal, Slovakia, Slovenia, Spain, Sweden, the United Kingdom.

Index

Armington elasticities 76, 102
Asia-Pacific expenditure shifts 173–7
Asian Currency Crisis 125, 126, 129, 144, 160
Asian International Input–Output (AIO) Tables 2, 30–31, 54–5, 77, 109, 178, 195
  updating procedure 203–6
automakers, aid to suppliers 100
'Automobiles to the Countryside' policy 161

Baldwin, R. 119
banks
  assessment of business risks 92–5
  China, impact of crisis 147
  and monetary circuit 85–9

China
  counter-crisis fiscal expansion 160–64, 165–6
  employment trade 56–9
  exports to US 28
  growth rate 145–6
  impact of economic crisis 28, 32, 63, 144, 145–8, 157–9
  inter-regional production structure 153–7
  output, impacts of economic crisis 32
  price shock exports 81
  vertical specialization 115–18
  see also triangular trade through China
Cline, W.R. 171
clothing industry, impact of financial shocks 83, 104
Coastal Area Development Strategy, China 153–5
computers and electronic equipment industry, multiplier effects 42
consumer goods, trade flows 21, 28
control totals, input–output tables 193
counter-crisis fiscal expansion, China 160–64, 165–6
credibility index 127–9
credit crunch 93
  impacts on China 147
current account imbalances 173–7
  rebalancing 169–89

demand
  and Asian economy 127
  domestic, effect on labour market 55–60
demand-driven I–O model 100–102
demand items, reactions to economic crisis 63
disruptive supply-driven shock, simulating 102–4
domestic demand, effect on labour market 55–60
domestic multiplier effect 31–2

economic crisis
  impact analysis 195–203
  impact on China 144, 145–8, 157–9
  impact on employment 51–71
  impact on Factory Asia 125–35
  impact on industrial output 28–40
  and vertical specialization 110–18
economy size and vertical specialization 115
employment, impact of global economic crisis 51–71
employment gain potential 56
employment give-out potential 56
expenditure allocations 175–6
expenditure shifts 173–7
exporter-specific variables and intermediate goods trade 132

exports 13–14
  China 147, 148–9
  destinations 14–21
  to USA 28–30

factor demands, effects of rebalancing 182
Factory Asia, impact of financial crisis 125–35
feedback effect 48–9
final demand sectors, input–output tables 193
financial crisis, *see* economic crisis
financial market stability and intermediate goods trade 131
financial sector, China, impacts of economic crisis 147
financial shocks
  chain of causalities 94
  impact measurement 75–81
  modelling 83–92
  real transmission channels 73–97
finished goods market and intermediate goods trade 131
fiscal expansion, China 160–64
flow variables, effect of shocks 93
forgone GDP growth rate 61–3

Ghosh model 75–7, 96, 100–102
global credit crunch impacts on China 147
global economic crisis, *see* economic crisis
Godley, W. 98
gravity equations and Factory Asia 125, 141–2
growth rate, China 145–6

Hayakawa, K. 125
'Household Appliances to the Countryside' policy 160–61, 168
Huanan region, China 156–7
  effects of counter-crisis fiscal measures 163
Huazhong region, China 156–7
Hummels, D. 107, 108–9

IDE-JETRO 149–53
imbalances 173–7; *see also* rebalancing
impact analysis
  global economic crisis 195–203
  of rebalancing 177–9
impact decomposition 32
Imported Real Supply-driven Impact Coefficient (IRSIC) 75–6, 78
importer-specific variables, intermediate goods trade 129–31
imports, China 148
Indonesia
  exports 28–30
  output 36, 39
industrial output, *see* output
input coefficient matrix 202–3
input–output analyses 191–203
  of impacts of economic crisis 30–40
  of post-crisis rebalancing 169–89
input–output models 51
  for employment analysis 52–4
input–output tables 77, 191–5; *see also* Asian International Input–Output Tables
inter-country multiplier effects
  labour markets 55–6
  production 32–9, 42
  see also triangular trade, multiplier effect
intermediate goods
  production values 126–7
  trade 126–35
  transactions model 138–43
international allocations of deficits 175
international I–O tables 77, 193–5; *see also* Asian International Input–Output Tables
inter-regional multipliers 155–7
inter-regional production structure 153–5
intra-regional multipliers 155–7
investment, reactions to economic crisis 63
I–O models, *see* input–output models
IRSIC (Imported Real Supply-driven Impact Coefficient) 75–6, 78

Japan
  intra-regional and inter-regional multipliers 155–6
  output, impacts of economic crisis 32–6

price shock exports 78
supply-driven shock effects 104

Keynes, J.M. 171
Korea, output, impacts of economic crisis 36
Krugman, P. 89, 171
Kurata, D. 149

labour markets
impacts of economic crisis 51–72
structural change 55–60
Lavoie, M. 98
Leontief inverse matrix 108
Leontief model 75, 96, 100–102
Li, R. 147

Malaysia
output, impacts of economic crisis 39
price shock imports 78
market access and intermediate goods trade 131
monetary circuit
basic model 85–9
effects of shock 93–6
and inter-industry supply chains 83–92
open model 89–92
multiplier decomposition method 47–50
multiplier effects 30–40
and labour markets 55–60, 63–7
triangular trade 40–42

negative multiplier effects 30–40
Ng, F. 119
non-tradable production 187

Ohlin, B. 171
output
Asia 28–40
China, impacts of financial crisis 157
overlap, structural 182–7
overlap indexes 184–7

parts and accessories, trade flows 21
Philippines, output, impacts of economic crisis 39
Pitigala, N. 106
Prasad, E.S. 169
price index 131
price shocks 77–83
production values, intermediate goods 126–7

RAS 205, 206
real transmission channels of financial shocks 73–97
rebalancing 169–89
impact analysis 177–9
structural implications 180–87
regions, China
and counter-crisis measures 162–3
impacts of financial crisis 157–9
inter-regional I–O table 149–53
inter-regional production structure 153–7
regional development 153–7
regional disparity alleviation policies 161–2
regional multipliers 155–7
Repullo, R. 89
risk assessment by banks 92–5

sector-specific price index 131
sectoral consequences of rebalancing 180–82
sectoral output, impacts of economic crisis 32–40
shock transmission 13–28, 197–203
China 146–8, 159
modelling 75–92
real transmission channels 73–97
triangular trade 13–28
Singapore, output 39
size of economy and vertical specialization 115
Somavia, Juan 51
Special Economic Zones, China 153
stock variables, effects of shocks 93–4
structural change in labour markets 55–60
structural implications of rebalancing 180–87
structural overlap 182–7
Suarez, J. 89
supplier aid by automakers 100
supply chain impacts of financial shocks 75–83

supply-drive I–O model 100–102
supply-driven shock 77–83
  simulating 102–4

Taiwan, output 36
Tao, L. 148
textile industry, impact of financial shocks 83, 104
Thailand
  output 39
  price shock imports 78
trade
  intermediate goods 126
  trade flows 14–28
  triangular trade, *see* triangular trade through China
  see also exports; imports
transfer problem 171–2
transmission mechanism, *see* shock transmission
Transnational Interregional Input–Output Table between Japan and China (IDE-JETRO) 149–53
triangular trade through China 1–2, 11–44
  multiplier effect 32–42
  and shock transmission 13–28
  and vertical specialization 116

United States
  current account deficit 173–4
  deficit reduction allocation 175
  demand and Asian economy 30–40, 127
  as export destination 14
  trade flows 21–8
  see also triangular trade through China

value-added items, input–output tables 193
vertical production chains 6, 7, 106, 108, 109, 110, 119
vertical production networks 5, 6, 106, 107, 111, 117, 119
vertical specialization 106–19
  China 115–18
  impact of economic crisis 110–18
vertical specialization indices 107–10, 121–4

wages
  exporter's, and intermediate goods trade 132
  importer's, and intermediate goods trade 129–31

Yeats, A.J. 119
Yonemoto, K. 148

Zhang, Y. 148, 149
Ziyang, Zhao 153